D0862725

CHOOSING THE *Jesus* WAY

ANGELA TARANGO

CHOOSING THE
Jesus WAY

American Indian Pentecostals *and the* Fight *for the* Indigenous Principle

The University of North Carolina Press

Chapel Hill

This book was published with the assistance of the
Authors Fund of the University of North Carolina Press.

© 2014 The University of North Carolina Press
All rights reserved

Designed by Michelle Coppedge Wallen. Set in Arnhem by Integrated Book
Technology. Manufactured in the United States of America

The paper in this book meets the guidelines for permanence and durability
of the Committee on Production Guidelines for Book Longevity of the Council
on Library Resources.

The University of North Carolina Press has been a member of the Green Press
Initiative since 2003.

Library of Congress Cataloging-in-Publication Data
Tarango, Angela.
Choosing the Jesus way : American Indian Pentecostals and the fight for the
indigenous principle / Angela Tarango. — First edition.
p. cm.
Includes bibliographical references and index.
ISBN 978-1-4696-1292-8 (pbk : alk. paper)
ISBN 978-1-4696-1293-5 (ebook)
1. Indians of North America—Missions. 2. Indians of North America—Religion.
3. Pentecostal converts—North America. 4. Assemblies of God—Missions—North
America. 5. Christianity and other religions—North America. 6. Christianity and
culture—North America. 7. North America—Religious life and customs. I. Title.
E98.M6T27 2014
299.7—dc23   2013038008

Portions of this work have appeared earlier, in somewhat different form,
as "Jesus as the 'Great Physician': Pentecostal Native North Americans within
the Assemblies of God and New Understandings of Pentecostal Healing," in
Global Pentecostal and Charismatic Healing, ed. Candy Gunther Brown, 107–26
(New York: Oxford University Press, 2011), reprinted by permission of Oxford
University Press, USA; and "Native American Pentecostalism," in *The Handbook
of Pentecostal Christianity*, ed. Adam Stewart, 147–50 (DeKalb: Northern Illinois
University Press, 2012), © 2012 by Northern Illinois University Press, used with
permission of Northern Illinois University Press.

18 17 16 15 14   5 4 3 2 1

THIS BOOK WAS DIGITALLY PRINTED.

JKM Library
1100 East 55th Street
Chicago, IL 60615

For my mother and father,

YOLANDA L. TARANGO and JESUS TARANGO JR.

Contents

Acknowledgments

Books do not write themselves, even though sometimes as scholars I am sure we wish they would. I have incurred many debts over the years, which I wish to acknowledge now.

This book came about because of the urging of Grant Wacker, who introduced me to the history of the Assemblies of God and hinted that there might be an "interesting history of missions to Native Americans there." Thanks Grant, for being an excellent mentor and for setting me on this course, which has at times been challenging, but also richly rewarding.

In the early days of my research and writing, the late Michael D. Green pointed out to me that the "key to this whole thing is the indigenous principle." I thank him for his guidance and friendship, as well as the guidance of others who read this work in its early stages, including Yaakov Ariel, Julie Byrne, J. Kameron Carter, Jan Cooper, Emily Mace, Laurie Maffly-Kipp, Samira Mehta, Kathy Morgan, Luis Losada, and Brendan Pietsch and the rest of my Duke University and University of North Carolina at Chapel Hill cohort who offered advice and encouragement.

Jennifer Graber and Tisa Wenger read the entire final manuscript, gave me copious feedback, and brainstormed ideas with me. I am deeply grateful for their help and friendship. Catherine Bowler helped me make sure all my Pentecostal history and theology was properly squared away. C. Mackenzie Brown helped me to clean up and restructure sections of the manuscript. Toni Wall Jaudon offered insights on religious practice over many a lunch when we both taught at Oberlin. I also thank my two anonymous reviewers for their feedback, which enriched the manuscript further.

I am deeply indebted to the director of the Flower Pentecostal Heritage Center in Springfield, Missouri, Darrin Rodgers, as well as the staff, including Joyce Lee, Sharon Rasnake, and Glenn Gohr. I am especially grateful to Glenn for his help in selecting the pictures for the interior of the book and the cover. The FPHC maintains a tremendous archive of Pentecostal history, much of which is digitized—something that many scholars who have to sift through so much material can appreciate. Through the FPHC I was connected with John Maracle, Rodger Cree, Joseph Saggio, Alma Thomas, and the late Ruth Lyon, all of whom shared with me their life stories, knowledge of the Assemblies of God's missionary work, and opened doors for me in Pentecostal circles. I would also like to thank the late Gary McGee, a fine historian of Pentecostalism, for his wisdom and guidance. The faculty and staff at the American Indian College of the Assemblies of God, in Phoenix, Arizona, were incredibly welcoming when I showed up unannounced wanting to tour the school and talk to them about the Native Pentecostal community that they serve. A special thanks goes out to the Native Pentecostal community for supporting me in telling its story. Any errors or misrepresentations in this book are my own.

The Department of Religion at Trinity University is a wonderful place to work, made all the more so by my colleagues including C. Mackenzie Brown, Rubén Dupertuis, Ruqayya Khan, Randall Nadeau, Sarah Pinnock, and Chad Spigel. Our indomitable departmental assistant Irma Escalante helped me with the many logistics in getting this manuscript to the publisher. I found Trinity's library staff helpful (more than once) when I was stuck in a jam trying to request particular books and sources. My good friends and Trinity colleagues Michele Johnson and Nicole Marafioti made up my small writing support group, and over food and wine we worked together to keep each other going. I am also grateful to the Trinity students who encouraged me and expressed interest in my work, especially Isaiah Ellis, who was my research assistant when I was polishing the final manuscript.

Funding for this project was provided by the graduate program in religion at Duke University, a grant from the Assemblies of God's Home Missions Department, a teaching/research fellowship at Oberlin College through the Consortium for Faculty Diversity in Liberal Arts Colleges, and a Trinity University summer stipend. Both the Department of Religion and the Office of Academic Affairs at Trinity provided the money needed to buy the copyrights for the photos for this book. I would also like to thank the staffs at the libraries of Oberlin College and Duke University, who helped me gather the information needed for my research.

An amazing editor is worth her weight in gold, and Elaine Maisner at University of North Carolina Press is that woman. She supported this project from the beginning and helped me keep my eyes on the finish line.

Caitlin Bell-Butterfield and Alison Shay answered all my questions and helped me to navigate the route towards publication. Ron Maner answered all of my copious technical questions and helped me pull the manuscript together.

I would not have made it through this process without my network of scholarly and nonscholarly friends. Stephen Marini "converted" me to the study of American religions while I was an undergraduate at Wellesley College and set me on the path that I travel today. During part of my research in 2010, I stayed in the guest room of Brandon and Nidia Bayne's home in Phoenix for several weeks, where, aside from doing research, Brandon and I ate waffles, watched World Cup soccer, and talked about American religious history. I am tremendously lucky to have the hospitality, friendship, and support of the Bayne family. Daniel Ramírez, Arlene Sánchez-Walsh, and Amos Yong are all fine scholars of Pentecostalism who encouraged me and offered advice throughout the process of writing this manuscript. A. G. Miller, David Kamitsuka, Pablo Mitchell, and the Departments of Religion and Comparative American Studies at Oberlin College guided me as well as gave me a teaching and research fellowship in my last year of graduate study. Candy Gunther Brown, Elesha Coffman, Seth Dowland, Rachel Maxson, Mandy McMichael, and Heather Vacek all gave me support, feedback, and pep talks. Sarah Ruble read pieces of the manuscript in its early stages, steadied me when I felt overwhelmed, and remains an extraordinary friend. Jenny Caplan cheered me on from the days when we were students together at Wellesley College and Harvard Divinity School and continued to do so through the writing of this manuscript. Emily Mace and Samira Mehta were always on call for writing woes and often dispensed wise advice. Finally, an enormous thank you to my "sister from another mother," Elizabeth Losada, who on so many occasions pushed me to keep writing and researching and to finish what I had started. There are many others whom I have not mentioned here and who have supported me with the gifts of friendship and help, and I am grateful.

When I first started graduate school, I was lonely, so I adopted a little black hound dog of uncertain background from a local shelter. The little dog grew up, went on long walks with me as a graduate student, moved with me to northern Ohio for my teaching fellowship, and has now settled in Texas with me. She is now old, with a grey face, arthritis in her knees, and silver eyebrows, but through it all, Chloe has truly been "woman's best friend." Along the way, we picked up a grey tabby cat I named Milo, who reminds me daily that just because I am human, I am in no way superior to him. They have accompanied me through this entire process, and their unconditional love keeps me sane.

Finally, I could not have gotten here without the love, support, and help of family. My brother, Jesus Tarango III, and my nephew, Jordan Wayne Tarango, reminded me to never get too big for my britches as I made my journey toward becoming an academic. This book is dedicated to my mother and father, Yolanda L. Tarango and Jesus Tarango Jr. When I was a little girl, my father used to buy me books every time I did something good or received good grades. His incentive program developed me into a verifiable book monster—you would never find me without a book as a child, and I read them so fast he could hardly keep up with buying them. I inherited my love of reading from my mother, who encouraged me to continue to push the boundaries of knowledge. It is to them that I owe my education—they worked hard so that they could send me to the best college possible, and later encouraged me and pushed me hard to be the best. They are my constant source of support, and I am lucky that I can count both my parents as my best friends. Even at times when I wavered, they kept the faith that I would finish "the paper." So thank you Mom and Dad; this one is for you.

CHOOSING THE *Jesus* WAY

Native Pentecostals, the Indigenous Principle, and Religious Practice

Later while preaching that meeting I received from God what I had been waiting to hear. He came to me, confirming His call upon my life, in a vivid visitation of His presence. "Now is the time for you to take the Gospel to the American Indians," He said. "You know now where they are. Go home and prepare yourself. Tell your husband and your church, and I will make the way plain for you." With this commission from the Lord, an intense love for American Indians flooded my soul. Now that I had a confirmation of my call from God, I knew I must take the next step—a step of faith.
—ALTA WASHBURN, *white evangelist to American Indians and founder of the American Indian College, circa 1935*[1]

I stood among the circular mounds and scattered cedar logs, a small Indian boy in crude Navajo garb, and looked across the small canyon. I shouted into the vast emptiness and heard the echo shouting back. Wonderingly I cried, "Who is talking to me; who dares mock Yel Ha Yah?" So I began my long search for knowledge—not for knowledge alone, but for an understanding of life itself.
—CHARLIE LEE, *Navajo evangelist/pastor and founder of the first indigenous church in the Assemblies of God, circa 1930*[2]

God called Sister Alta Washburn and Brother Charlie Lee. One was a dark-haired, petite midwestern woman with only a ninth-grade education; the other, a famous young Navajo artist. They came from vastly different places, but during the middle decades of the twentieth century, their lives and work intersected. They were unlikely partners in a movement that shaped the largest American Pentecostal denomination, the Assemblies of God (AG). As agents of change, their calls to become missionaries to American Indians profoundly altered their lives as well as the lives of others.

In 1918, the first missionaries from the AG set out to work among American Indians. Those missionaries, laboring among Northern California Indians in the Shasta Lakes region, pioneered the beginnings of the AG's home missions.[3] The AG's emphasis on world missions initially overshadowed this project, and it took many years before home missions gained momentum among Pentecostal believers. Yet for the AG, realizing the goal of indigenous churches proved to be a long and painful struggle—especially in home missions. Working-class white Americans dominated the ranks of early Pentecostal missionaries, usually hailing from the Midwest or the South. Minimally educated, few white missionaries boasted Bible school degrees or any other form of higher education. These early missionaries went to reservations with little understanding of Indian culture or life, and many carried the baggage of white paternalism. Some were loath to give converts any form of power within the individual missions. Allowing Indian missionaries and clergy control over their own churches and acknowledging that God could work within Indian culture proved easier in theory than in practice.

Yet this slowly changed. By the 1950s, missionary work among American Indians gained momentum, and by the 1960s a distinct American Indian leadership had emerged. That Indian leadership pushed for the establishment of an all-Indian Bible College and for voting rights on the governing councils of the AG. By 2007, it had achieved both goals, and the AG had established 190 churches or missions among them. American Indians currently make up 1.5 percent of the overall AG population.[4] This number is in line with the overall percentage of Native peoples in the United States, which the U.S. Census reports to be 1.5 percent.[5]

Indian Pentecostals' struggle for indigenous leadership so defined them that it became, in a sense, the practice that helped them realize what it meant to be Native and Pentecostal. They rooted their method in a distinctly realized Pentecostal theology—the indigenous principle—which allowed them to push for more Native autonomy within the AG. Although Pentecostalism changed American Indian converts, they also changed the AG. These were not people who passively converted, embraced Pentecostalism, and followed the lead of the AG. Instead, they actively engaged the AG and demanded their own autonomous space within the denomination.

Indian Pentecostals were crucial actors within the AG. When the AG dragged its feet in the building of a Bible college to train its Indian pastors, a sympathetic white missionary named Alta Washburn built one with the support of both Indian leadership and like-minded white missionaries.

When white missionaries failed to actualize the indigenous principle in Indian congregations, a maverick Navajo preacher named Charlie Lee took control of his church in order to lead by example. When the AG gave Indians their own national Indian representative but denied the position power, financial backing, or voting rights, the men who inhabited the position pushed for tangible power. In the summer of 2007, the current national Native American representative, a Mohawk named John Maracle, became the first American Indian elected to a seat on the AG Executive Presbytery. As much as the AG changed its Native converts, Native Pentecostals forced the AG to change, showing how a small minority group could carve out its own place within American Pentecostalism despite considerable, almost formidable, obstacles.

The Indigenous Principle as Practice

This book argues that American Indian Pentecostals and a few liberal-minded white female missionaries took the theology behind the AG's missionary work—the indigenous principle[6]—and gave birth to a new form of religious practice that allowed them to negotiate their own complicated place within the AG. In doing this, they embraced a colonizing theology and transformed it into a form of resistance that allowed them to exercise autonomy within Pentecostalism. The indigenous principle developed into a practice through Native Pentecostals' own missionary work and through their development of Native leaders and clergy, their support for Native Bible colleges, and their fight for national leadership and recognition within the denomination. By understanding the indigenous principle as the main catalyst for Native Pentecostals' religious practices within the AG, we move away from the typical missionary narrative of the colonized and colonizer and instead delve deeper into how Native peoples shaped their own religious identity, autonomy, and theology within a majority-white denomination.

This book does not intend to follow the format of classic denominational history, but it does engage many of the contours of the AG in order to bring out the rich ways that American Indians lived and practiced their Pentecostalism. The AG, in many ways, is just one way to look into the prism that is Native Pentecostalism, and I chose it for three main reasons. First, it has the most extensive archive of a Pentecostal group's interactions with American Indians. Second, the AG has a well-developed Pentecostal theology of missions, including missions to Native peoples, which allows the reader to see how they interacted with a distinct missionary theology. Third, the AG is a clearly structured Pentecostal organization—in that way it is easier to work with in comparison to nondenominational independent Pentecostal churches, which often have distinct differences in theology or missionary methods. Scholars need to be very careful to not lump all Pentecostal groups together, because while all Pentecostals share similarities, some are unique in their theology as well as how they approach their own religiosity. Moreover, not all Native Pentecostal practices are the same as those practiced by Native members of the AG, but I chose the AG as a case study in order to see the intersection of practice, theology, and Native autonomy. Therefore, I choose to root the book in the history of the AG and its theology in order to give a fuller rendering of Native Pentecostalism through the lens of one particular denomination.

Theology plays a distinct and important part of this book. American Indian Pentecostals are in no way unique in taking a theology created by white Christians for evangelization and modifying it for their own means. Perhaps the most widely known example of this can be found in the religious history of African Americans. Scholar Michael McNally notes that, "although the mission to slaves was in part an extension of a power system that upheld slavery, the Christian tradition became a resource with which African Americans tapped into sacred power; fashioned a meaningful, shared culture; and criticized the moral contradictions of a slaveholding Christian society."[7] McNally goes on to question why scholars of Native American religions have overlooked this possibility up until recently. He answers this question by offering an important criticism of the field: "When absent of meaningful interchange with native Christian communities, archive-bound scholarship has taken for granted a notion of religion that is out of step with what most native people practice as a more all-embracing lifeway."[8] In other words, scholars must move beyond their own formal notions of religion and seek out what Native Christians understand as religion if we are to eventually have as rich an understanding of their engagements with Christianity as we have with African Americans. Although my scholarship is historically and archivally based, I made a conscious effort to go through the material with an eye for Native engagement, resistance, and the indigenous remaking of Pentecostalism. By doing this, I hoped to discover how Native Pentecostals shaped their own lifeways and their own religious practices beyond the traditional Pentecostal practices of tongues, healings, visions, and prophecy.

The theology behind the indigenous principle is not specifically geared only to Native Pentecostals but undergirds all Pentecostal (and most other forms of evangelical Protestant) missionary work. In short, the indigenous principle is the Pentecostal theology of missions. It is more often talked about in world or international missions within the AG, but it applied to home missions too, which would include groups like American Indians and Hispanics in the United States. The main idea behind the indigenous principle is this: Christianity should be rooted in the culture of the missionized, and in order to accomplish that, the missionary should do everything he or she can to create a self-perpetuating indigenous church among the converts that will be run, financed, and supported by the local Native peoples.[9] In short, a good missionary who embraces the indigenous principle will understand that the ultimate goal is not only to eventually cultivate local leadership but also to leave ethnocentrism and colonial ideas back in the home country and to accept the native culture he or she is working in as equally valid. It is, of course, easier said than done.

The modern form of the indigenous principle and the term itself were articulated by the Pentecostal missiologist Melvin Hodges, who worked as an AG missionary in Latin America. When Hodges came back to teach at the AG Central Bible College in Springfield, Missouri, in the 1950s, he began to write and teach the indigenous principle to a new generation of Pentecostal missionaries, one of whom was Navajo missionary Charlie Lee. After leaving Bible school, Lee took what he had learned from Hodges, returned to the Navajo reservation, and much to the surprise (and perhaps chagrin) of the AG, began to preach the gospel in Navajo and build the first indigenous American Indian church. Because the indigenous principle was a theology that applied to all AG missions, not just the missions to American Indians, many other ethnic groups that were missionized by the AG utilized the indigenous principle in creative ways, especially in Latin America. My history, however, focuses on Native Pentecostals and how they shaped their interpretation of the indigenous principle. American Indian Pentecostals took the theory and theology of the indigenous principle and in their struggle to realize both, theory and theology became truly *indigenous*—meaning, they reflected the actual reality of Pentecostal Indians' lives; in doing so, the Indians shifted the principle's original meaning into a practice lived out by Native converts. The indigenous principle was no longer just an idea, a theology imposed by missionaries upon their converts—it instead became a tool that those Native converts used to fight for autonomy within Pentecostalism; as such, a colonizing theology was reimagined as a form of resistance by Indians.

To some, the idea of Pentecostal American Indians, or even Christian Indians, is likely to be anomalous, even mind-boggling. Americans have long held a fixed idea in their minds of Native peoples as frozen in time—bedecked with feathered headdresses, shooting arrows from the back of sturdy mustangs, and practicing "heathen" rituals in front of a fire—and, indeed, this is the image that many white Pentecostals had when they arrived on the reservation to missionize Native peoples. Although Native peoples have been exposed to Christianity for centuries, and even though many practice some form of Christianity (either strictly or alongside traditional Native practices), there has been a resistance both in the popular imagination and within some subsets of the scholarly community to seeing Christian Indians as "real Indians." The implication here is that practicing Christianity is deeply problematic, because it is the adoption of the colonizer's religion, a religion that, no doubt, has been destructive to traditional native religions and rituals. Yet Native Christians exist, and many Native people have made the choice to become Christians and to engage specific denominations or religious movements that often try to sideline them as a minority voice. This is the case with American Indians within Pentecostalism—the believers in this book count themselves among the saints, just as any white Pentecostal would, but they often find that they have to fight harder to validate their religious experiences and practices within the AG because they are Natives.

Native Christianity is deeply layered, constructed, and practiced by its believers, as scholar James Treat points out:

> Native Christians have constructed and maintained their own enigmatic religious identities with a variety of considerations in mind. Like native traditions, Christian institutions can mediate social power and material resources and provide avenues for the development and recognition of religious leadership. Like native traditions, Christian liturgical forms can facilitate community reconciliation and allow for the fulfillment of ceremonial obligations. Like native traditions, Christian teachings can articulate beliefs and values that provide direction in daily life and in overcoming personal struggles, and that form the basis for prophetic critique and political action.[10]

Being a Native and a Christian does not mean that one is any less Native, a truth affirmed by many of the Native believers within the AG. It also does not mean that a believer wholly embraces the colonizing and ethnocentric discourse of many white-run denominations without mounting subtle and important challenges to white power, as many Native Pentecostals did. Finally, being a Native Christian does not mean that one does not seek to be a prophetic voice that challenges Christianity to meet new and previously unimagined needs. As Treat affirms in his book, Native Christians are a sizable presence among Indian people and need to be studied in order to understand the rich complexity that is modern Indian life.

This book moves forward and beyond the issue of whether Christian Indians have a valid and indigenous religious form of Christianity. I believe that they do, and my job is to show the reader how deeply textured and complicated those practices are among Native converts within a majority-white denomination. This brings us to the issue of practice; first of all, I want to focus on how using practice to understand Native Pentecostals helps expand how scholars approach Native Christians in general. Focusing in on practice is one way to change the dominant discourse in understanding Native Christianity. By doing so, I move the "focus away from missionaries and their intentions to what Native people made of the Christian tradition, in turn equipping us to appreciate the complexity and variety of ways of being both native and Christian."[11] This allows me to step away from the battle over whether an Indian can be a Christian and instead explore how Native Pentecostals actually practice their Christianity.

I draw many of my ideas on Native Christian religious practice from Michael McNally's work. McNally urges missionary historians to move away from the issue of belief and conversion, because both are so closely tied to the ugly history of Christian colonization and imperialism. By using practice instead to understand Native religious agency, McNally urges a "framework oriented to religious practice [that] can more ably encompass the varieties of native Christianity and more nimbly discern the capacity of native Christianities to negotiate tradition and change within the difficult circumstances of colonization."[12] So instead of parsing out the implications of conversion within Native cultures, my work focuses instead on how Native peoples live out their own religious identities, and how they take an outside religious idea (the indigenous principle) and mold it into a practice that reflects their own reality.

This holds with the ideas of Leigh Schmidt, Laurie Maffly-Kipp, and Mark Valeri, who have worked extensively on practice within American religions and who state that "the exploration of practice is, at bottom, an examination of the intricate exercises of power, the procedures of enforcement, the spaces of negotiation, as well as the subtle tactics of resistance."[13] Because Native Pentecostals were denied power and autonomy by the AG, and because they were treated as second-class converts, it was their practice of the indigenous principle that allowed them to subvert the power of the denomination, to confront paternalism, ethnocentrism, and racism, and to engage the denomination by using the AG's own theology of missions against it. How could the AG continue to deny them power and agency, when the very theology on which it built its missionary work urged missionaries to embrace native converts and treat them as equals? By calling the AG to account for its failing in living up to the indigenous principle, Native Pentecostals were appealing to the AG to live up to its own idealistic Pentecostal roots. If the Holy Spirit was to be able to fall equally upon all peoples, did that not include American Indians too?

In order to accomplish an understanding of the indigenous principle as lived, or as a practice, I understand that the mundane aspects of missionary life (both Native and white) need to be treated with the same authority as the more spectacular instances of Native leadership and defiance. In this way, I try to showcase Native Pentecostals and their white supporters in their everyday tasks—"the spaces of their experience,"[14] as historian Robert Orsi puts it. By focusing on the everyday battles that Native Pentecostals waged for more autonomy and power within the AG, I also show how "theologies are not made in a single venue only—in the streets or in the churches, at shrines or in people's living rooms."[15] Theology, in this case the indigenous principle, is lived in ways that are surprising to even those who live it. As my study shows, Native Pentecostals practice the indigenous principle in a variety of ways, within both the personal and public spheres. Building churches, encouraging Native leadership and education, and cultivating a national platform are all forms of religious practice that Native Pentecostals undertook in their everyday lives, because the indigenous principle informed all of these actions.

The indigenous principle is transformed in its lived practice into a communitist[16] theology. Coined by Native scholar Jace Weaver, the term *communitist* is "a combination of *community* and *activist*."[17] In such theology, Weaver asserts, "The community itself 'stands at the very center' of such an interpretative system."[18] For Native peoples, the community is the most important aspect of Native life. The same could be said for Pentecostals, who highly value their local church community, some would argue, to the detriment of the larger community. For Pentecostal Indians, the experience of salvation itself is deeply personal, but it is the push for the indigenous principle and Native Pentecostal leadership that leads them to engage the AG in a communitist way. Understanding the indigenous principle as a religious practice means that the Native Pentecostal community is at the heart of that practice—a community that values indigenous leadership and wishes to nurture it. Therefore, we must understand the push for the indigenous principle holistically as communitist within the Native Pentecostal community in order to discover how Native Pentecostals formed principle into practice.

Why look at the push for the indigenous principle as a form of religious practice? When most scholars think of practice within Pentecostalism, no doubt they refer to the traditional Pentecostal practices such as speaking in tongues, prophecy, and being slain in the spirit, as well as the overall Pentecostal tendency to embrace a spontaneous (and yet often routine in its spontaneity) and raucous liturgy. Many scholars are curious to discover how Native believers might fuse their own traditional Native customs with Pentecostal ritual in terms of the uses of drums in the liturgy, or forms of dance—and some scholars have begun to study the implications of this sort of liturgical contextualization.[19] Yet this is not what this book is about—chiefly because its main goal is to reconstruct the history of how Native Pentecostals changed the AG, just as much as they were changed by the denomination, and because the focus of the study is national, whereas a study of liturgical contextualization would be best undertaken at a more local level because it would depend on ethnographic research. Therefore, by looking at how a theological idea—the indigenous principle—is transformed into a lived practice by Native believers, a history of engagement, resistance, and the struggle for power can emerge despite the serious problem of often scanty and biased source material.

Although my study reaches beyond the issues surrounding colonization and race, there is no ignoring the reality that, in the early decades of Pentecostal missionary work, white missionaries found Native peoples to be culturally inferior to white Pentecostals. They were seen as uneducated, backward, superstitious, heathen, and even "of the Devil." Racism and ethnocentrism prevented some white missionaries from seeing that Native converts were perfectly capable of serving as evangelists for the AG. Indeed, the AG has a troubled history with minority peoples in the United States—its treatment of African Americans was appalling for most of the twentieth century, and it approached missions to Hispanics with much of the same ethnocentrism and racism that it brought to missions to American Indians.[20] For this reason, it is important to remember that as scholar Andrea Smith says, "The relationship between Native and white evangelicalism is simultaneously one of reinscription and contestation."[21] There is a constant push-pull between the Native Pentecostals I study and the AG. In some ways they adapt to certain aspects of general Pentecostal identity, and in other ways they fight their own denomination for power and authority. Native Pentecostals were always aware of their own precarious position within the AG, aware that they had to "toe the line" as well as "push the envelope" if they ever wanted to see any form of meaningful change as to their place within the denomination.

Beyond the indigenous principle as a religious practice, there is another compelling aspect to the story of Native Pentecostals within the AG that will not be surprising to missionary historians. It is that white female missionaries were often the biggest supporters of their Native counterparts, proving that gender played a crucial role in how white missionaries viewed the indigenous principle. Pentecostal historian Gary McGee rightfully points out that it was female missionaries who often set up and operated Bible schools in the earliest years of Pentecostal world missions and notes "that women held important posts in most of these schools, variously as founders, administrators, and teachers, [which] reveals the substantial part that they played in the shaping of early Pentecostal reflection on mission, mission education and missionaries."[22] In missions to American Indians, examples include Alta Washburn and women like Alma Thomas, who helped Sister Washburn to make her vision for an all-Indian Bible school a success.

Alta Washburn's place in this history is pivotal; without her, the American Indian Bible Institute (now the American Indian College) would not have become a reality. Pentecostalism has allowed women prophetic leadership since its inception, although women always gained more latitude if they worked as missionaries. Few women within the AG found success as domestic pastors.[23] Although the AG leadership was (and still is) largely male, women have taken on a variety of roles, including those of pastor and missionary.[24] In some respects, Sister Washburn's place in this history is unsurprising because the mission field (in both home and world missions) had long offered American women a variety of leadership roles.[25] Yet she is extraordinary for the grit and perseverance that she displayed. In her autobiography Sister Washburn does not take much of the credit for her work—like most Pentecostals, she gives the glory to

God. She exhibited some of the very best traits of Pentecostalism: pragmatism, a deep concern for the poor and voiceless, willingness to take on leadership, and a stubborn drive to do the best she could for the people that she served.

There is no doubt that Washburn drew a small circle of dedicated followers because of her personal charisma; she was clearly a force to be reckoned with. But still, why was it that a white woman would become the biggest ally of Native Pentecostal leaders? I propose that it is not only because Sister Washburn was an extraordinary woman, but because as a missionary to American Indians, a historically underserved missionary field, she was able to escape the AG's attention for a long time, and therefore was allowed more autonomy, room to innovate, and freedom than would have been the case for a conventional pastor or even a world missionary. This freedom allowed her to innovate in a manner consistent with the early Pentecostal women leaders that McGee mentions, even though her greatest work came almost five decades after the first generation of female Pentecostal leaders, and at a time when options as an AG pastor were rather limited for women. There is also the aspect that female missionaries have a long history of being progressive when it came to serving on missions to American Indians. One well-known example is discussed in Bonnie Sue Lewis's work *Creating Christian Indians*, which shows how white female Presbyterian missionaries helped develop Native leaders for the Presbyterian Church, an example that is eerily similar to what occurred in the AG.[26]

This book intends to be a hybrid—a new way of approaching both American religious history and Native American studies that is useful to both disciplines. When I first approached the study of Native Pentecostals, it was such an understudied field that I found myself alone, in the void. There is little work done on Native American Pentecostals in the United States—much of the work that currently exists has been undertaken by Canadian scholars Bob Burkinshaw and Clinton Westman and the American anthropologist Kirk Dombrowski and has chiefly focused on indigenous peoples north of the lower forty-eight states of the United States.[27] Aside from Andrea Smith's formidable study, little work exists on modern Native evangelicals in general. No large-scale study of a modern evangelical denomination and its engagement with Native Americans has been published, although several newer historical works have appeared in recent years that challenge the old and now-fading dominant missionary narrative that Native converts to Christianity were always bowing to the inevitable juggernaut of colonialism. Instead, this new scholarship, much of it undertaken by younger scholars of American religion, posits that Native Christians often found autonomy and power within Christianity, yet there remains a lacuna of scholarship on Native Christians in the twentieth and twenty-first centuries. Therefore, my book finds itself in a unique place and consequently approaches its subject matter pragmatically. It borrows from multiple disciplines. From American religious history, I root the work within the history of Pentecostalism, engage the ever-expanding theories of religious practice, and challenge traditional missionary history. From the discipline of Native American studies, I draw upon the work of authors such as Philip Deloria and Robert Berkhofer to explore how Native peoples are portrayed and "imagined" in missionary publications and to center the work within general Native history and the history of U.S. Indian policy. The point of the book is to see how the collective practices of Native Pentecostals within the AG were shaped into a small but cohesive movement that challenged the authority of the denomination's white dominated leadership.

The bulk of the book spans from 1918 to the early 1980s, although the conclusion alludes to events in the 2000s. The reason for this is to focus on the first generation of Native Pentecostal missionaries—a generation that is for the most part now gone. My goal was to make the voices of this generation as clear as possible, so that future historians of Native Pentecostalism could use this history to understand the current trends in modern Pentecostalism—and the role that Native peoples play now. I do not bring the book entirely through the 1980s and 1990s because my main goal was to tell the story of the mid-twentieth century Native Pentecostal pioneers. It will take another work (and another set of methods) to bring the history of Pentecostal Indians in the AG up to date.

Finally, it is important to acknowledge that all the actors in this book had an unshakable belief in the power of the Holy Spirit. This unique personal relationship with God allowed them to take risks that many nonbelievers might have found daunting. Pentecostal Indian converts felt that the authority of the Holy Spirit is what allowed them to speak up for autonomy and power for their own people within the AG. White missionaries who were sympathetic to American Indians used their belief in the Holy Spirit to innovate for changes that other white missionaries may have felt uncomfortable with. Together they formed a dedicated group that make up an extraordinary, if small, chapter in the history of American Pentecostalism.

Problems of the Supernatural

Pentecostals expected contact with the supernatural. According to historian Grant Wacker, a "longing for direct contact with the divine in a number of ways" characterizes Pentecostalism.[28] The movement's emphasis on healing, speaking in tongues, prophecy, and a personal relationship with God meant believers experienced God as present in their everyday lives. Accounts of divine revelation and miraculous healings permeate this study, and those descriptions of the supernatural create another analytical dilemma for my work.

I take Pentecostal (both white and Indian) beliefs seriously as expressions of an authentic religious experience. The anthropologist Glenn Hinson points out that Pentecostal believers' lives revolved around the experiences of the divine, which heavily influence how they related to each other: "To ignore these matters is to deny the saints' experiential world and thus to craft a portrait that speaks more to academic understandings than the lived reality of believers."[29] Understanding the lived reality of believers in this history is crucial, because without it we run the risk of losing large portions of the story.

For this reason, I straightforwardly present the believers' explanations of the miraculous. Most often, the miraculous appears in the forms of physical healing, but it also occurs in other ways, such as Alta Washburn's revelations from God. (According to her autobiography, God spoke to her often.) In the case of Rodger Cree, a Mohawk evangelist, he experienced a vision of an Indian woman crying out in hunger and pain that led him to his first missionary posting in the Hudson Bay region of Canada.[30] Pentecostal history requires that I capture how Pentecostals related to the divine—how the Holy Spirit was ever present in their lives. If I removed the miraculous and divine from this story, I would remove much of the richness and uniqueness of the Pentecostal experience, which differentiated Pentecostals from other Christian groups: it was an experience that touched all the senses and one that "epitomized the uninhibited expression of raw religious emotion."[31]

My acceptance, however, of Pentecostal explanations of the miraculous does not mean that I do not search for other forms of understanding in the sources. Most AG missionaries (both white and Indian) ascribed the motivations behind their work to God's will and the revelations of Holy Spirit. That they believed this does not mean that, as a historian, I cannot tease out other motivations revealed by the sources. The key to telling a history that is meaningful to both believers and historians is to elucidate underlying motivations while respecting Pentecostals' own interpretations of their actions. Native and white Pentecostal believers reported miracles throughout the sources. The importance lies not in understanding whether the miracles *actually* happened, but in understanding *how* the miraculous enriches the historical underpinnings of the AG's mission history. In other words, I seek to understand what roles the miraculous and the divine played in the everyday, mundane lives of both Indian and white missionaries.

The issue of the miraculous is one of the key factors that helps explain why Pentecostal Christianity took hold among some Indian populations. First of all, for some Indians, Pentecostalism filled a need. Traditional Indian religions were rich in their variety, yet they did exhibit some commonalities. Almost all traditional Indian religions included both physical and spiritual healing.[32] The same should be said for Pentecostalism, which emphasized not only bodily healing from illness or hurt but also spiritual healing from the mental terrors of life. Historians of Pentecostalism in Latin America observe a similar connection—Pentecostal healing and belief helped people overcome alcohol and gambling problems and stabilized the family structure.[33] North American Pentecostal Indians fit into this same pattern. Pentecostal healing gave them one way to cope with the hardships of reservation life, such as substance abuse, physical abuse, poverty, and the breakdown of the traditional family structure in the modern reservation system.

Along with healing, Pentecostalism offered closeness to the divine. In Pentecostalism God was ever present and personal, and he revealed himself in various ways—through prophecy, visions, and prayer. Again, as with the important role of healing in Native traditions, vision quests or revelations were common in traditional Indian religions.[34] Indian evangelists often spoke about points of revelation or visions that they experienced, such as Rodger Cree's observation that a ball of fire came down upon his head when he first started speaking in tongues or Charlie Lee's search for God on the top of a mesa while herding sheep.[35] Such encounters with the divine were common in Native traditions, but they understood these examples within a Christian context. Thus, divine experiences and healing powers, essential features of Pentecostalism, likely made it an attractive form of Christianity for American Indians, because it absorbed already familiar forms of religious practice and allowed them to form their own new practices as Pentecostals.

Sources

The primary sources that I use in this work largely come from the Assemblies of God archives at the Flower Pentecostal Heritage Center in Springfield, Missouri. I amassed a variety of materials including a few autobiographies, fundraising letters, official letters, official missionary files, surveys, minutes from a variety of planning meetings, and the General Council minutes. I interviewed one of the last missionaries from the first generation of Native leaders, Brother Rodger Cree. I also interviewed Alta Washburn's close friend Sister Alma Thomas, as well as the former editor of the *Pentecostal Evangel*, the late Sister Ruth Lyon. I have also interviewed and remained in contact with the current Native American representative, Brother John Maracle. Yet, even with these sources, this project would not have been possible without the archived articles of the *Pentecostal Evangel (PE)*.

Anyone who studies American Pentecostalism knows the importance of periodical sources in the reconstruction of its history. The flagship periodical of the AG, the *PE* is published weekly and covers a wide variety of AG news while also serving as an evangelistic tool. Because other sources have gaps and are especially likely to omit names and dates, I relied on the *PE* to reconstruct a timeline of important people and events in the history of the home missions to American Indians. The *PE* also captured the voices of Native leaders, now long gone, because it was the main platform from which they could speak to a general Pentecostal audience. Native leaders often published articles in the *PE*, including testimonials as well as their hopes for the success of the AG missions program.[36]

Along with providing a timeline and an outline of important events, the *PE* is useful because the reporters wrote in an accessible, testimonial manner. This orientation toward the popular means that Native Pentecostal voices are showcased in its pages, because the AG had a vested interest in sharing these stories as evangelistic tools.[37] The emphasis on egalitarianism within Pentecostalism meant that everyday white Pentecostals wanted to hear the voices of American Indian Pentecostals, and this interest clearly created enough demand among the readership that the *PE* paid attention.

Of course, there are potential pitfalls when using the *PE* as a source. As the official mouthpiece of the AG, the *PE* presented only accounts approved by denominational leadership—that usually meant accounts favorable to the AG. Testimonials filled the pages of the *PE*, but no apostate stories appeared. This bias means that one has to read carefully for any signs of discontent among missionaries and Pentecostal Indians. Their opinions, when given, always appear edited.[38] It is also important to remember that Pentecostals rarely take credit for their actions; they always give credit to God. Yet careful reading between the lines, coupled with the information from the other sources, fleshes out a fuller story.[39] It is also important to note that at times the *PE* gives misspellings of place names and people, or even the wrong names, and at times some of the information is incomplete. When I can I have noted this in the manuscript, but sometimes, with almost no other way to cross-check the information, I had to simply rely on the *PE*.

In this work, I wrestle with the same problem that many other works of Native American studies have confronted: whites who were interacting with American Indians recorded the majority of the information. How does a historian accurately gauge the Native story through white sources? Although the white Pentecostal elite controlled the *PE*, fortunately it also published the writing of Indian Pentecostals. I have also benefited from modern-day Indian Pentecostal leaders who were willing to share their stories with me and by testimonials, autobiographies, and the letters of some past leaders. So, although many of the sources are filtered, I have sifted through them while keeping in mind my priority to privilege voices of American Indian Pentecostals. I focus mainly on the Indian leaders within the AG because they were the Pentecostal Indians who were present in the sources. Whenever possible, I try to bring out the voices of the Pentecostal Indian laity, but those sources in the literature remain few.[40]

Terminology

Finally, I have a few thoughts on the use of specific language in this work. I chose to use the terms "American Indian" and "Indian" because they are the terms used by the sources, and to use another term would be jarring to the narrative structure of this book. When talking about the non-white actors in this work I often switch back and forth between "Native" and "Indian." When capitalized, "Native" is specifically referring to Native Americans; when lowercase, "native" refers simply to native peoples in general. Wherever possible, I give the tribal designation of the Native actors. In the case of the Tohono O' Odham tribe of southern Arizona, I use the other tribal name "Papago" in order to stay in synchrony with the sources. Finally, when I use the designation "Pentecostal Indians," it is important to remember that I am specifically referring to those within the AG. Other Native Pentecostal, charismatic, and evangelical believers who do not belong to the AG exist, but this history refers only to those who identify with the AG.

I use the designation "brother" and "sister" when referring to both the white and Native Pentecostal actors in this history to remain consistent with the sources and to stress the communal, egalitarian Pentecostal ethos—one that in theory extended beyond markers of race or social status. When I can, I give the first names of all actors in this story, but often the sources give only the last names. For female missionaries, this is especially true—they usually were identified only by their husbands' names in the *PE* and typically lacked a missionary file if they were appointed to work alongside their husbands. In those cases, I identify the missionary only as "Sister" with her last name. When referring to God in this book I used the gender pronoun "he" to remain consistent with the sources.

Finally, a few words on what this book does not include. This book focuses on Native Americans affiliated with the Assemblies of God in the lower forty-eight states of the United States. A few Canadian evangelists are included, but that is because they spent most of their careers in the United States. There is an extensive history of Pentecostalism among Canadian first peoples, but this work does not directly deal with it. This book focuses exclusively on AG Pentecostalism, and while there are Native Pentecostals in the Church of God (Cleveland) and in independent Pentecostal churches, they are not included for methodological reasons. Also, while the AG carried out extensive missionary work to Native peoples in Alaska, that history is so different from that of Native people in the lower forty-eight states due to distinct differences in culture and geography that it deserves a separate book-length treatment. Finally, I made the decision to not include the AG missions to the Lumbee people of North Carolina, who have Native leaders and their own Bible College, on the advice of AG Native Pentecostal leaders. The reason for this decision is similar to my decision to not include Alaska in this study—including the Lumbee would have made this a two-volume work, as the Lumbee deserve a separate book-length treatment because of the extensive nature of Pentecostalism among the tribe.

Overview

This book is organized both chronologically and thematically. Chapter 1 focuses on the AG and the roots of its missionary program to American Indians. This chapter goes into a great deal of detail explaining the indigenous principle and its importance to Pentecostal missionary theology. It closes by highlighting the beginnings of AG's missions to American Indians. Chapter 2 explores the lives of both Native and white missionaries from the 1930s to 1960, their conversion narratives, and their different approaches to evangelization and church planting. Chapter 3 considers the response of Native missionaries in the 1950s and 1960s to white critiques on traditional religions, their redefinition of Pentecostal healing on their own terms, and their portrayal of themselves as both Indians and Pentecostals. Chapter 4 tells the story of the Native students of American Indian College and its white missionary founder, Alta Washburn, and how the fight for an all-Indian Bible school was a move toward forcing the AG to acknowledge the importance of the indigenous principle. It also explores the leadership of Navajo evangelist Charlie Lee, who founded the first indigenous AG church among a federally recognized tribe. Chapter 5 focuses on Cherokee evangelist John McPherson, the first national American Indian representative for the AG, and how in the 1970s the Native leadership worked to force the white AG leadership to acknowledge that Native leadership was essential to spreading the gospel among Native Americans. In the epilogue, I reflect on how understanding a particular theology as a *practice* can inform American religious history and change how scholars of Native history approach the often troubling and complicated waters of missionary history.

Closing Thoughts

Working with groups of people who remain alive and who continue negotiating complicated religious identities presents a sticky problem. Andrea Smith publicly grapples with this problem in her work: when scholars step into modern religious communities to study them, they inevitably become tied to those communities. This is, perhaps, the main reason that scholars do not work on modern Native missionary history—it raises difficult questions of churches, Native people, and the scholars themselves. Even though this history relies heavily on archival sources, I remain well aware that I have written a history that Native Pentecostals themselves might read and that the AG will notice. For that reason I strive for both fairness and historical accuracy.

The perspective of the researcher is also something that cannot be ignored. I will note that I am the great-granddaughter of an early Mexican American Pentecostal preacher. My mother remembers her grandfather, Rogelio Lopez, as the pastor of a tiny Pentecostal church in East Los Angeles on Brooklyn Ave. My maternal grandmother, who was raised Catholic, converted to Pentecostalism in an AG church, along with her sisters, when my mother was a young adult. Although I was raised, and remain, a progressive Catholic, I remember from a very young age my grandmother reading her Bible at the breakfast table while drinking her coffee in the morning. For many years I had no idea that my maternal grandmother and aunts were any different from my family, other than that they were "alleluias," did not go to mass, and were forever giving me different copies of the Bible. There was rarely any antagonism between the Catholic and Pentecostal halves of my family that I can remember, and I was raised far from my mother's family's institutional Pentecostal influences.

On the other hand, I was also touched by the indigenous traditions of my father's family—my father's mother smudging her home to cleanse it for the new year is one such example, along with my father's own insistence that I understand the reality of indigenous people's lives in this country, and my own indigenous roots below the border. When I was nine years old, my father took me to Canyon de Chelly, and there a Navajo tour guide took us through the canyon and told us how the U.S. government starved his people out and forced them on the Long Walk. For these reasons, I would be remiss to say that I have not been shaped, in some ways by both halves of my own religiously and racially complicated family. I believe that this is to my advantage, because I know from personal experience how religion and collective identity is malleable, messy, and extremely hard to categorize. These experiences allow me to leave some questions unanswered and the story partially unfinished—because that is how the people whom I am writing about would view their own lives. This history of Pentecostal Indians is only a snapshot, a glimpse into a greater history that continues to be lived out by believers, and I feel that it is important to acknowledge that reality. I am also as concerned as AG Indians with the need for a fair and accurate picture of a marginalized religious culture. I undertook this study mainly for a scholarly reason, but one specific personal conviction underlies it all: my mother and father taught me from a young age that the true history of this country is one that must include all its peoples. In this I have tried to add my own small contribution to that goal.

Finally, I turn back to the opening quotations in this introduction. Both address a personal, supernatural faith. One is a young woman's confirmation of a calling from God; the other is a little boy's quest for the truth. Both are recounted from the vantage point of later life. Their belief in the prospect of an indigenous church and a Christ that could heal all—red or white—propelled them forward into extraordinary lives that they could not have foreseen. Alta Washburn and Charlie Lee were both in many ways ordinary Americans, living ordinary lives of belief, pain, and toil. Yet they showed that, through faith, hard work, pragmatism, and sheer force of will, ordinary Americans could shape the course of something much greater than themselves and change the course of a major American religious movement.

CHAPTER 1

The Indigenous Principle

Pentecostal Missionary Theology and the
Birth of the Assemblies of God's Home Missions
to American Indians

"I am still on the Lord's side. I am located here at La Moine, [*sic*] Cal. I moved here to get right among the Indians. With the Lord's help I have reached quite a few and have given out the Word of life to them. . . . There are some God has touched and I pray that they will receive the promise of the Father. I request your earnest prayer for us and the dear Indian people."[1] Brother Thompson's report of his missionary work to American Indians was the first of its kind in the pages of the *Christian Evangel*, the forerunner of the *Pentecostal Evangel* (*PE*). The simple language and misspelling of the place name (it is Lamoine, not La Moine) highlights his social location as a rather ordinary American—one who had chosen to be one of the first-known white Pentecostal missionaries to Native peoples in the United States.

This is the story of ordinary believers, both white and red, men and women, and how they harnessed the power of the Holy Spirit to transform everyday lives, institutions, and theology. This is a story not only of paternalism and ethnocentrism, cultural misunderstanding and racism, but also of innovation and leadership, pragmatism and inspiration. Chiefly, however, this is the story of belief, of the transformative fire of Pentecost, of the toil of being a disciple, and of holding a religious movement to its deepest principles. This is the story of American Indian Pentecostals and their white supporters, and how a small minority group challenged a religious movement.

This book focuses on the AG's home missions program to American Indians, how American Indian converts rose to leadership positions, and how those leaders took the theology of the indigenous principle and shaped it into a religious practice—it is what undergirded their rallying cry for Indian leadership, autonomy, and spiritual authority. This work focuses on the voices of the American Indians who were shaped by, and who shaped, the Assemblies of God; however, we must also consider the structure and history of the denomination before the issues of racial, cultural, and religious identity can be explored.

In order to provide a working overview of AG history and the theology that led to the evangelization of American Indians, I divide this first chapter into three sections. First, the chapter considers the birth of the Assemblies of God and the establishment and organization of its Foreign and Home Missions Departments. The chapter continues with an examination of the early theology behind the indigenous principle—the Pauline ideal that churches should be rooted in the culture of the missionized. The indigenous principle is the key to understanding this work. It represents the theology that Indian Pentecostal leaders utilized to argue for their greater involvement in the AG, and it is a theology that they lived, embodied, and practiced in their struggle for religious autonomy. The chapter closes by tracing the beginnings of home missions to American Indians in the years from 1918 to 1950, before large numbers of white evangelists arrived on the reservations.

Historians have written much on global Pentecostalism and its emphasis on world missions but little on the American home missions experience. Few historians seem aware that the AG features a long history of missions to American Indians. To be sure, at the turn of the twentieth century, American Indians were no strangers to Christian missionaries. By the time Pentecostalism appeared on the reservations, American Indians had experienced several centuries of interaction with Christian missionaries. Those missionaries, especially Protestant ones, had been deeply influential in the shaping of federal Indian policy, including shaping the policies surrounding the creation of reservations and the allotment of those reservations in the late nineteenth century. Missionaries supported the building of boarding schools, both federal and religious, to Christianize Native children and encouraged adult Indians to give up their "heathen ways" so that they could become like white Americans.[2] By the early twentieth century, American Indians were wary of Christian missionaries and often resisted them in the hope of preserving their cultures. In this climate, Pentecostal missionaries arrived on the reservations.[3]

The three sections of this chapter explore the beginnings of the AG's main difficulty during the early decades of the twentieth century: the juxtaposition of Pentecostal ideals about indigenization with the need for denominational organization. These ideals resulted in a strong American Indian leadership in the AG during the middle to late decades of the twentieth century, but the realities of denominational organization and personnel—both presumptively paternalistic toward Indians—resulted in white control, a problem that ran counter to indigenizing church ideals from the 1950s to the 1980s. The essential problem that the AG faced in its missions to American Indians emerges: could the AG stay true to its roots and belief in the power of the Holy Spirit and allow the Gospel to empower all peoples, regardless of race or nationality? Could it allow indigenous people real, tangible autonomy and power? Accomplishing this goal would have required a truly radical departure from the history of Christian missions to American Indians. The result is a complicated history of a denomination steeped in religious idealism, but also shaped by its own time and place. Thus, the indigenous principle did not trump the deeply rooted ethnocentrism and paternalism within the AG, but it gave Native Pentecostals a tool with which to hold the denomination accountable. White AG missionaries thought their work of spreading the Gospel lay at the heart of their identities as Pentecostals, but it was their American Indian converts who helped save the soul of the denomination by demanding that it live up to its foundational and most cherished beliefs.

The Beginnings of the Assemblies of God

In 1906, during the great Pentecostal revival at the Azusa Street Mission in Los Angeles, California, scores of believers received the gift of tongues. They thought that they were actually speaking the language of a foreign land and therefore could evangelize foreign peoples. Caught up in the fervor of the moment, many early Pentecostal believers traveled overseas and tried to use their newfound gift for spreading the gospel. *The Apostolic Faith*, the periodical that documented the great revival, reported this phenomenon. "A band of three missionaries, Bro. Andrew Johnson and Sisters Louise Condit and Lucy M. Leatherman, who have been baptized with the Holy Ghost and received the gift of languages, have left for Jerusalem. . . . Bro. Johnson has received seven different languages, one of which is Arabic. Sister Leatherman speaks the Turkish language."[4] These three missionaries constituted only a few of the many believers who thought that God had sent the gift of tongues for the purpose of world evangelization. Eventually, however, believers understood the gift of tongues to be something other than the gift of an actual language. Yet early Pentecostal believers remained undeterred. In their eyes, even if God had not given them the ability to speak foreign languages, God or the Holy Spirit had still given them a new and exciting faith to proclaim, and they fanned out across the United States and the globe to spread the word of revival and Pentecost.

As a denomination, the Assemblies of God came into being partly if not largely because of the Pentecostal missionary impulse.[5] The early years following Azusa Street were chaotic and decentralized, with believers moving from revival to revival, congregation to congregation. Missionaries with neither formal ties to a congregation nor financial support launched themselves on faith missions.[6] Yet early Pentecostalism lacked organization. The gifts and authority of the Holy Spirit meant that most of its early leaders were men and women called to the faith rather than those who had formal training to be leaders. The resulting lack of organization presented numerous problems for early Pentecostals.

In 1913, the mostly white and loosely organized Pentecostal leadership in the Midwest sent out a letter to other pioneers in the movement and advertised in Pentecostal periodicals that it wanted to organize a general council of all Pentecostals.[7] These leaders drew mainly from four Pentecostal groups: Charles Parham's following in Texas and Arkansas, the Zion City group founded by John Alexander Dowie, William H. Durham and William H. Piper's missions from Chicago, and Pentecostal believers who had left A. B. Simpson's Christian and Missionary Alliance.[8] These groups differed in theology from the Holiness groups that had initially popularized early Pentecostalism. Instead of coming from a Methodist, Wesleyan background, the groups that initially made up the AG came mainly from Baptist, Presbyterian, and non-Wesleyan Reformed traditions influenced by the Keswick teachings.[9] These groups did not agree with the Holiness idea that sanctification was a "perfecting work of grace." Instead, "they wanted to return to a position more characteristic of the Reformed tradition in which sanctification was understood as a process that commences at conversion, but was never 'perfected' in this life."[10] They also held to a second distinct experience in the order of salvation that they called baptism of the Holy Spirit, always evidenced by speaking in tongues as the Spirit gave utterance. These differences also meant that the AG drew from the white Midwest and South rather than African American Pentecostals who were steeped in the Holiness tradition.

Pentecostal leaders flocked to Hot Springs, Arkansas, in the early spring of 1914 to take part in the council.[11] Before this call for a council, some semblance of organization existed in midwestern, white, Higher-Life Pentecostalism, mainly through the publication of periodicals, the camp meeting circuit, and other conventions. The lack of a formal organization, however, meant that Pentecostals had no appointed leadership to speak for them.[12] This council allowed the movement to standardize its beliefs and goals so that Pentecostals could be more effective at spreading the gospel. The council began with four days of meetings that focused on awakening the Holy Spirit. On Monday, 6 April, the council organized itself for formal meetings and set forth its explicit purposes, later published in the Pentecostal periodical *Word and Witness*.[13] These were to clarify doctrine and reduce theological differences in the Pentecostal ranks; to emphasize missions, both home and foreign; to find ways of funding the missionary project in the most efficient manner possible; to charter churches under one name and one leadership; and to develop a Bible school network.[14] These motivations led to the founding of the Assemblies of God.

With such purposes firmly in mind, Pentecostal leaders elected E. N. Bell as the chair of the new council and J. R. Flower as the secretary.[15] After some deliberation, the council extended voting rights only to male members of the leadership, and a preamble and resolution of constitution emerged. This document declared the council's purpose: "Neither to legislate laws of government, nor usurp authority over said Assemblies of God, nor deprive them of their Scriptural and local rights and privileges, but to recognize Scriptural methods and order for worship, unity, fellowship, work and business doctrines and conduct, and approve of all Scriptural truth and conduct."[16] The statement evidenced the Pentecostal tendency to minimize a formal denominational leadership. The designation "Assemblies of God" originally referred to the variety of Pentecostal churches that came together for the council, but the name became permanent. Along with adopting the resolution, the council elected a small group of men to an advisory body known as the Executive Presbytery.[17] The members of the first Executive Presbytery acted on behalf of the General Council in overseeing home and foreign missions.[18] The first Executive Presbytery consisted of twelve men, most of them influential leaders in the movement. Though they were members of the Executive Presbytery, they all also ran successful ministries elsewhere.[19]

Once the council selected an Executive Presbytery, the AG began to concentrate on other pressing issues. First, it dealt with the need for an educational network where believers could gain a biblically sound education. The General Council began to solicit ideas for what became an extensive AG Bible school network. But with little organization and funding available, it decided to make use of closely aligned schools. The General Council selected the Bible school of Robert Benjamin Chisolm in Union, Mississippi, and T. K. Leonard's Gospel School in Findley, Ohio.[20] In addition, the AG adopted J. R. Flower's *Christian Evangel* (now the *Pentecostal Evangel*) as its weekly paper.[21]

The first General Council also took an official stance on the role of women, directly influenced by the new chairman, E. N. Bell, who outlined his beliefs in the early Pentecostal periodical *Word and Witness*.[22] Bell found no scriptural precept that allowed women to exercise independent leadership or to serve as church pastors. He did, however, believe that women enjoyed the right to prophecy, and he agreed that the meaning of "prophecy" could remain broad.[23] Following this argument, the General Council decreed that women retained the right to serve as missionaries and evangelists but denied them pastoral ministry or any office that would place them over men.[24] This official stance ensured that the early Assemblies of God functioned under a white male power structure. Female Pentecostals thus found themselves locked out of many options enjoyed by the earliest male leaders and would often find room to innovate only as missionaries.

The Beginning of Foreign and Home Missions

In the early years, missionary work, particularly world missions, is what drove the need for continued Pentecostal organization. From 1914 to 1918, the General Council met yearly and agreed upon major issues of doctrine, including its affirmation of tongues as evidence of baptism in the Holy Spirit. After 1918, the growing denomination concentrated on building its internal structure—particularly its missions, both foreign and home, as well as publishing and education. According to mission historian Gary McGee, "The period from 1914 to 1926 represents the most unstable years in the history of the Assemblies of God missions program."[25] McGee categorizes early missionaries into four subgroups. First are those touched by the Pentecostal fire who immediately departed for foreign lands without any training in language or culture, special education, or even dependable financial backing. The majority of these missionaries returned home once they encountered difficulties too hard to overcome.[26] The second group left for the mission field without any training but recognized the need for language and cultural study; these missionaries learned the needed languages and sought to understand the foreign culture of the country that they had selected.[27] The third group consisted of veterans from other Protestant missionary organizations. It included trained missionaries who had received the baptism of the Holy Spirit while in the field and then came to the Assemblies of God. McGee points out that this band provided much of the needed stability and organization for the foreign missions movement in the early years.[28] The fourth group of missionaries, who had been educated in the early AG Bible institutes, came a few years later.[29]

The movement away from complete faith missions toward a formalized system of mission support signified the AG's evolution from its roots as a boisterous early Pentecostal sect to greater structure and stability, as did the development of the AG publishing system. The Gospel Publishing House, the official press, had been instrumental to the denomination's growth and to its missions program. By 1919, the Gospel Publishing House had combined the Pentecostal periodicals the *Word and Witness* and the *Christian Evangel* to create the *Pentecostal Evangel*, the flagship periodical of the fellowship.[30] The *PE* mainly served to keep the early Pentecostal fervor over the baptism of the Holy Spirit alive, but it also functioned as a useful tool for early missionaries. The *PE* was the one official periodical that most AG members received, and missionaries were able to place their pleas for money in its pages. The AG distributed the *PE* as widely as possible, so that missionaries could use it as an evangelistic and fundraising tool. The Gospel Publishing House published thousands of tracts and hymnals for missionary use in both foreign and home missions. It also published Sunday school lessons for pastors and their Sunday school teachers. By 1925, the Gospel Publishing House had produced "111,000 pieces of Sunday School literature per quarter, two children's papers with a circulation of 37,000, and printed more than 5 million copies of Assemblies of God publications."[31]

The desire for greater stability led to a permanent educational institution. In 1922 the General Council secured a tract of land on the north side of Springfield, Missouri.[32] There, they built the campus for what became the Central Bible Institute (CBI), the first General Council–approved school of the AG. The General Council designed a curriculum focused on training missionaries and pastors and began to construct dormitories and classrooms. CBI welcomed all who believed that they had the proper calling and Pentecostal experience to undertake training for the ministry, regardless of their educational backgrounds.[33] The General Council also decided that CBI would be the model for all AG Bible institutes, so the AG developed multiple schools using CBI's curriculum.[34] Yet even with the building of CBI, the majority of early foreign and home missionaries (including those who evangelized American Indians) lacked a Bible school or Bible institute education. Usually they simply learned what they needed to learn on the mission field.

As noted, from the onset of the Pentecostal movement, missionaries evangelized other cultures. By 1919, the growing number of foreign missionaries prompted the AG to develop a separate Foreign Missions Department overseen by the Executive Presbytery.[35] J. R. Flower led this first Missions Department and began the difficult task of determining both a budget and the direction for the AG's foreign missions program.[36] Flower had to define a distinctly Pentecostal approach to missions. Would Pentecostals engage the world, as their Protestant counterparts did, by building orphanages and schools? Or would they focus solely on evangelization, in the belief that conversion and baptism of the Holy Spirit were the two most important elements?[37] Although most Pentecostals focused on evangelization, a few early missionaries, such as Lillian Trasher, operated orphanages or schools.[38]

During the first years of Flower's tenure, the geographic distribution followed the trend already established by Holiness missionaries.[39] Missionaries established outposts in foreign missions around the world, and when they achieved critical mass, they formed district councils. Flower divided the foreign missionary field using the model of districts for AG churches in the United States. The earliest foreign districts included North China, North India, Japan, Egypt, and Liberia.[40] As missionaries proliferated around the world, new districts formed. The creation of districts allowed for better organization, which enabled the AG to distribute its missionary personnel and funds more effectively.

The greatest problem facing the Foreign Missions Department in the early years involved money. Because most Pentecostals went on faith missions, they needed funds from supporters back in the United States, and funding was often undependable. For instance, publishing revenue from the *PE* originally supported the foreign missions. As the number of foreign missionaries grew, however, the publishing revenues could no longer carry all the cost.[41] As a result, Flower decided to revise the financing strategy. He estimated that missionaries needed $40 a month to cover basic expenses, $15 for each child, and $500 for travel funds to and from the field. In 1922, Flower set the goal of raising $233,800.[42] Meanwhile, the job of secretary-treasurer of the Foreign Missions Department had become too much for one person, so they divided the position. Flower stayed on as treasurer, and William Faux became secretary.[43] Flower continued to advocate for more standardization in foreign missions, pushing through guidelines that stressed the Pauline example of indigenous churches in foreign missions. He also mandated that missionaries meet the Foreign Missions Committee in Springfield, urged them to attend Central Bible Institute, and empowered the Foreign Missions Committee to set the standards of training and screening.[44] While some missionaries chafed at the new requirements, Flower believed that the new standards would improve the quality of AG's missions work.[45] Flower's early standards and innovations provided the basis for the AG foreign missionary enterprise. Although the structure and organization set up by Flower promoted efficiency, it also made innovation and inclusion of newcomers more difficult in the coming years.

While the Foreign Missions Department developed a detailed and well-documented mission statement and set standards for foreign missions, historians have largely ignored home missions. Unlike foreign missions, home missionaries did not benefit from an existing framework. Initially, "home missions" simply designated missionary activity that took place in the United States among groups outside the reach of mainstream Christianity. Officially, it remained under the auspices of the Foreign Missions Department from 1914 to 1937.[46] The reasons for not supporting a separate department for home missions remain unclear. However, we can surmise that given the AG's laserlike focus on foreign territories, the home front lacked appeal. Foreign missions were exciting—Pentecostal missionaries expected to encounter a new culture and new language and deal directly with "the godless heathen." Home missions, on the other hand, meant traveling to an impoverished part of the United States to work among people who were already suspicious of Christian missionaries, who had long suffered from institutionalized forms of racism and classism, and who in many cases were already Christians—just not of the "right" variety. Foreign missions were full of hope—they had a chance to evangelize people that had been untouched by Christianity. Home missions, on the other hand, forced Pentecostals to open their eyes to the injustices in their own society.

Yet some AG missionaries did feel called to domestic fields. American Indians were not the only group chosen for evangelization by Pentecostals. Home missions grew among the mountain people of Appalachia, Mexicans living in the southwestern United States, prison inmates, Gypsies, and eventually the military, the deaf, Alaskan natives, African Americans, and Jews. Over the twentieth century, the groups changed and evolved, but the outlook of the home missions remained the same: to serve and evangelize minority, disabled, and isolated groups in the United States.[47]

Articles in the *PE* before 1937 reveal that home missions cropped up here and there but lacked effective organization. Where home missions existed, the missionaries dealt with the unique problems of each situation on their own. This protocol, or lack thereof, resembled that of many world missionaries at the onset of the Pentecostal movement. But by the 1930s, foreign missions flourished among the AG and had an organized structure as well as goals. Home missions did not develop a cohesive structure and goals until almost two decades had passed.

In 1921 the General Council established a fund for home missions within the Foreign Missions Department. It also encouraged the *PE* to run articles and ads that solicited funds for home missionaries.[48] By 1927, many who were involved in home missions believed they warranted their own department. Yet with foreign missions, publishing, and education taking up much of the available funding, a separate department of home missions was not approved because of a lack of money. Some AG leaders also resisted the idea of establishing a separate home missions department, because they implicitly assumed that all Pentecostals would evangelize their fellow Americans.[49] In 1937 delegates reached a compromise, and the General Council created a new Department of Home Missions joined with the Education Department.[50] This decision led to a decades-long involvement between the two departments. The man chosen to oversee the Department of Home Missions was Fred Vogler, whose tenure led to more structure for home missions.[51] Vogler established guidelines for the Home Missions Department, whose missionaries would work in cooperation with the district where they were stationed. The AG encouraged the missionaries to attend Bible schools and established a permanent fund to support them.[52] Under Vogler's careful eye, home missions gained publicity in the *PE*, which helped with the recruitment of missionaries from

Bible schools and among talented evangelists who possessed passion but no Bible school education.

By the early 1950s, Vogler developed a national appointment process for home missionaries, which allowed the AG to ensure that they were qualified. We know little of the guidelines, but we can safely assume that they resembled those listed on the AG's ordination application from this period. The application asked for basic personal information, education, literacy, when one had been baptized in the Holy Spirit and if one had received the gift of tongues, if one agreed with the tenets laid down by the General Council, and if one affirmed the fundamental truths of 1 Corinthians 1:10 and Acts 2:42.[53] The first national missionary appointment took place in 1952, and the missionary was an American Indian—Charlie Lee of the Navajo Nation, graduate of the Central Bible Institute and the Santa Fe Indian School, nationally renowned artist, maverick Pentecostal evangelist, and fervent believer in the indigenous principle.[54] The AG appointed a man who would forever change the face of Pentecostal missions to American Indians and who would force the AG to examine what it really meant by the indigenous principle.

The Indigenous Principle

That an American Indian could be the first nationally appointed home missionary testifies to two truths about the AG's earliest home missions. First, home missionaries had established themselves on some Indian reservations well before the AG organized a department of home missions. Second, at least some home missionaries proved open to training indigenous converts—their goal was to send promising young Native leaders to Bible school so that they could return to their own people as missionaries. In order to understand the indigenous principle and the later struggles of American Indian Pentecostals who tried to realize it, we need to examine its theology and history in the Protestant missionary enterprise and its articulation in a Pentecostal framework.

Indigenous church methods were unique neither to Pentecostalism nor to Protestant Christianity. The root of the idea for the indigenous church came from the letters of Paul. Pentecostals referred to verses in Acts 13:43–49, 14:3, 16:4–5, and 20:28 as the "Pauline example," which provided the biblical foundation for their ideas regarding indigenous churches.[55] The first influential theorist of the indigenous church was Rufus Anderson, the secretary of the American Board of Commissioners for Foreign

Missions (ABCFM), the first major American Protestant foreign missionary council. Anderson's service to the ABCFM began in 1820 when he was still at Andover seminary, but he did not assume responsibility for the foreign missions program until 1832. His long career lasted into the final decades of the nineteenth century.[56]

Because Pentecostal missiologists often referred to Anderson as their inspiration for the indigenous principle, it is useful to explore his work, even though he predated the Pentecostal movement by half a century.[57] Anderson's perspective on missions followed a strict sequence: the missionary plants a church among native people; the missionary trains and educates a Native pastorate; the missionary gives Natives the responsibility for running the church; and finally, the missionary hands over control of the church and leaves.[58] According to historian William Hutchison, Anderson's work, based on two major premises, proved innovative. Hutchison states, "One of these [premises], the expected triumph of Christian religion and civilization, represented the conventional wisdom of his time and required little argument—merely occasional incantation at the expected level of militancy."[59] The second premise is more important for understanding the direction and parameters of Anderson's work for indigenous churches. Hutchison puts it this way:

> Anderson's program was a thoroughgoing trust in the working of the Holy Spirit. His lifelong campaign against the imposition of Western cultural and religious patterns, and in favor of independent native churches, bespoke no appreciable sympathy for foreign peoples or cultures; it rested on an insistence that the Gospel, once implanted, can be relied upon to foster true religion, sound learning and a complete Christian civilization—all in forms that will meet biblical standards and fulfill the needs of a given people.[60]

In other words, Christianity, as the inherently superior religion, would grow and by itself civilize the "uncivilized" natives if properly planted, according to Hutchison's interpretation of Anderson. For these reasons, Anderson believed that teaching natives English or founding missionary schools or hospitals as a civilizing influences represented a waste of missionary effort.[61]

While Anderson's theories sound remarkably modern and served as the distant inspiration for the AG's later articulation of the indigenous principle, a few caveats are in order. While Anderson successfully voiced these theories, he proved unable to enforce them among all of the numerous

ABCFM missionaries. He also never directly addressed the issue of paternalism, as later AG missiologists did—indeed, during Anderson's time, missionaries did not understand paternalism as a problem. Finally, Anderson's theories meant that natives would be able to run their own churches at the parish level, but he made no provision for their ascending in the church hierarchy. While native pastors in India, for example, could run their own churches, they remained under a white bishop or church board. Still, Anderson's ideas proved progressive for his era, and they foreshadowed the struggle other Protestant groups in America experienced when they confronted the problems of the indigenous church.

Early in the twentieth century, the Pentecostal movement faced the difficulty of articulating a position on foreign mission work. Coming at the end of the "Great Century" of Christian missions, Pentecostals looked to Scripture. With the precedent set by the Pauline example of church planting and with Anderson's advocacy for indigenous missions to guide them, Pentecostals tried to craft an indigenous principle[62] for their own mission theology. According to McGee, three reasons explain why Pentecostals decided to adopt the indigenous principle and expand it beyond Anderson's ideas. First, the early Pentecostals who united to become the Assemblies of God were, as a group, anti-authoritarian. They based their approach to missions on Acts, where they read of "independent congregations, directed by the Spirit, evangelizing their vicinities."[63] Therefore, they did not approve of a powerful missions board directing missionary actions. While the AG did eventually develop a missions division, for the first thirty years it mainly served as a fundraiser rather than as an overseer of the ministries of individual missionaries. Pentecostals believed, like Anderson, that a person only needed the Spirit and a working knowledge of the Bible.[64]

The earliest twentieth-century influence on the AG's development of an indigenous church theology came from the writings of the pre-Pentecostal Roland Allen.[65] Allen published a small book titled *Missionary Methods: St. Paul's or Ours?* In the book, he used the ministry of Paul as an inspiration and explanation for how to apply indigenous church planting to missions work. His ideas resembled Anderson's, but he was the first to write a detailed explanation of the indigenous principle that invoked the work of Paul. His book is also the first to directly confront issues of paternalism and colonization within indigenous church theology.

Allen heavily influenced later Pentecostal missiologists, especially Melvin Hodges. His book opens with a detailed exegesis of St. Paul's ministry from the New Testament. Allen leaves no stone unturned, carefully detailing everything from how to deal with miracles and demons to the more mundane aspects of financing missionary work.[66] Allen served as a missionary to China at the beginning of the twentieth century, and in his work he proved to be an adamant supporter of native autonomy and leadership. He rightly highlights the problem with white Protestants' fixation on appointing native bishops in a missionary area such as China.

> Before we have native bishops we must have native priests, and before we see native priests we must see native Christians. The roots of an indigenous Church are in the first converts. The training of the first converts is the important matter. The tree will be what the seed promises. If we plant brambles we cannot gather grapes. We cannot allow ourselves to be deluded with the idea that the appointment of native archdeacons, rural deans, or bishops will undo the training of the Church or amend mistakes made at the very beginning.[67]

Allen then launches into a scathing critique of modern missionary work, especially of the inability of missionaries to train converts to become church leaders: "We can gather in converts, we often gather in large numbers; but we cannot train them to maintain their own spiritual life."[68] St. Paul, according to Allen, did not have these difficulties, because he "founded 'Churches,' whilst we found 'Missions.'"[69] It might seem odd that a missionary would speak so disapprovingly of missions, but Allen had his reasons—the main being that the structure of missions was counterproductive to promoting autonomy among the people they served.

Allen points out what he thinks to be the main problem of missions: "The theory is that the Mission stands at first in a sort of paternal relationship to the native Christians: then it holds a co-ordinate position side by side with the native organization; finally it ought to disappear and leave the native Christians as a fully organized Church. But the Mission is not the Church."[70] In setting up and financing the mission, Allen states that missionaries lose their way, and they inadvertently (or consciously) become tools of colonialism and division among the native people whom they are trying to convert. Therefore, they are often counterproductive.

> There is thus created a sort of dual organization. On the one hand there is the Mission with its organization; on the other is the body of native Christians, often with an organization of its own. The one is not indeed separate from the other, but in practice they are not identified. The natives always speak of "the Mission" as something which is not

their own. The Mission represents a foreign power, and natives who work under it are servants of a foreign Government. It is an evangelistic society, and the natives tend to leave it to do the evangelistic work which properly belongs to them. It is a model, and the natives learn to simply imitate it. It is a wealthy body, and the natives tend to live upon it, and expect it to supply all their needs. Finally it becomes a rival, and the native Christians feel its presence as an annoyance and they envy its powers; it becomes an incubus, and they groan under the weight of its domination.[71]

The mission, according to Allen, then undermines its own purpose because the people whom it serves become disillusioned.

Allen argues that the only way to combat these problems is to model missionary work after St. Paul's own example. St. Paul, for instance, tended to not stay in a new place for too long. He would make converts, preach the word, help establish the roots of a local church, and then move on, usually within six months. He kept in touch with the churches by letters and exhorted his converts to become missionaries, and many of them did, as well as leaders in their own local churches. Allen notes that the people with whom he and other missionaries were working were no less receptive or capable as those in St. Paul's day, but that modern missionaries are more wedded to the missions system, their idea of denominational structure, and the proper order of how a mission was to be set up. To do what St. Paul did was risky—he had faith that somehow Christianity would take root and flourish without too much help, and that is the tactic that Allen wanted to see missionaries adopt.[72]

Allen's ideas were risky and radical for his day because they disavowed colonialism within missions and scathingly critiqued paternalism. For instance, toward the end of his work, Allen wholeheartedly eschews fostering native dependence on missionaries. "We have managed their funds, ordered their services, built their churches, provided their teachers. We have nursed them, fed them, doctored them. We have trained them, and have even ordained some of them. We have done everything for them except acknowledge any equality. We have done everything for them, but very little with them. We have done everything for them except give place to them. We have treated them as 'dear children,' but not as 'brethren.'"[73] Native converts were not children. They were not people to be patronized, manipulated, and left in dependence on white missionaries. Instead, if white missionaries were to truly be Christians, they would give native converts the autonomy and space to create their own communities, away from white denominational structures. What is amazing about Allen's ideas is that this most radical aspect was mostly ignored for about half a century, until Melvin Hodges took Allen's ideas and translated them to the Pentecostal missionary experience. Before exploring Hodges's work, however, it is incumbent upon us to explore the work of Alice Luce, who also drew inspiration from Allen.[74]

Alice Luce served as an influential white missionary to Mexican Americans and Mexicans in the Southwest.[75] According to McGee, she read Allen's work not long after its publication in 1912. "Although she initially felt that his suggestions were unrealistic, later reflection caused her to recognize 'the diametrical distinction between our methods of working and those of the New Testament.'"[76] In January 1921, Luce incorporated Allen's ideas into her missionary philosophy, printed as a series in the *PE*. In the series, she undertook a critical reading of Paul's letters in order to develop a Pentecostal approach to missions. In her analysis, she emphasized the power of the Holy Spirit, pointing out that it was essential that missionaries be called by the Spirit and only those who were truly called would have the ability to make clear and biblically sound decisions.[77] She also stated that such a missionary would heed the "checks of the Spirit" as well as the advice of others and would focus on preaching "only Christ."[78] Her most important remarks, however, came in the third installment of her series on church building. There, Luce stated, Paul's "aim was to found in every place a self-supporting, self-governing and self-propagating church."[79] According to Luce, missionaries must strive toward building such churches, even if they eventually fail. And if they fail, Luce argued, it could be owing to a variety of reasons, including the pride of the missionary or the inability of the missionary and his or her converts to really become Pentecostal and therefore be guided by the Holy Spirit. Failure was not an inherently bad thing—it could lead to a humble reexamination by the missionary and converts that might result in eventual success.[80]

Finally, Luce took Anderson's belief in the superiority of American civilization and culture and subverted it, by urging missionaries to "work harmoniously with others, whatever their nationality" and by noting that "we do not read of [God] making any distinction whatever founded merely on race or nationality."[81] She went on to state:

> Many say that these young assemblies need foreign supervision for a long time. Possibly so, but that is not because we are foreigners, but

because we are older in the faith, and have experienced more of the Spirit's guidance than they have. . . . The babes in Christ always need the help of those who are older and more spiritual; but let us make our greater experience, or spirituality, or capacity for supervision the criterion and *not our nationality*. And when the Lord raises up spiritually qualified leaders in the native churches themselves, what a joy it will be to us to be subject to them and to let them take the lead as the Spirit Himself shall guide them.[82]

Luce closed her argument by emphasizing the interdependence of missionaries and converts, noting that neither can operate without the other.[83] Luce's assertion that missionaries were not superior to their native converts because of their nationality but because of their spirituality proved both progressive and troubling. Luce was one of the first AG missionaries to distance herself from the idea of American imperialism and cultural superiority. Yet she replaced it with a Christian spiritual superiority, based on the length of time one had enjoyed the Spirit's guidance. Because the AG missionaries had more time in their faith than their newly converted charges, this still translated into an American spiritual superiority and paternalism. Luce never directly combated paternalism, leaving the problem for later missiologists to solve. Scholar Arlene Sánchez-Walsh rightly points out that "Luce's views on her mission field appear to be contradictory."[84] Luce was highly maternalistic in practice according to Sánchez-Walsh, as she tended to advocate for autonomy among her converts but also insisted on having converts carefully directed by white missionaries, for fear that they would defect to one of the Oneness congregations that were becoming popular among Latinos in the late 1920s.[85] Luce's example shows how hard it was for a missionary, even those who wrote about fostering indigenous leaders and churches, to actually fully practice the indigenous principle. As with most things in life, it was easier said than done.

While Luce exercised a tremendous amount of influence over the AG's missionary endeavors, the most important influence came from the Latin American missiologist and former missionary, Melvin Hodges. His work *The Indigenous Church* was originally a series of lectures delivered at the 1950 Missionary Conference in Springfield, Missouri.[86] Hodges's work saw publication in a small booklet. Gaining popularity quickly, Hodges started training missionaries to be followers of his indigenous principle while he was teaching at Central Bible Institute.[87] In many ways, Hodges's work echoed Anderson's, Allen's, and Luce's, but it was the first systematically to bring together all aspects of indigenous mission theory in a Pentecostal framework. It was also the first within Pentecostalism to discredit paternalism and nationalism. In Hodges's view, paternalistic missionaries who thought they knew best never actually received the gifts of the Spirit. Hodges was the first AG missiologist to say openly that the very nature of paternalism was un-Pentecostal and detrimental to mission work. A true Pentecostal missionary had to trust in the Spirit and the ability of his converts.

In *The Indigenous Church*, Hodges argued aggressively against the evils of paternalism, even to the point of offending his fellow missionaries. This bluntness emerges in the following passage, where he expounds the need to build an indigenous church: "We must found a truly indigenous church on the mission field because the Church of Jesus Christ in China, in Latin America or in Africa, is not, or should not be, a branch of the Church in America. It must be a Church in its own right. We should plant the gospel seed and cultivate it in such a way that it will produce the Chinese or the African Church. We must train the national church in independence rather than dependence."[88] Missionaries unwilling to give up their power and the purse strings to local leadership formed one of the main hindrances to an indigenous church, according to Hodges. He also inveighed against missionaries fostering dependence in the church by providing for the people and by not letting them have any say in the management of the church or fundraising. He notes, like Allen, that the mission system was deeply problematic to the growth of indigenous churches because it created financial dependence. "A frequent hindrance to the development of the indigenous church is the introduction of outside funds into the structure of the work, resulting in a church that depends on foreign aid for its support and advancement."[89]

Belief that Americans were spiritually superior (as in the argument that Luce put forward) simply led to cultural colonization, and Hodges, like Allen before him, urged his fellow Pentecostals to do away with that idea.

> An understandable but excessive fondness for the "American way" may make missionaries feel that American methods are the only right methods. The work must be administered according to the American plan, and Bible schools must be patterned after programs in the United States. Even the chapel must be built according to the American idea of architecture. Nationals find it difficult to fit into this

pattern. Therefore, year after year missionaries continue to adminis-trate according to their own ideas, and the indigenous church does not develop.[90]

Throughout his work, Hodges argued that native peoples, with the help of the Holy Spirit, were completely capable of running their own churches. It harmed the AG missionary system if missionaries failed to train the con-verts to do so. Paternalism, nationalism, or a belief in spiritual superiority should never hinder this goal. To allow that to happen, in Hodges's view, undermined the very nature of Pentecostalism as a religion for all people.[91]

Hodges urges his readers to think beyond the dominant paradigm when it came to missionary work. "We think our way is right simply because our predecessors followed it or other missions established it. Yet experience is teaching us that the modern pattern of missions is not sufficient to meet the demands of the day."[92] Hodges asks AG missionaries to look beyond the way things have always been done and instead focus on the efficacy of actually setting up an indigenous church—even if it challenges the domi-nant paradigm of AG missionary work. His argument focuses on the idea that missionaries should be open to trying out new ideas and actions in the mission field so as not to get stuck in a rut.

Hodges also acknowledged that it might be hard for a missionary to give up control over a mission that he or she may have worked so hard to establish. He notes that "after placing men in positions of authority or allowing the church to do so, the missionary should be careful not to snatch up the reins of authority again and bypass national leaders."[93] To do this, would be disastrous for the growth of an indigenous church, which Hodges goes on to elaborate.

> We teach that the church is to be self-governing, but when some important problem comes up, we simply tell national leaders what to do instead of presenting the matter for their decision. We disre-gard their position, set them to one side, and do as we think best. Although we talk about nationals taking responsibility and assuming leadership [sic], yet in reality we do not permit it. Nationals come to assume that when a decision of importance must be made, we will do as we please. As a result, they fail to follow us in our decisions, pro-ducing a corresponding lack of coordination in the work. At the same time resentments develop and schisms form between nationals and missionaries.[94]

As a writer, Hodges is characteristically blunt and pragmatic. Having served as a missionary in Latin America, he had received real-world experience that he translated into a missionary theology. While both Luce and Allen were also missionaries, and while Allen came out more against colonialism and paternalism than Luce did, neither displayed the sort of practical, matter-of-fact frankness that characterized Hodges's work.

Hodges's work met resistance from those in the mission field who were used to working independently, and who preferred the system that was already in place. Many missionaries did not agree with Hodges, and it took the AG a long time to implement the indigenous principle in its foreign missions work and an even longer time in its missions to American Indians. But Hodges gave his students and followers a carefully argued articulation of how the Gospel should be realized in missions work. Those who absorbed Hodges's work proved influential in helping Pentecostalism bring local Native churches into being.

Hodges had a particularly strong influence on Charlie Lee, the young Navajo artist-turned-preacher. While at Central Bible Institute in the late 1940s, Lee took Hodges's classes and wholly absorbed his teachings on the indigenous principle. When Lee returned to the Navajo reservation in 1952, he avidly embraced Hodges's ideas, much to the dismay of his white missionary colleagues. In 1976, after twenty-five years of toil, Lee realized his dream: the first fully indigenous AG American Indian church on a federal reservation. The success of this church, in turn, forced the AG to confront its deepest held principles and beliefs regarding the power of the Holy Spirit in missionary work.

Early Missions to American Indians: 1918–1950

We know very little about early AG missionary work to American Indians. Aside from a few brief articles in the *PE*, we find no other records. This section, therefore, depends on the *PE* for its reconstruction of where and when the earliest efforts took place. Although I must describe these early years in general terms, they nevertheless reveal two important early trends in AG missionary work to Indians: the geographic concentration of Indian missions in the West and Southwest (with the exception of the Mohawks in upstate New York), and the development of local Native leadership, encouraged by white missionaries, despite missionary paternalism.

During the early years of AG missions to Indians, evangelists seemed to go wherever they wanted. Their efforts toward Native peoples lacked direction until the end of the 1930s and did not really flourish as a movement until the 1950s. The first reference to a mission to Indians occurs in the *PE*'s predecessor, the *Christian Evangel*. In 1918, Clyde Thompson reported that he was living among the Indians of northern California near Lamoine (Shasta Lakes region).[95] Other than asking for prayers for success, Thompson gave no information on the tribe or the conditions, as the reader can see from the excerpt that opens this chapter.[96] After this one brief mention, Thompson does not again appear in the *PE*, but it is clear that his mission to Indians in northern California survived, or that he at least inspired other workers. In 1927, the *PE* reported about an outreach in Humboldt County among the Hoopa.[97] Aside from one short article on a mission to a tribe in the Battle Mountain region of Nevada, missions to California Indians were the only ones of their kind for sixteen years.[98] This emphasis on converting northern California Indians resulted from the strenuous efforts of the missionaries J. D. Wells and D. L. Brown, who wrote several articles on their plight. The articles emphasized their poverty, mistreatment at the hands of the federal government, and "spiritual darkness." The *PE* published the articles in order to raise funds for Wells's and Brown's work.[99] Although contextual information in their articles is scant, these two men apparently moved among the small bands of northern California Indians scattered in the region. In 1931, the *PE* reported that there were AG mission stations among only eight groups of Indians in the United States.[100] Other than the outreach to Indians in Nevada, the *PE* cited no other outposts. Thus, it is reasonable to assume that the other seven of those eight stations were scattered among the Indians of rural northern California.

At the same time, the AG's official focus fell on evangelizing the western tribes.[101] Two reasons appeared. During the early twentieth century, Indians emerged as romantic phenomena of the American West, a view that became cemented with the popularity of cowboy and Indian movies by midcentury.[102] Second, most of the Eastern tribes either had been removed from their ancestral lands or had not yet recovered from hundreds of years of cultural destruction. In a practical sense, then, the AG needed to focus on the western tribes, because they were the largest intact groups. The one exception was the missionary work in upstate New York among the Mohawk, which led to strong Mohawk leadership in the AG. It appears, however, that in the earliest years of Pentecostalism, the bulk of this work was accomplished by itinerant nondenominational evangelists, some of whom were disciples of Aimee Semple McPherson.[103]

Beginning in the 1930s, reports in the *PE* show that the longest-running missions and those that developed through early Native leadership centered in the western and midwestern states. In 1937 the AG decided to target the largest of the American Indian tribes, the Navajo.[104] Two missionary couples sent to live with the tribe reported in the *PE* of Navajo poverty and superstition. They sought, of course, to use the *PE* to raise more funds and recruit more missionaries for Indian work.[105] In 1941 the *PE* carried a report on a mission founded in 1934 in Washington State on the Little Boston Indian reservation.[106] Also during that same year, the *PE* reported the beginning of a mission among the Kiowa people in Oklahoma.[107] Similar articles followed, including a report of a mission among the Apache on the San Carlos reservation, begun in 1935, which diligent missionaries had grown and fostered.[108] In 1947, white evangelists launched a mission among Indians on the Fort Hall reservation in Idaho and another in Montana.[109] By 1949, reports surfaced of missionary work among tribes in Minnesota, Wisconsin, and North Dakota.[110]

The 1940s, a decade of slow but steady growth among missions to American Indians, saw the emergence of a few important Native leaders and their most ardent white supporter. In 1947 the *PE* notes that George Effman and his wife were conducting evangelistic work among an Indian tribe in La Push, Washington.[111] What the *PE* does not say is that Effman was a Klamath Indian from the area near the border of California and Oregon. The earliest AG missionaries who worked in this region likely evangelized him.[112] Effman was not the only influential Native leader who emerged in this period. In April 1948 the *PE* recorded the first "Indian Conference," a gathering of missionaries and American Indian Pentecostals on the San Carlos Apache reservation. The speakers included the young Navajo Charlie Lee, who had been saved at an Apache revival, and who, according to the *PE*, was "blessed with a fine voice to sing the gospel."[113] The young Navajo student became an influential leader, but at that time, Lee was simply a young Pentecostal exhorter, a Navajo who had not yet fully realized his own identity as a Pentecostal Indian.

Three other major Pentecostal Indian leaders emerged in the 1940s. Although they went unmentioned in the *PE*, their ordination files and autobiographical writings tell their stories. One was Andrew Maracle, a Mohawk missionary to his own people and the uncle of John Maracle, the first American Indian to hold a seat on the AG's Executive Presbytery.[114] A second was John McPherson, a Cherokee evangelist, who in 1979 became the first national Indian representative.[115] Rodger Cree, also Mohawk, was a third. Cree's family was evangelized by a Canadian disciple of Sister Aimee Semple McPherson during Pentecostalism's early decades. None of these first generation Indian missionaries were still alive in 2009 except for Cree, who remained active in evangelistic work to his people.[116] All of these men—Effman, Lee, Maracle, McPherson, and Cree—ranked in the vanguard of Native leadership. They all received the Gospel at missions established early in the AG or other Pentecostal outreach to American Indians. All of this happened long before Melvin Hodges's indigenous principle became a stated, public goal in the 1970s. The early emergence of these Indian leaders shows that some white missionaries encouraged their Native converts to join the ministry. So while paternalism plagued the missionaries of the 1950s and 1960s and was, no doubt, also prevalent among some of the earliest white missionaries, some also practiced the ideas behind the indigenous principle and helped develop early American Indian leaders.

Though most of the missionaries from this period were men and the American Indian leadership remained almost exclusively male, the most important white supporter of the indigenous principle and Native leadership was a woman. Alta Washburn arrived on the White River Apache reservation in 1948 after feeling a deep and supernatural call to ministry among American Indians.[117] She became their most ardent white defender and for her era proved radically progressive. Washburn never would have defined herself as a feminist, but her unshakable belief in the power of the Holy Spirit allowed her to argue in favor of Native leadership more forcefully than any of her white male colleagues and certainly more than any contemporary Pentecostal woman. Throughout the 1950s and into the 1960s, readers of the *PE* never even knew her first name—she appeared as "Mrs. Clarence Washburn"—but her importance to the development of Native leadership cannot be overstated. Like Lee, Washburn functioned as a major figure in the AG, and also like her Native brothers, she was initially overlooked by the growing hierarchy in Springfield. Yet she joined forces with American Indian leaders to confront the AG and forced it to be true to its own indigenous principle.

Conclusion

The early years of the AG brimmed with contradictions. The denomination came out of a movement that eschewed denominationalism. Pentecostals considered the idea of faith missions to be of utmost importance, and a missionary program developed to oversee them. Early Pentecostals created a detailed theology regarding the indigenous principle but found it difficult to implement in both foreign and home missions. Early Pentecostals were idealists who longed for the blessings of the primitive church, but they also approached the world in a remarkably pragmatic way. They wanted the Holy Spirit to lead them to be true Christians—people who would bring Christ to all, but without the cultural insensitivity that previous Protestant missionaries had shown. And yet, time after time, AG missionaries stumbled. While they longed for otherworldly guidance, their problems were stubbornly of this world, and they needed to deal with real-world prejudices and jealousies.

The earliest years of Pentecostalism, with its defiance of the rules set by the American Protestant mainline, were raucous and exhilarating. The first years allowed for a degree of racial mixing, the occasional leadership of women, and the ability of ordinary people to become extraordinary after experiencing the gifts of the Holy Ghost. For Pentecostals, this was an empowering era, one that looked forward with idealism and hope. While that era quickly faded away as Pentecostal groups split and separated themselves into denominations, the spark of anti-authoritarianism that the Holy Spirit gave to converts remained. Even as the AG became a denomination with all the bureaucracy and problems characteristic of a denomination, the individualist spirit of its people remained and, indeed, helped them hold the denomination to its ideals.

The most important of those ideals was the indigenous principle. Pentecostal theologians who were looking for a way to understand and approach missions adopted this idea, which Rufus Anderson had developed in the nineteenth century. Fully developed in Pentecostal form by Melvin Hodges, the indigenous principle was important in the evolution of the earliest American Indian missionaries. Without some knowledge of it, white missionaries would not have encouraged promising Indians to go to Bible school or consider careers as pastors or missionaries. Yet, while some individual white missionaries practiced the indigenous principle out of belief or pragmatism or both, the denomination as a whole did not make it official practice until many decades later.

The indigenous principle, however, was a theology that would come alive in the hands of Native converts who dedicated their lives to its realization. In order to achieve it, they fought to develop Native leadership, establish places of education for promising leaders, and tried to found indigenous churches. Their actions of trying to apply the indigenous principle to their lives became a religious practice—the fight for the indigenous principle is what distinguished Native Pentecostals' core identity as Pentecostals. While they spoke in tongues, experienced ecstatic conversions, and eventually carved out their own place within the AG, it was the fight for the indigenous principle that became the defining beacon in their lives and ministries.

Before Native Pentecostals, however, could move toward realizing the indigenous principle, they faced the twin evils of ethnocentrism and paternalism, which were aggravated by other factors, including the need for money. The need for funds forced the AG to develop denominational oversight in both its foreign and home missions. While both mission departments remained loosely organized for the first few decades of the denomination's life, they were eventually galvanized into structured departments that not only raised money but also determined standards for education and ordination. As the Department of Home Missions became more formalized and structured, it also suffered more from paternalism.

While the AG was dealing with these early contradictions, white missionaries trekked to the remote reservations of the American West and established mission stations, gained converts, and encouraged early indigenous leadership. We know little about these early pioneers, much less than we do about their overseas counterparts, but they established the traditions for AG missionary work to American Indians. Those early, unknown missionaries trained the first generation of Native leaders, men who came to the forefront of the indigenous church movement in the late 1960s and 1970s. But before the AG could move forward, it had to work on the problems of paternalism and cultural misunderstanding. So, although Melvin Hodges could teach the indigenous principle during those years at Central Bible Institute, many white missionaries out in the field struggled to overcome paternalism and ethnocentrism. Somehow, they had to come to terms with their purpose as missionaries—a purpose that would remain undefined until the American Indian leaders began to assert themselves as Pentecostal Indians who deserved a voice in forming their chosen religious identity.

CHAPTER 2

The Indigenous Principle on
the Ground *American Indians, White*
Missionaries, and the Building of Missions

Born with a leaky heart and not expected to live long, Luther Cayton was deemed chosen by God because "God spared his life and he now has no heart trouble. His bones were so brittle they would break with his own weight, but God also healed this condition."[1] Cayton, a Cherokee whose father was a holiness Methodist minister, eventually ended up serving as a missionary to his own people within the AG. Similarly, his contemporary James Phillips, an Apache, also came to Pentecostalism after a serious accident—he had broken his jaw while out on a drinking spree. Phillips was saved after much urging by his convert wife while in the hospital. Shortly thereafter while he "was working in a mine near Salt River Canyon and helping in the Assembly at San Carlos as he had time, the Lord called him to minister to his own Apache people."[2] Brother Phillips began a ministry among his fellow Apache miners.

Early in her ministry to the American Indians of the desert Southwest, white AG missionary Alta Washburn experienced a rare moment of doubt. As her husband carefully navigated the treacherous dirt road that snaked through a desert canyon in northern Arizona, Sister Washburn lay on the floorboards of the car, crying out to God, confessing all her fear and doubt. She wept, "Oh God, what are we doing here? This country is so strange and terrifying. And Lord, I'm not sure the Indian people will accept us. How can I preach to them when I can't speak their language? I'm frightened and discouraged Lord. Please strengthen and increase my faith right now Lord."[3] In Sister Washburn's mind, her doubts and frightened prayers were products of Satan's "taunts." She continued lying on the floor until she heard a response from God, who assured her that her life's work and calling were to spread the Gospel among the American Indians. Heartened, Sister Washburn sat up and told herself, "I had heard from my Lord. Nothing could keep me from obeying Him and fulfilling His call on my life."[4]

The first generation of both white and Native Pentecostal missionaries often experienced a moment of "saving grace," usually a two-step process of becoming born again and then being baptized in the Holy Spirit. Additionally, they all received a "call," a divine confirmation that they were needed in missionary work to bring God's word to American Indians. Sometimes these calls were dramatic such as Rodger Cree's vision of a Native woman crying out to be saved;[5] others were more mundane, such as Alma Thomas's sudden realization while she was having her morning coffee.[6] And even after the call, some needed yet another moment of divine reassurance, like Alta Washburn as she rode in her car to the Apache reservation.

In order to paint the picture of all the various ways that the indigenous principle came to be present "on the ground," this chapter explores two basic aspects of missionary work: why Natives and whites became Pentecostal missionaries in the first place, and the mundane details of building their missions. Doing this highlights the differences between Native stories of salvation and white stories of being called and reflects the differing approaches they took in building their missions and specifically their differing interpretations and implementation of the indigenous principle.

The initial implementations of the indigenous principle among white and Native missionaries during the 1940s through the 1960s were, at best, disorganized and fluid on the ground. It was during this chaotic and uncertain period that distinct differences emerged between the two groups in how the indigenous principle was utilized. Native missionaries embraced the indigenous principle simply because they saw it as the most efficient way to build churches among their own people and because it gave them autonomy and leadership potential in the AG. In contrast, white missionaries split into two main camps: the pragmatists and the idealists. The pragmatists, such as Sister Washburn, came to the indigenous principle because they saw the results it brought in missionary work among Indians. The idealists, who came to predominate, thought it was a great idea in theory but were hesitant to implement it fully. This second attitude, which I term a "halfway" indigenous principle, outwardly encouraged Native conversion but faltered in nurturing the leadership potential of the Native converts, thereby undermining the development of local indigenous churches and national indigenous leadership. It is this half-way indigenous principle that created problems and roadblocks for Native Americans in the AG well into the twenty-first century.

Finally, paternalism and ethnocentrism remained a problem for white AG missionaries to American Indians and are the two key factors in understanding why white missionaries tended to adopt the halfway approach to the indigenous principle. In order to explore these issues more fully, this chapter includes a brief study on all-Indian camp meetings. They were developed by white Pentecostal leaders to encourage Native conversion and leadership but set up in a manner that gave Native leaders little power over running the meetings and conflicted with the traditional powwow circuit. All-Indian camp meetings became the most popular way to evangelize Native peoples, but they also are indicative of how white missionaries did not fully embrace the indigenous principle.

American Indian Missionaries and Conversion

Once an Indian converted to Pentecostalism and subsequently experienced the Holy Spirit, his or her life often changed sharply. Pentecostal Indians embraced a new identity, one that often put them at odds with their Indian background and dramatically altered their lifestyles and relationships with family members. Many also found a calling to be missionaries to their own people. This section presents four different conversion narratives in order to show the preconversion background of these prominent Indian missionaries, why they chose the "Jesus Way," and how that choice led them to put into motion the indigenous principle by creating Indian leadership and autonomy in the AG.

The conversion narratives in this section represent first-person testimonials taken from the pages of the *PE*, autobiographies, and recorded interviews. For all of these men, conversion served as the major turning point of their lives. This indicates the importance that Pentecostals placed upon conversion and the personal testimonial. All four of the men likely told their conversion narratives hundreds of times during their ministries, and these testimonials follow common patterns. The predictable nature of the typical conversion narrative presents certain problems. According to Grant Wacker, all conversion narratives take the form of a "relentlessly stylized, three-step sequence."[7] This sequence includes the initial problem, the event of conversion, and the benefits that occurred after conversion. Virtually all Pentecostal conversion narratives fit into this structure.

Because believers recount them as a reflection of a spiritual journey, the authors "cast their words in a dramatic before-and-after framework in which the Pentecostal experience marked a transition from darkness into light. We simply never find an admission that things might have been the same, let alone better, before the transition."[8]

Another major problem for the historian is that testimonials in print are invariably "shorn of their real-life context."[9] While the testimonial offers the narrative of a life and emphasizes specific events that fit into this narrative, usually there is no way of knowing the full context in which conversion occurred. Only the memory of the convert—a suspect memory that has reconstructed the event to make it fit into the language of Pentecostalism—survives. Even with these problems, however, an examination of the testimonials of Pentecostal Indians is needed. The conversion narratives show how they constructed their own memories and, in doing so, their identities.

Charlie Lee grew up herding sheep in the shadow of the Shiprock on the Navajo reservation in the Four Corners region of northwestern New Mexico. From a young age, Lee was a spiritual seeker—he wanted to know the meaning of life and, as a Navajo, turned to his elders for answers. According to Lee, "My wise old grandfather tried to draw from the resources of his own years of experience to bring some measure of satisfaction to my inquisitive mind, but still the searching went on."[10] His grandfather and grandmother taught him about the Navajo gods and traditional beliefs, but it was not enough. At a government boarding school, Lee discovered that he was a talented artist. His talent attracted notice, and school officials sent him to the Santa Fe Indian School, a boarding school that specialized in the arts. His paintings, traditional renderings of Navajo life and animals, began selling remarkably well. By the time Lee graduated, he had exhibited his paintings at the Indian Ceremonial in Gallup, New Mexico, the State Art Museum in Santa Fe, the Philbrook Art Museum in Tulsa, the Heard Museum in Phoenix, and the de Young Art Memorial in San Francisco. He had also won two first prizes at the 1946 New Mexico State Fair, one for animal figures and one in the home life category.[11] Dealers all over the Southwest bought his paintings, and the Smithsonian Institution purchased one as an example of modern Navajo art.[12] Fame and fortune had unexpectedly smiled on the young Lee.

Lee realized that he was extraordinarily fortunate because his artistic ability had given him a viable way to make a living. Yet he was still seeking answers and felt a call to serve his people. Boarding school had introduced him to mainline Protestant Christianity. To him this was simply the "white man's God," an impersonal and detached deity who could not give him the answers he needed. The summer after graduation from high school, he visited an Apache friend at the San Carlos reservation in Arizona, where he encountered AG missionaries and Pentecostal-style worship. Lee reported, "For the first time in my life I saw a group of Indians worshipping God with enthusiasm and sincerity. They not only testified to the saving grace of God, salvation through the shed blood of Jesus Christ, but also emphasized the infilling of the Holy Spirit."[13] Upon attending several services, Lee experienced a conversion that he explained as "a personal confrontation with a Being, not a religious process of being initiated into an organization. It was a confrontation with an individual personality—Jesus Christ."[14]

When Lee converted, he moved beyond making a commitment to Jesus. "But to me this salvation which I heard about was more than a thing to help me. I began to reason this way: I want to help my people; lift them out of their ignorance and darkness. The best thing I can offer them is the story of Jesus because that is of eternal value."[15] Brother Lee believed that God had handed him a "burden" to shoulder—a "burden" for his own people. Shortly after his conversion, Brother Lee gave up his art, and in 1948 he enrolled at Central Bible Institute in Springfield, Missouri.[16] Although he continued to paint as a hobby, his art now funded his ministry to the Navajos and helped fund the building of a church. At CBI he learned about the indigenous principle from Melvin Hodges and decided to apply it to a mission to his own Navajo people. In 1951, Brother Lee returned to his beloved homeland and began to preach the Gospel in Navajo—a radical move considered risky by other AG missionaries.[17]

Excellence, tenacity, and ingenuity best defined Brother Charlie Lee and his missionary work among the Navajos. As an artist, his colleagues considered him one of the best of his generation. As a missionary, he lived out his life according to the indigenous principle. Brother Lee eventually built the first fully indigenous church in the AG even though no one in the AG expected him to be so successful. Brother Lee was different from many of his Indian contemporaries because he came out of a stable traditional family and enjoyed a flourishing career before conversion. By white conventions, he was a "model Indian" for his time: an accomplished artist who could appeal to both white and Indian audiences while still retaining a traditional Navajo style in his paintings. This pattern also marked his missionary work. Brother Lee was one of the first Indian converts who fully and publicly embraced both the Indian *and* Pentecostal halves of his life. For Brother Lee, choosing the "Jesus Way" did not mean that he had to repudiate the "Navajo Way."

Although Brother Lee had contact with traditional Navajo religion, he never fully embraced it as his contemporaries Jimmie Dann and Andrew Maracle had done. Dann was a member of the Shoshone tribe and a devoted Sun Dancer, while Maracle was a Mohawk who participated in the Log Cabin religion (also known as the Code of Handsome Lake). Although their backgrounds and beliefs were dissimilar, the same circumstances brought them to their Pentecostal conversions. Both Dann and Maracle failed to find answers within traditional religion, and both turned to alcohol. For Jimmie Dann, conversion formed his major turning point. For Andrew Maracle, the healing that followed conversion sealed his belief in the power of the Holy Spirit.

Jimmie Dann grew up on the Shoshone reservation in Fort Hall, Idaho. Exposed to the Sun Dance as a youth, he sought spiritual power so that he might heal and lead his people from their poverty and troubles.[18] The fact that Dann grew up exposed to the Sun Dance in the pre–World War II era meant that he came from a very traditional Shoshone family, as the dance itself was banned on the reservations until after the war and only undertaken in secret by traditionalists during this time period.[19] Stationed in the Pacific theater during World War II, Dann worried about death. He asked himself, "If I am killed, will the Great Spirit take me to the Happy Hunting Ground?"[20] Dann struggled to find answers to his questions. Throughout the war, he kept practicing his traditional beliefs to protect himself. As he explained it: "On the islands where our unit was stationed I often slipped away alone and sang the songs of our tribal dances, begging the Great Spirit to keep me from harm."[21]

Although Dann survived the war unscathed, he grew more disillusioned with his traditional beliefs and, after returning home, turned to liquor. Before the war, Dann had felt called to be a medicine man or a tribal leader, but now, unsure of what he believed, he turned away from all religion.[22] In 1946, white AG missionaries appeared on the Fort Hall reservation. Angry that the "white man's religion" had arrived, Dann did all he could to drive them out, physically threatening the missionaries and disturbing the worship services. Twice, Dann faced the authorities for his actions.[23] Three years later, a now-married Dann went out one evening with his wife. For lack of anything else to do, she suggested that they visit the AG mission.

He noted, "Hate for the missionary still burned in my heart. But when we reached the church, a great desire for cleansing from sin came over me and in spite of myself I turned my car into the churchyard."[24] That evening, Dann converted to Pentecostalism and received Holy Spirit baptism. He wrote that God had placed a "burden" on him: "Now for the first time I could do something for my people. I could tell them of Jesus."[25] Brother Dann later attended Southwestern Bible Institute and became a prominent traveling evangelist.[26] His conversion narrative fits the classic Pauline pattern of a persecutor turned Christian convert.

Born in 1914, Andrew Maracle faced a harsh life on the Six Nations Reserve in Ontario, Canada. His mother died in childbirth along with her baby. Because his father was a logger who traveled often, friends and family separated Maracle and his seven siblings and sent them to live with whoever could care for them.[27] In childhood, Maracle moved frequently among family friends and even strangers. At his first long-term foster home, Maracle became acquainted with the Longhouse religion and became an avid practitioner. The Longhouse religion gave his young life meaning. Maracle recounted: "Traditional dances were a form of worship and expression of thanksgiving for the seasons and their first fruits. To waste was wrong! Each individual was taught 'he was a way or law unto himself.' We were told to 'Listen very, very carefully.' I became infused with spiritual, cultural and political knowledge. I also clung tenaciously to my Mohawk language."[28] For Maracle, Mohawk identity imposed an obligation to embrace and defend traditional religion as well as his language. He became an adamant "defender of the faith" whenever he encountered Christianity. He harassed the missionaries on the reservation until one day he wandered into an AG mission looking for a meal. By the end of the evening, he had converted and found himself "cleansed of sin."[29]

Conversion did not immediately change Brother Maracle's life in the clear-cut way it changed Brother Lee or Brother Dann. He did not immediately become a missionary like his contemporaries. Instead, he continued working as a day laborer while testifying at church in the evening. The major turning point for Brother Maracle was a near-fatal accident in upstate New York. A large metal roller he was hauling with a horse team broke loose, spooked the horses, and landed on him.[30] When Brother Maracle woke, he found himself in a hospital, paralyzed from the neck down. The doctors told him he would never move again. Determined that God would help him, Brother Maracle lay in the hospital for six weeks praying. Then his cousin Lansing Maracle and his pastor came from Canada to visit. The pastor said: "'Brother Maracle, we are going to pray for you. Do you believe that God is going to heal you?' My answer came without any hesitation. 'I don't believe only God can but I believe He will heal me!' Pastor Freez reached out to place his hand on my head to pray, but before he made contact, another hand touched me and was gone! Praise 'His' wonderful name. I was instantly healed by the power of God."[31] Brother Maracle's doctor came to check on him the next morning and pronounced him healed. The doctor stated that Brother Maracle's recovery was indeed a miracle. After his healing, Brother Maracle found a new purpose in life. He enrolled in the local Zion Bible College in upstate New York so that he could become an AG missionary.[32]

While Brothers Lee, Dann, and Maracle hailed from traditionalist backgrounds, some AG Indian missionaries came from Christian homes. Rodger Cree grew up in a Pentecostal home, a farm on a small Mohawk reservation thirty miles from Montreal. In 1928, a traveling French Pentecostal preacher named Brother St. Arneault, a protégé of the Pentecostal evangelist Aimee Semple McPherson, had converted his mother.[33] Shortly thereafter, Cree's father followed her example. Cree's mother told her son that his father immediately gave up hard living. "He was a weekend drinker—he got mean and my mother would want to leave and go back to her mother. That happened several times. When he became a Christian it was such an instantaneous change . . . his salvation was so powerful that he never drank again. He stopped using tobacco."[34] Cree grew up in a loving home, which he described as "peaceful."

Like other Native evangelists, Cree encountered racism at an early age. He summed up the experience with a quip: "The French and Indian Wars never really ended."[35] He recalled that French Canadian children regularly tormented Indian children on their way to school. Angry after French children chased him into a deep snow bank and taunted him, Cree decided that he and his brother would teach the French Canadian children a lesson. As he told it:

> So we decided that this couldn't continue, so my dad had a fish knife, its got a bent to it. Course we didn't tell our parents or anything. So we took that knife to school. Sure enough once we got near the school, they thought "here come these Indian kids we are going to have our fun, and drive them off the road." So instead of our running, we ran towards them. I grabbed my brother's hair, and I had that knife, I had

that knife and showed I was going to scalp them. It was amazing . . . how quickly those kids disappeared into the doorway of that school. We were never bothered again.[36]

Pentecostalism was still a young movement when Cree was a boy. His church was a small independent Pentecostal one that the local Methodist church vehemently opposed.[37] Although he grew up in the Pentecostal tradition, Cree was not born-again until he attended a New Year's Eve service in Montreal at age seventeen. Eight days later, he received Holy Spirit baptism. He recalled, "I saw a ball of fire that was lodged in the ceiling—when that ball of fire touched my head, I began to speak in a different language, altogether. Supernatural."[38] A desire to go into the ministry seized Brother Cree, and he enrolled at a French Canadian Bible college, despite his hatred of the French. There, through the power of the Holy Spirit, he said that he learned to overcome his own racial prejudice. He recounted: "I remember going to school and walking and I heard someone say (in French) 'the savage has come.' The Holy Spirit kept me from turning around. . . . I learned how to deal with those people."[39] During his second year in Bible college, Brother Cree experienced a vision of an Indian woman crying out in sickness; he decided right then to become a missionary to his own people.[40] His first mission was among the Cree people of the Hudson Bay area of Canada, a posting that Brother Cree felt was providential, given his last name. He went on to become a traveling evangelist and missionary both in Canada and in the southwestern United States.[41]

Like Brother Lee, Brother Cree never felt that Pentecostalism conflicted with his identity as a Mohawk Indian. He fiercely defended the view that Indian culture is defined by language and customs, not religion, saying, "When you are Native, you don't have to do cartwheels, or play the drums, or put on regalia. You know who you are, your identity. You cannot dress it up."[42] Brother Cree and Brother Lee embraced language as a key marker of their Native culture and sought to proclaim the Gospel in Native languages, enabling themselves and others to construct identities that were both Indian and Pentecostal.[43]

Brothers Lee, Dann, Maracle, and Cree all came to Pentecostalism from different tribal affiliations, different childhood backgrounds, and different religious experiences. They all converted as young men, and each felt the call to missionary work among his own people. While each conversion was distinct, some striking similarities also marked them. All of these men had hoped to help their people, but before their conversions they did not know how. Pentecostalism gave them hope and the ability to reach out to their fellow Indians as missionaries. Brothers Dann and Maracle both struggled with alcoholism and anger toward their lives as Indians; Pentecostalism gave them a way to resolve that anger. Brother Cree dealt with hatred toward the French; Pentecostalism gave him a way to heal his hatred. Brother Maracle was not the only man who reported a major miracle; Brother Cree and Brother Dann also experienced dramatic physical healing later in their careers.[44] All four defined Pentecostalism in terms of healing: physical, mental, and spiritual. Jesus had moved from being "the white man's God" to the "Great Healer." Brothers Lee, Dann, Maracle, and Cree took their experiences to their people, hoping to find a way to save them not only from sin but, more importantly, from hundreds of years of injustice, racism, and mistreatment.

Besides healing, Pentecostalism offered these four men autonomy and leadership. As Wacker has stated, "The testimony clothes individual lives with timeless significance."[45] Brothers Lee, Dann, Maracle, and Cree all wanted to help their people in some manner, and in their eyes, Pentecostalism gave them the means to change the world. Upon conversion, white Pentecostal believers encouraged all four men to attend Bible college, which they did. While they were students at those colleges, colleagues encouraged them to become missionaries. Within the AG system, these Indian men gained opportunity because of the belief in the primacy of the Holy Spirit. In Pentecostalism, one needed only the power of the Holy Spirit to preach God's word; because all four had experienced such power, they held as much authority as any other Pentecostal, white or Indian. Like their white counterparts, they needed only a few gifts in order to go out and preach: a working knowledge of the Bible, a willingness to speak in public, and an ability to innovate. Pentecostal Indian leaders also embraced the supernatural. Sociologist Margaret Poloma explains how important this point is with respect to the modern Pentecostal clergy, noting that clergy are "also often mystics of the sort who may hear God speak in an audible voice, see visions and dream religious dreams, give prophecies, and act on the basis of prophetic meanings."[46] Native evangelists were mystics of exactly that type—they readily accepted the Pentecostal miraculous and wielded the authority of the miraculous to achieve their successes. While the testimonies of these four men fit in a familiar Pentecostal framework, they also show the motivations of men who truly believed that the Holy Spirit had chosen them to help their people. This belief carried them through all the difficulties they encountered in their lives and ministries.

White Missionaries and "The Call"

It is hard to get an exact accounting of the demographics of the early white missionaries, because few formal records exist. By piecing together information from deceased missionary files (and not all missionaries had one) and information from the *PE*, a general picture emerges of white Pentecostal missionaries from this period. Married men made up the majority of early white Pentecostal missionaries, while their wives assisted them in their call to the American Indian home missions field. A few unmarried women, as well as Sister Washburn, who appears to have been one of very few married female missionaries who were not assisting a husband, completed the missionary demographic. (Washburn's husband usually held a regular job and supported and assisted her missionary endeavors.) Most of the missionaries were "old-stock whites."[47] They came from working-class backgrounds and hailed from the American Midwest or South, two regions where American Pentecostalism already had entrenched itself by the mid-twentieth century. Sister Washburn fits this profile. Born in West Virginia, she spent most of her young adult life in Ohio before she permanently moved to the American Southwest.[48] Other examples include Brother Norman Rehwinkel, a white missionary to the Great Lakes tribes, who grew up in Milwaukee, Wisconsin,[49] and Sister Pauline Nelson, a white missionary to Southwestern tribes who was born and reared in Aurora, Missouri.[50] These are only three of those who served as AG missionaries, but they are representative of the white missionaries of this period.[51]

Most white missionaries to Native Americans were modestly educated.[52] Commonly, evangelists such as Sister Washburn had completed only the ninth grade,[53] while many others did not possess even that much schooling. Brother Burt Parker, for example, completed only the sixth grade.[54] A few, such as Sister Virginia Kridler, finished high school,[55] and almost none attended a Bible college. This pattern reveals the missionaries' time and place as much as their social status. The majority of the AG missionaries who evangelized during the 1950s and 1960s had been born close to the beginning of the twentieth century. By the 1930s and 1940s, the AG was just beginning to get the Bible college network off the ground, so it is not surprising that many of the early missionaries did not have the opportunity to attend.[56] Finally, an advanced education was not essential to white missionaries' work, according to the democratic and pragmatic nature of Pentecostal missions. As long as missionaries were literate, possessed a working knowledge of Bible basics, and were not afraid of public speaking, their success rested more on personality, ingenuity, and ability to connect to others.

Finally, the men and women who became missionaries shared a common motivation. All white AG missionaries understood themselves as called by God. Sister Washburn was serving a small church in Ohio during the 1940s when she heard of the trials and tribulations of missionary work among American Indians through the letters of AG friends engaged in such missions. In her autobiography, Sister Washburn recounted how she felt a growing "burden" to work among Native Americans. In typical Pentecostal style, she prayed for guidance and, in her mind, received an answer. "'Now is the time for you to take the Gospel to the American Indians,' He said. 'You know now where they are. Go home and prepare yourself. Tell your husband and your church and I will make the way plain for you.' With this communication from the Lord, an intense love for American Indians flooded my soul. Now that I had a confirmation of my call from God, I knew I must take the next step—a step of faith."[57] Because of her faith in God's call, Sister Washburn faced her husband and family and persuaded them that they needed to leave their cozy home and comfortable pastorate in Ohio for an unknown life in the Arizona desert. Sister Washburn and her family probably possessed some inkling of the hardship that they were about to face, but on arrival at the San Carlos Apache mission, the reality of their situation hit them. Sister Washburn recalled, "The first night after we had gone to bed, we heard a loud Boom Boom coming from drums in the distance. The dreadful noise was accompanied by loud shouts and chants. It sounded much too close."[58] The noise was coming from a traditional Apache "sing"—a healing ceremony for the sick. Realizing what she and her family would encounter, Sister Washburn reflected, "Mixed emotions filled our hearts as we were now in the land of our calling. . . . This was the real thing. We realized we had to prepare ourselves with God's help for a transition to this strange environment and people."[59] At that moment, Sister Washburn realized that her burden for missionary work among the American Indians would be a heavy one indeed.

Obstacles and hardships that the calling presented were common and even celebrated in Pentecostal literature, such as self-published autobiographies like Washburn's or the *PE*. Partisans saw these difficulties as a test of one's faith in God and in the guidance of the Holy Spirit. Consider the missionary work of Pearl Habig and Lorraine Hampton, two single Pentecostal women who felt a call in 1951 to the Arapahoe and Shoshone reservation in Wyoming. The two women arrived on the reservation at an inopportune moment. "It was sub-zero weather and Christmas was near. It seemed an inauspicious time to begin their efforts."[60] Both women doubted their call, but decided to put their faith in God. Their reward was a small but active group of converts. Again and again in Pentecostal literature a "burden" or "call" to missionary work was understood as coming from God. Following that call was therefore a test of faith. A missionary's "call" was theologically nonnegotiable. Few who answered the call ever looked back.

White Missionaries on the Reservations

Armed with the belief that they were doing God's work, white AG missionaries arrived on Indian reservations with little sense of what lay ahead. The first obstacle they faced was church building, in both the literal and figurative sense. Missionaries had to find places where they could hold services and then determine how to tailor the Gospel to their audience. Because extra buildings proved scarce on the reservations, missionaries found themselves improvising, often preaching in private homes, under tents or brush arbors, and sometimes in the open air. The struggle to construct church buildings proved difficult because they received no salary. They survived only on donations from the faithful. High rates of unemployment on the reservation only compounded the problem. Even after they won converts, white missionaries could not expect that their converts would have much to donate financially, although they could (and often did) donate time, talent, and labor toward the construction of a building. Missionaries pragmatically had to include their Native parishioners in the actual physical building of churches, because they knew that outside construction contractors did not exist on the reservation. The churches often looked like other structures on the reservation—modest rather than imposing. When the people could not afford to finance the church, white missionaries turned to public appeals to other Pentecostals, often through newsletters to their supporters and articles in the *PE*. How white Pentecostals built churches among Native peoples shows how they attempted to live out the ideals of the faith mission, the complex ways that they viewed their Native converts, and how some came to embrace the indigenous principle.

AG missionaries, like many other Protestant evangelists who embraced faith missions, were practical people who did not let anything get in the way of their determination to spread the Gospel. From the Papago reservation in Arizona, Sister Naomi Johnson reported that

> about six weeks ago we were granted a plot of land by the Papago Indian Tribal Council as a site for our church. We have been using a brush arbor in the summer and a tiny tent in cool weather, but our tent is too small to accommodate even thirty-five people so we are hoping to get our building up very soon. The Assembly at Healdsburg, California, and the First Church in Amarillo, Texas, have given enough so that we can start at once on the foundation. We trust that the Lord will send in sufficient funds for the rest as the need arises.[61]

Missionaries commonly worked on a new church without sufficient funds to complete it, as in Sister Johnson's case. "Trusting in the Lord" often meant that missionaries hoped fellow believers would send a check or building materials, once word of their need got out. In the example of the mission to the Oneida Indians, Sister Mildred Kimbell reported in the *PE* that in April 1959 her new church had opened even though it remained unfinished. She stated, "At present we are hoping to get a well dug which will cost about $500. Pray that God will help us. The building cannot be completed until we get water."[62] Sister Kimbell was fortunate if her only major need was a well. Often, for lack of funds, missionaries built only the skeletons of churches, leaving them without proper windows or insulation.[63]

Occasionally financial relief came from unexpected external sources. In the case of Brother Charles McClure on the Cattaraugus reservation in New York, local AG churches helped finance the modernization of his church, including a proper plumbing system that allowed for running water and restrooms. The local gas company, however, donated one of the most fundamental needs for a mission in upstate New York: free gas for the heating system.[64] Missionaries discovered that utilities, which most Americans considered necessities, were hard to come by on the reservation, where there was little infrastructure to support running water, heat, electricity, or the drilling of much-needed wells. Raising enough money to put in the basics was difficult enough for the missionaries; they also had to acquire extra funds to pay for the "luxuries" such as pianos, hymnals, proper pews, extra Bibles, and sheet music for the choirs.[65] With money so tight, missionaries wasted very little, even when it seemed to outsiders that what they had was unusable. Sister Emogean Johnson reported that for a long time she used a revival tent as a church while ministering to the Navajos and Hopis in Arizona. After much wear and tear, according to

Sister Johnson, "We spent much time mending rips in the old tent. It was a common sight to see my husband's head sticking out through the top of the tent as he mended."[66] Eventually the tent became unusable, and the Johnsons sold it to a Christian Navajo for the price of one sheep. The tent was reborn as a shelter for the local Navajo spring lambs in order to protect them from the cold and predators.[67] On the reservation, nothing went to waste—not if the missionaries or their converts could put it to good use.

Although donations from non-Native Pentecostal believers built many churches, in some cases Indians were able to fund their own churches. In 1950, Hoopa converts paid off the $800 needed for improvements to their church.[68] Because the tribe operated successful sawmills, its members were prosperous before the tribe was terminated in 1954. Few tribes, however, were as economically prosperous as the Hoopa, so others built their churches by sheer will and hard work. On the Gila River reservation in Arizona, the local Pima converts built a tiny church with their own hands. *PE* reporter Edna Griepp described the process: "Water was hauled in and mulch was made out of the desert soil. The ladies mixed the mud and packed it between the boards to make the "sandwich church," while the men did much of the building. Not a skilled carpenter was around to make even as much as a window frame."[69] The Pima converts took pride in their work and proved grateful to have a church building, even though the mud church was "crude," according to the local white missionaries and the *PE* reporter.[70]

Occasionally missionaries reported that a miracle enabled them to build a church or fund a new revival tent. On the Rosebud reservation in South Dakota, for example, white missionaries reported that they needed a new tent, but funds were limited. The missionaries came across a local rancher who "told of his covenant with God about a tent. His pasture land was drying up due to lack of rain. He had asked God to send rain before Sunday, promising that if the needed rain came he would purchase a new tent for Indian missions. Torrential rains came, bringing new life to the parched pasture land. 'Now,' he said 'I'm ready to buy that tent.'"[71] The rancher received his rain, and the local missionaries secured a new tent, seemingly through the miraculous workings of the Holy Spirit. Such miracles helped solidify the missionaries' faith.

For missionaries on the Southwestern reservations, access to water was almost a bigger problem than not having a church. White missionaries reported to the *PE* that their converts needed water so that they could make long trips from the distant parts of the reservation to the mission. Without wells at the AG missions, converts would not go to church because they feared that their horses (which were how many people on the reservation still traveled in the 1950s and 1960s) would perish from thirst or their cars would overheat in the desert. Wells proved expensive and required heavy equipment. The AG Arizona district superintendent, J. K. Gressett, improvised a solution after it cost $1,000 to drill a well at a local mission station. "Brother Terry Smith and I bought a complete well-drilling rig on a truck for less than half the cost of that one well. We operate the drill ourselves, donating our work and hoping that the actual cost can be met by help to the missionaries."[72] Knowing that a successful mission in the desert could not operate without water, Brother Gressett just bought his own drill. Ingenuity triumphed.

Once missionaries built churches on the reservations, they faced one last hurdle: the problem of success. Successful missionaries often discovered that they were "crowded out" of the small, plain churches that they had constructed with limited funds. In order to allow their mission work to grow, they had to expand—and expansion, like initial church construction, cost money. In the case of Sister Helen Burgess, a white missionary to the Navajos in Arizona, her popular Sunday school had outgrown its building. In the pages of the *PE*, she pleaded with readers for $2,500 to renovate her church and buy a small bus for transporting converts from distant parts of the reservation.[73] Similarly, on the Shoshone and Paiute reservations, which Brother Roy Nelson and his wife served, the growing congregation became too large for the small hall that they rented. Brother Nelson appealed for $1,200 so that they could complete the construction of a much larger building.[74] According to the pages of the *PE*, the problem of church growth became more pressing in the late 1960s and early 1970s. By then, most of the major missions to American Indians had been operating for at least a decade.

The *PE* is filled with a variety of these church-building stories regarding the missions to American Indians. While the stories do give the reader some idea of what actually occurred at the missions they also reaffirm some of the basic tenants of Pentecostalism's restorationist impulse. Notice that many of the stories emphasize the miraculous—money that appears from an unlikely source to help pay for building materials or needed services. Such reports from the missionary field served one main purpose. Chiefly, miracle stories tied to successful church building affirmed to both the white missionaries and the readership of the *PE* that they were indeed doing God's work, since he blessed them with the needed money, help, or labor to complete it. The *PE* was also the main vehicle missionaries could use to raise money from the faithful, who might read about a needy church and feel inclined to send a check to help out the missionaries. So while these church-building stories tell the reader some detail of what was actually happening on the reservation, we must remember that they also served both a spiritual and a pragmatic purpose.

The church-building stories also position both the white missionaries' and Native converts' images in the pages of Pentecostal literature. Missionaries are portrayed as hardy, full of ingenuity and zeal for the gospel. Native converts are also portrayed as hardworking and faithful, often in the face of poverty or hardship. It is likely that many missionaries and converts displayed these traits, and there is no reason to believe that what is reported in the *PE* is untrue, but one must keep in mind that the *PE* reports only stories that are beneficial to the Pentecostal cause and that emphasize its unique traits. Almost no apostate stories appear in the *PE*, and missionaries do not extensively speak of the daily, boring grind of attempting to win reluctant converts. As we continue to explore the variety of ways that white missionaries portray Native converts in this chapter, we must remember that the *PE* is always colored by its Pentecostal perspective.

The major issue that faced white missionaries was how to spread the Gospel among both receptive and unreceptive Indians. As with physical church building, missionaries had to be innovative in order to reach potential converts and overcome the obstacles of race, class, language, and culture. White missionaries on the reservation were well aware that the tribes would not totally welcome them, so they targeted segments of the population that might be receptive to the Gospel. In that case, they adopted tactics similar to the white missionaries of the nineteenth century—convert those who were influential in the hope that they would sway others. In the process, some white missionaries discovered that they would have more success among the local tribe if they both converted local people and encouraged them to take up Pentecostal missionary work and leadership. It is this aspect of missionary work that led to a glimmer of the indigenous principle on the ground among pragmatic white missionaries.

Missionaries focused on both the youngest and oldest members of the local Indian population assuming that they would be more amenable to embracing Christianity and that they would also influence their family members. While ministering in the Phoenix area, Sister Washburn evangelized a young Pima girl named Julianne Sampson. Julianne had several physically imposing older brothers who openly disliked "preachers."

Sister Washburn feared the young "Pima giants" but continued ministering to little Julianne. One evening, the Sampson brothers showed up at Sister Washburn's church for a meal and stayed for the evening service. According to Sister Washburn, a miracle occurred. "Before long the Sampson brothers were brought to their knees at our altar under the conviction of the Holy Spirit. They wept tears of repentance, their massive bodies quivering as they sobbed out their confessions of sin before the Lord. What an impact their salvation made on our congregation and on the people of their Salt River reservation. Notorious for their drinking and fighting they had now become as gentle as babes."[75] The Sampson brothers became a major asset to Sister Washburn's ministry and to the AG network of indigenous home missionaries. Talented musicians, they lent their skills to local evangelists and traveled around the country to Indian revivals. All of the brothers married Pentecostal women and attended Bible school. One brother, Virgil, graduated with a Bible school degree and became a successful Native evangelist until he died in a car accident.[76] Sister Washburn's strategy had succeeded.

As Sister Washburn discovered, Native converts made good missionaries, evangelists, and church workers. The missionary couple Brother Gene and Sister Betty Steele also experienced this insight when they evangelized Rose, a young blind Navajo. Rose seemed unlike most Navajo converts. Because of her blindness, she had a vocational education, having attended a government school for the blind, where she learned Braille and secretarial skills. Once Rose converted, she enrolled in Bible school in order to develop her skills for evangelism. The Steeles remarked, "Since she is efficient in reading and writing Braille, playing the piano and organ, and singing and witnessing for the Lord, we look forward to her completing Bible school and having a fuller ministry among her own people."[77] They realized that someone like Rose aided their ministry.

Sometimes missionaries focused on those who were influential within the tribe. Medicine men represented one such group. Throughout the 1950s and 1960s, the *PE* joyfully reported conversions of medicine men or traditional tribal elders as proof of the power of the Holy Spirit over heathenism. One story in the *PE* celebrated the conversion of an eighty-one-year-old Apache medicine man named David Ethelbah. The local missionaries acknowledged that Brother Ethelbah was a leader in the Apache community and encouraged him in his evangelization work on the White River reservation. A *PE* reporter commented, "The people of the community continued to respect Brother David as their leader since he was a former medicine man. His influence for God makes him a blessing to the Cedar Creek Indian Church."[78] Missionaries understood that it was easier for Indians to hear about Jesus and Christianity if it came from one of their own—especially if that convert held prestige and influence within the community. It was also an important coup for any missionary who could claim that he had converted a medicine man. There are multiple examples of this in the *PE*, and for the previously mentioned reason, they must be read carefully.

It is not surprising that Pentecostals would focus on medicine men. Every other form of Christian missionary who came before them had done the same—the idea was to discredit traditional Native religion. The problem is that while the *PE* shows that it was important to Pentecostals that they focus on converting medicine men, we do not know the actual extent of the conversions themselves. The medicine men may have converted to Pentecostalism and disavowed traditional religions, or they may have embraced Pentecostalism and continued to practice their own beliefs when the missionaries' backs were turned. From the information in the *PE*, the reader has no way of knowing what actually happened. Yet we can, for sure, state that Pentecostals sought to do battle with the forces of traditional religion, in the idea that they were leading Native traditionalists from the dark and into the light.

Besides focusing on certain members of the tribe, white missionaries reached other specific segments of the population. Imprisoned Indians constituted one such group. Brother Oliver Treece, a missionary stationed on the San Carlos reservation, spent time at the local jail, which housed Apaches who had committed various crimes. The jail held both men and women, as well as the young children of incarcerated mothers. According to Brother Treece, "As our helpers begin to sing and testify about the love of Jesus, some prisoners crowd about the doors and windows; others stay back in their corners. . . . At the close of the service gospel papers and tracts are given to all and special prayer goes up to our Father in heaven."[79] Brother Treece was not overly optimistic in his reports. Unusually candid for a white missionary, he acknowledged that most of the prisoners did not stay on the right side of the law, saying, "Many of the prisoners promise to come to church as soon as they are released (and thank God, some do) but many forget their promises and the next time we see them they are in jail again."[80] He remained hopeful, however, because, in his opinion, "God does not forget them. His ear is ever open to their cry, and His Word will not be fruitless."[81] For Brother Treece, the hard work among the jailed

Apaches was worth it if he managed to "sow" just one seed that would lead someone to turn his life around.

White missionaries also evangelized Indians employed in the rodeo and cattle industries. During her first missionary assignment, Sister Washburn heard about missionaries who pioneered cattle roundup evangelization among the cattle-ranching Western Apaches. Led by Sister Jean, these evangelists attended the yearly cattle roundup on the reservation, watched the day's events, and shared a meal with the Apache cowboys. At the end of the meal, Sister Jean and her helpers launched into singing and playing music in order to draw an Apache crowd. Then the evangelization began. According to a letter sent to Sister Washburn, "By this time, the cowboys had removed their dusty, trail-worn hats. We detected an atmosphere of reverence for God's holy presence. We knew conviction of the Holy Spirit rested heavily upon the hearts of those Apache cowboys and others gathered in that [sic] tribal stockyards."[82] Sister Jean reported that many souls found salvation that day, and even more hearts were touched. Other missionaries continued Sister Jean's work at local roundups and rodeos into the 1960s, when it became a formalized AG endeavor. For example, in 1965 Brother Swank reported that he and a large group of local missionaries attended the All-Indian Rodeo in Sells, Arizona, in hope of evangelization. The group set up a booth and distributed copies of the PE along with many different tracts and pamphlets. They also played recorded readings of the Scriptures that they had taped in a variety of Indian languages. The missionaries noted, "This was quite an attraction, for we noticed many of the older people, especially, listening to these. One old man in particular listened for two hours."[83] Music and singing rounded out the program at the AG booth. Rodeos could be a fruitful field in the search for converts.

Conversion, followed by evidence of baptism in the Holy Spirit (that evidence usually being speaking in tongues), was the most important marker of Pentecostal success. The PE is filled to the brim with conversion narratives of all kinds of peoples, and American Indians are no exception. By carefully reading these narratives, we know that missionaries targeted certain groups of American Indians for conversion, in the hope that they would be able to influence other members of their tribe or family to convert. Such a technique is common to all Pentecostal missionary work. Yet the problem with the conversion stories within the PE is that they tend to be reported with a particular audience in mind: the general Pentecostal readership of the magazine. This means that it is hard to read anything specific into the conversions except that they did fit the Pentecostal ideal.

Despite these issues, nuances in the stories reported within the *PE* suggest to the reader that winning converts to Pentecostalism was not easy and often required a great deal of ingenuity, pragmatism, and determination.

While many of these white missionaries encouraged Native people to serve their churches once they converted to Pentecostalism, they did not make the indigenous principle a centerpiece of their evangelism. If anything, they came to it from a pragmatic standpoint. Because Indians were more likely to listen to other Indians who had authority within their tribe, Indian evangelists were a good thing. White Pentecostals were more concerned with the actual act of conversion and encouraging converts to embrace the markers of Pentecostalism (e.g., speaking in tongues, visions, prophecy). What is noticeable in these accounts of church building from the early period is that the indigenous principle does not dominate their particular practice of Pentecostal evangelization, in the sense that the missionaries do not immediately set up structures that would allow the local churches to become fully indigenous—that is, develop strong leadership or financial independence. This highlights one of the main differences in how the two different groups of missionaries approached the indigenous principle: for white missionaries it was a matter of pragmatism, but for Native missionaries it became the driving practice that undergirded their approach to Pentecostalism.

Holy Ghost Powwows

During the middle decades of the twentieth century, the Pentecostal camp meeting or revival still served as a common means of evangelization. By the middle 1950s, white missionaries reworked the camp structure to meet the needs of their Indian converts. That gave birth to the most popular means of AG Native evangelization: the all-Indian camp meeting, which became a major contributor to the development of indigenous missionaries. Camp meetings, according to reports published in the *PE*, offered places where Indian evangelists and missionaries first became widely known to the greater AG public. They were sites for fellowship and community among converts. It allowed them to affirm their Pentecostal identity and gave them an alternative to traditional Native American powwows and celebrations. In essence, the all-Indian camp meeting became a sort of "Holy Ghost powwow." Yet the planning and execution of all-Indian camp meetings also exposed paternalism and ethnocentrism among the white missionaries and the problems of a halfway indigenous principle.

White missionaries were suspicious of traditional Indian powwows or celebrations because they felt that those gatherings, always an important part of Indian life, led to sin. In order to give their Indian converts an alternative to the powwow, missionaries planned camp meetings to take place at the same time, typically in the summer. In 1957, when the all-Indian camp meeting movement was just beginning to take form, white missionaries to the Apaches decided they needed to counter the influence of the powwow. "The Apache Indian Camp, in Mescalero, New Mexico, was held at the same time as the Indian Celebration. The Celebration is an annual affair among the Indians and is a time of idol worship, dancing, and sin. It was inspiring to see the Christians separate themselves from this and attend the services of the camp where they enjoyed God's blessing upon their lives."[84]

Instead of going to the celebration, Pentecostal Indians gathered at the Apache Indian camp, which allowed them to be with Pentecostal Indians in a setting that was similar to, but also different from, a traditional powwow. AG home missionaries organized all-Indian camps by tribe or region. By the late 1960s, because of lobbying and influence by Native AG missionaries and evangelists, white AG missionaries allowed Indians at these gatherings to embrace aspects of Indian culture they deemed non-threatening to the Pentecostal message. Thus, the actual camp meeting took different forms depending on the region and tribal influence. Some missionaries held meetings under the traditional tent, but often Indians themselves improvised a structure. In the Southwest, where the largest camp meetings took place among the Navajo and Apache, Indian converts would build a brush arbor. Often, the meeting grounds included whole herds of sheep, goats, and cattle, along with the family dogs. Indian children were encouraged to amuse themselves by playing with the dogs, participating in sports, and racing their ponies.[85] PE reporters and outside observers who visited the camps noted that all the animals, pony races, and camping Indians created a joyful, if madcap, scene. "The camp presented a picturesque scene a visitor such as I would not soon forget. Family life went on between services. There were tepees, covered wagons, pickups, trucks, tents under clumps of juniper trees and brush shelters. Over open fires the people were cooking their Navaho fry bread or Hopi hot bread, frijoles and tortillas. Children were being scrubbed outdoors. Small washings flapped on pinon trees. One woman was ironing with an old flat iron."[86] Conditions at the camp were rustic; there was no electricity, and clean water usually had to be hauled to the site. Indians came by whatever means they could, often in groups in the beds of pickup trucks, by covered wagon, or even by walking. They arrived from far-flung portions of the reservations, where they might be the only Pentecostals for miles, in order to meet fellow Indian converts. At the meeting, they sometimes found themselves battling the elements. In the Southwest, it was the heat of the desert summer, which typically stayed in the triple digits. Bugs, scorpions, and venomous snakes added drama.[87] At one camp among the Lower Brule Sioux in South Dakota, a tornado destroyed the meeting tent and picked up the missionary's wife, carrying her twenty-five feet in the air.[88] Saving souls was daunting; the elements made it harder.

While the Indian camp meetings did take place under difficult circumstances, the editors of the *PE* emphasized the hardships and poverty of the Indian converts. *PE* reporters used words such as "crude" or "primitive" to describe the structures in which the Indians lived during the meetings. Highlighting their poverty, the editors of the *PE* noted that even in the 1960s many Indians walked or came by horseback. Reporters described Indian food as exotic cuisine that "regular" Americans did not eat, although frijoles and tortillas were common fare in the Southwest. Such descriptions served two purposes. By focusing on the poverty, the editors of the *PE* highlighted the Indians' faith—that even though Indian converts had to overcome major hardships to attend camp, they came anyway, thus testifying to the power of the Holy Spirit. Second, by emphasizing the poverty of Indian converts and their "exoticism," the white editors reaffirmed that the Indian converts, while Pentecostals, were different from white Pentecostals. This subtly emphasized white missionaries' beliefs that, while American Indians were redeemable, they were also still somewhat savage and other.

The program at all-Indian camp meetings resembled traditional Pentecostal ones. The missionaries separated children and young adults from their families during the day, and they took part in their own Bible study classes and workshops in doctrine. They encouraged the children to play sports and sometimes even had special children's worship services. By the late 1960s, a handful of the camp meetings specifically targeted Indian youth and separated them from their families.[89] The adults spent the day in Bible study, both in English and in the local Indian language, since many of the elders did not speak English. Throughout the day, the adults took breaks to cook food or tend their animals. They spent the evenings in worship services that usually emphasized singing in Native languages.[90]

Because of the emphasis on preaching in Native languages at Indian camp meetings, white missionaries, who usually spoke only English, found themselves heavily dependent upon Native evangelists and missionaries.[91] Almost every camp meeting featured at least one prominent Native missionary who preached. But though white missionaries depended on the Native preachers, the latter rarely *ran* a camp meeting. The white district superintendents, in collaboration with the white home missionaries, planned them. This pattern stemmed both from logistical reasons and from the undercurrent of pervasive paternalism. To be sure, there were few Native evangelists or missionaries during the 1950s and 1960s, so these men traveled from one camp meeting to the next.[92] Because of a demand for their services, they were unable to be involved in the planning. But white missionaries' paternalism also played a role. While white missionaries were often eager to work with Indian missionaries and evangelists, they were not typically willing to hand over their power in the actual planning and execution.[93]

All-Indian camp meetings offer a lens to view the AG work with Indian converts. They clearly show the main trends of the AG's work among Indians: the willingness to innovate in order to save souls, but also the entrenched ethnocentrism and paternalism that plagued AG missionary work. White AG missionaries were willing to accommodate Native lifestyles, to the point that they permitted their converts to bring goats and sheep to camp meetings (likely for food purposes: with lack of refrigeration on site, it was easier to have meat to slaughter fresh), made allowances for children to race ponies (as long as no gambling was involved), and arranged for the elders to hear the gospel in their own language. White missionaries consciously modeled the camp meeting after the traditional Indian powwow, for it was both a religious and a social gathering.

Yet camp meetings were a source of conflict for Indian converts because they created a confrontation with traditional culture. By scheduling camp meetings at the same time as traditional tribal gatherings, the AG missionaries forced a choice. They implied that they did not trust their converts to be able to resist the "temptations" of a traditional environment. Powwows were not only religious gatherings but social functions and business gatherings as well. By scheduling camp meetings to coincide with the powwows, white missionaries showed that they did not believe that their converts could eschew the religious elements and attend a powwow purely for economic and social reasons, such as buying or trading a horse, purchasing jewelry or rug-making supplies, or even visiting with neighbors or relatives. Finally, while Indian evangelists and missionaries were extremely important for a camp meeting's success, they rarely held positions of power. All-Indian camp meetings began among the AG as an experiment and became so successful that they proved the most popular way to evangelize Native Americans. Yet they also showed the undercurrent of paternalism that would continue to plague the AG and expose the halfway indigenous principle that so many white missionaries ended up falling into.

Native Missionaries, Lay Leadership, and the Indigenous Principle

On entering the mission field, most Indian evangelists and missionaries had to confront the practical problems involved in saving souls. Limited funds and the racism of greater American society hindered Native missionaries more than their white missionary brothers and sisters. Together with their white colleagues, they wrestled with the same mundane problems, including how to build churches on reservation land and attract potential converts. But they enjoyed one distinct advantage over their white counterparts: as Indians, they possessed a better sense of the culture and society that they were serving. Within the realm of church building and evangelizing, they often enjoyed a great deal of autonomy. Once on the reservations, particularly remote desert reservations, and left alone by white district officials, Native missionaries had to rely on themselves to build churches and win converts. They took advantage of their autonomy and became creative in their approaches. In doing this, they also embraced a distinctly pragmatic Pentecostal attitude toward innovation. This innovation allowed them to put into place certain structures and missionary programs that helped them realize the indigenous principle, and they did so more forcefully and systematically than their white counterparts.

The building of Brother Charlie Lee's church in Shiprock, New Mexico, illustrates one distinct advantage Indian missionaries had, despite their lack of resources: they knew how to overcome the obstacles that the tribal governments put in the way. On graduation from Central Bible Institute in Springfield, Missouri, in 1951, Brother Lee returned to the Shiprock region of the Navajo reservation, where he grew up. He set out preaching in Navajo but worked more than a year before gaining any converts. Navajos lived in small family units, scattered sparsely around the reservation. Brother Lee had no land of his own on the reservation, and there was no place for a church. He and his wife lived seventy miles away from the

Shiprock area in Cortez, Colorado, and endured a long desert commute over dirt roads.[94] Brother Lee understood that in order to acquire land for a house and a church, he would have to deal with the powerful Navajo tribal council, which during the early 1950s remained split between "progressives" and "traditionalist" factions. Only a Navajo-speaking missionary could have gone before the tribal council, because the elders conducted the council meetings in the Navajo language. The tribal council had the power to give Brother Lee the land needed for a church and parsonage, but after three attempts he received only enough land to build a house, as was his rightful claim as a Navajo.[95]

Although he could afford to build only a two-room house, Brother Lee completed the building and started to hold services there. He continued lobbying the tribal council, which had denied him the permit to build a church because it claimed that there were already enough churches in the Shiprock area.[96] Still, Brother Lee persisted, and while he did not openly challenge the tribal council's power, he continued evangelizing and holding meetings in his house. Finally, during his third petition a Navajo elder stood and spoke on behalf of Lee. "'Now,' he said, 'this young man has returned and wants to start a church, and we are fighting him. He is entitled to have a piece of land but he has been considerate enough of our authority to channel his request through our Tribal Council. I think we ought to let him have his request.'"[97] The tribal council granted him the permit to build a church, rewarding Lee's persistence. In 1957, Brother and Sister Lee moved into their small church and continued their ministry. By 1961, they had as many as three hundred Sunday school students, and Lee's work in spreading the Gospel in Navajo began to attract the attention of the white AG leadership.[98] Lee's patience and willingness to work with both the tribal government and local elders gained the respect of the Navajo people. He also showed the AG that indigenous leaders could address the difficulties of reservation evangelization more effectively than their white counterparts.

Brother Lee was not the only Indian missionary who used his cultural knowledge to build a church for his people. Arthur Stoneking, a Winnebago evangelist, did the same when he built an all-Indian church in the American city with the largest urban Indian population, Los Angeles. Brother Stoneking arrived there shortly after his discharge from the United States Navy—he had fought in the battles of Okinawa and Iwo Jima in 1945. He married a Pentecostal woman and converted shortly thereafter at the First Assembly of God in Maywood, California.[99] Brother Stoneking knew of the federal relocation program that had placed many Indians in urban areas, and he sought to reach out to them.[100] He knew it would be a daunting task, first, because of the size of the city and, second, because most Indians did not like to mingle with members of other tribes. The third problem that Stoneking faced was identifying fellow Indians in the city. He approached these difficulties with typical Pentecostal aplomb combined with a distinctly Indian approach to evangelization.

At the time that Brother Stoneking was hoping to found an urban Indian congregation, he was also driving the school bus for the Maywood Christian School. This job gave him the opportunity to identify local Indian children. Through the children, he contacted the parents. Once he had enough interested people, Brother and Sister Stoneking organized a Bible study in their home, where they converted several families and began the work of building a church.[101] By 1959, even before he had his own church building, Brother Stoneking had established an indigenous Sunday school led by five Indian lay leaders of the Navajo, Maricopa, and Choctaw tribes.

The Bell Gardens Assembly of God aided Brother Stoneking by allowing his Indian congregation to meet in its building on Sunday nights. The same congregation later gave Brother Stoneking an empty lot for his church.[102] On 21 June 1964, a crowd of 450 came to the dedication of the new all-Indian church in Bell Gardens. The congregation represented more than thirty tribes, and three different choirs sang in various Indian languages.[103] Brother Stoneking's choir eventually became one of the most successful ministries in his church. By the late 1960s the choir was traveling the Indian camp-meeting circuit, testifying and singing in a variety of Native languages.[104] Brother Stoneking also signed a contract with a Long Beach radio station, KGER, where on Saturday evenings his parishioners preached in their Native languages and then translated the program into English. Eventually, his radio program became so popular that Christian stations in Tucson, Gallup, and Phoenix adopted it.[105]

By emphasizing the similarities among Indian cultures, Brother Stoneking was able to build a successful mission in an urban area where Indians were living in different neighborhoods without the familial or tribal networks that had sustained them on the reservations. The Indian Revival Center substituted for the community that Indians had known on the reservations they had recently left. Within this community, composed of a variety of tribes from almost everywhere in the nation, they found fellow Indians who understood their hardships and homesickness. While

Brother Stoneking built his church on these common Indian experiences, he was able to launch his successful radio and music ministries only because of tribal differences. Since his church was so diverse and many of the congregants spoke traditional languages, Brother Stoneking used this knowledge to launch successful evangelization efforts that appealed to Indians from different tribes. The diversity of the church members could have pulled the Indian Revival Center apart, but it led instead to its growth and popularity, as local Indians flocked to it after hearing its radio programs or seeing members of the All-Indian Revival Choir testify in their own languages. By encouraging his congregants to speak in their Native tongues, he went beyond the English-only evangelization of many of his white counterparts and nurtured the Pentecostal Indian identity of his flock.

Brother Stoneking relied heavily on lay leadership in order to build an indigenous church, but he was not the only missionary, white or Indian, to encourage the laity. Lay leadership had always been essential in Pentecostal congregations, and missionaries established typical AG lay-leadership groups in their Indian churches. These included the Men's Fellowships, Women's Missionary Conferences, and Christ's Ambassadors for youth. While all of these forms of lay involvement were distinctly Pentecostal, Indian converts brought to them their own emphases and points of view.

By 1964, six different Men's Fellowship (MF) groups were active among Indian congregations.[106] Although typical AG MF groups emphasized spiritual concerns, the Indian MF groups often found that their churches most needed their manual labor. The lack of funds and muscle power that made building churches on the reservation so difficult meant that missions benefited greatly from MF workers. At the Canyon Day Apache Mission, Apache members of the MF "planted trees all around the mission property, decorated the interior of the auditorium, built a new altar and platform and put matching plywood in the walls . . . they also plan to build tables and benches in the Sunday school platform."[107] MF members put skills often acquired as day laborers to use maintaining the mission church. The men also volunteered in other areas. In addition to teaching Sunday school, preaching, and testifying in their native languages, one MF group from Brother Lee's Shiprock Mission found a particular calling in jail ministry. According to the *PE*, Navajo members of the Shiprock MF proved more effective than white missionaries in prison ministry because "many of the men had occupied cells in the jail before their conversion, so now they can testify to the saving grace of the Lord."[108] As former inmates, some Navajo MF members understood the problems that their jailed fellow Navajos faced and were able to evangelize more successfully.

The female equivalent of the MF was the Women's Missionary Conference (WMC), which tended to both the practical and spiritual needs of the mission. Just as the Navajo men had contributed much to the church through the MF, Apache women, as members of the WMC, reinforced their identity as Pentecostal Indians through their service work. During their meetings, the members of the WMC of Canyon Day, Arizona, spent time in Bible study and prayer as well as sewing and maintenance work for their church. They also saw to some of the mundane aspects of church life by cleaning the sanctuary and sewing colorful quilts to hang on the walls. Moreover, the Apache women innovated in ways that were distinctly Indian.[109] In an article on Apache lay work, one *PE* writer noted: "Our women won forty ribbons at the Apache Indian Tribal Fair for their sewing, cooked foods, etc., and our Assemblies of God booth won first prize. This gave them an opportunity to witness and pass out over four thousand tracts in the two days."[110] This statement shows how Apache WMC members changed Pentecostal evangelization methods. Typically, missionaries, especially white ones, discouraged their Indian converts from attending traditional tribal gatherings because they could lead to sin. The Canyon Day Apache WMC, however, subverted this logic and turned a traditional gathering into a means of evangelization. By entering the various cooking and sewing contests, they acknowledged their Apache identity, participated in a traditional tribal celebration, and claimed their right to be present at the tribal fair. As Pentecostals, they used their attendance to evangelize fellow Apaches. Like the Navajo members of the MF, the Apache members of the WMC used their service work to show that they identified as Pentecostal Indians.

The Christ's Ambassadors (CA) program provided leadership experience for young adults. By the early 1960s, a handful of Indian AG congregations, including Sister Washburn's All-Tribes Mission in Phoenix, had adopted CA groups. The All-Tribes CA group consisted of enthusiastic young evangelists who spent their time in outreach ministry among urban Indians. They concentrated particularly on the local Indian hospital and jail.[111] The members of the All-Tribes CA distinguished themselves in their work at the Phoenix Indian Boarding school, where they met on Sunday nights and led worship among the Pentecostal students. Their leadership both allowed the Pentecostal students to continue to practice their faith while they attended federal boarding school and helped the students form ties among the local Pentecostal community.[112]

The AG discovered that lay leadership organizations could indeed flourish among well-established Indian congregations in ways that were similar to those in white churches, but in other ways these groups became distinctly Indian. The MF, WMC, and CA all performed their expected functions: members of the MF maintained their church buildings and evangelized local men, the women of the WMC served their churches by performing "women's work" such as sewing and cooking, and the CA evangelized the community. But the Indian members in each of these bodies shouldered new duties in order to serve their fellow Indians. The members of the MF aided and evangelized Indian inmates in jails where they themselves once might have been prisoners, the women of the WMC entered cooking and sewing contests at traditional tribal gatherings as a means of evangelizing, and the CA worked among their peers at the local boarding school. These adaptations not only allowed the groups to reinforce their identities as Pentecostals and Indians but also brought them autonomy within the AG system. Their service as congregation members of AG churches and missions gave meaning to their work with the lay groups, and they found that they could exercise authority and bring about innovation among their fellow Indian Pentecostals. Therefore, they lived out the ideals of the indigenous principle—Native peoples contributing and growing their own churches and not relying on white missionaries to do so. Through Native leaders' innovation on the missionary field and the lay leadership of their congregants, glimpses emerge of the lived indigenous principle as practiced by everyday American Indian Pentecostals.

Conclusion

The problems of cultural misunderstandings and white paternalism in mission work are hard to assess fairly because everyone is a product of her or his own time and place. The white AG missionaries who embraced their "burden" and left their familiar American homes for work on unfamiliar Indian reservations were not really that much different from the average working-class American. On the reservation, they encountered strange people, strange food, strange customs, and strange languages, and yet they were in their own country. The white missionaries carried with them the ethnocentric attitudes of white Protestant Americans, but they also were pragmatic and, at times, innovative. They squarely faced multiple demons including their own poverty, ignorance, illnesses, and self-doubt. In the midst of this sea of misunderstanding, white missionaries constructed an incomplete model for evangelization that Native missionaries improved upon. They tried to implement the indigenous principle, but most settled for only a "halfway" approach.

American Indian AG missionaries, on the other hand, understood the particular difficulties that faced them in their fight to spread the Gospel. Life for most American Indians in the 1950s and 1960s was harsh, whether on or off the reservation. Indian missionaries personally knew the scourges of government dependency, alcoholism, and racism. More than white missionaries, they knew intimately how these problems affected the lives of Indians. For example, during one evangelistic tour, Brother John McPherson noticed a group of Indian women going out to pick cactus flowers for food. When he asked if the flowers were particularly tasty or nutritious, the women replied in the negative, but added that it was the only food available. Brother McPherson wrote:

> I prepared to preach the message that night, but my mind kept going back to the conversation with those ladies. It's hard to receive the gospel when your belly is empty. . . . While we enjoy the comfort of a lovely home, many of the people of the reservation live in squalor. Somewhere today while we enjoy our evening meal there is an Indian family dipping a dried tortilla in a bean pot. While we drive our new car to a lovely edifice for worship, that Indian family is making its way down a rattlesnake infested trail to a mud church without even a floor. More than just numbers of statistics, this kind of poverty has names and faces that present themselves again and again in my reverie.[113]

For many Indians, life was tough. AG Indian missionaries understood this, and desperately fought to change it.

Once converted, Pentecostal Indians defined themselves as born-again believers whom the Holy Spirit had selected specifically to serve their own people. The AG offered a place for them; they received an education and exercised their autonomy to innovate on the mission field. During the early years, Indian missionaries sought to implement the indigenous principle and did their best to encourage their congregants and set up structures that would allow the indigenous principle to be realized. Once they arrived on reservations or in Indian neighborhoods, they built congregations and encouraged lay leadership and congregational participation, thereby extending to their people the autonomy that they had found in the AG system. By showing white missionaries that they could indeed run their own churches and be responsible for their own religious lives, they embodied the indigenous principle and showed that it could be realized. It was more than theory, and it could be lived out in new ways that spoke to the American Indian experience.

Yet American Indian missionaries ran up against a problem, and that problem was that white missionaries to Indians had a different conception of missionary work and Pentecostalism. White missionaries were interested in winning converts and training local people as evangelists or missionary helpers, but they did not push as hard as Native missionaries to develop strong indigenous leadership. They did not understand that they had to develop local leadership, which would eventually turn into regional leadership, and would then become national leadership, which was the goal of Native missionaries by the 1960s. In contrast, by the late 1960s American Indian missionaries' practice of the indigenous principle was pushing forward in earnest. Their whole goal was to organize indigenous churches and train an indigenous clergy. Although the Pentecostal Indian leadership as a whole benefited from the general autonomy of the AG home missions network, they began to demand a voice within the institution. Displeased that they possessed no official voice to speak for them at the General Council, Indian missionaries asked for a nationally appointed Indian representative long before the AG was willing to consider the option.[114] The indigenous principle grew from being a practice among Indian Pentecostals to a political force within the denomination that had to be reckoned with.

Aside from the issue of political empowerment, Christianity for Native missionaries was not just something that one converted to—it was something that the believer actually owned, and it had to be understood in authentically Indian terms. Meanwhile, the majority of white missionaries seemed to regard Native-run churches that were rooted in an indigenous Christianity as something that was impossible because of the economic, cultural, and educational hurdles that existed for American Indians. Even more so, they disagreed with Native culture as a whole and sought to eliminate much of it, whereas Native missionaries tried their best to preserve some aspects of their own culture. This fight over Native culture, traditional religion, and particular understandings of healing reared its ugly head in this time period and is explored in depth in the following chapter.

CHAPTER 3

The Lived Indigenous Principle

New Understandings of Pentecostal Healing,

Native Culture, and Pentecostal Indian Identity

Late one evening in 1943, John McPherson, a young Cherokee solider, went out drinking with his wife. As he stumbled from one bar to the next, he spied a Pentecostal preacher on the street corner exhorting sinners to come to Christ. Although McPherson grew up in a Salvation Army home and his wife was the daughter of a Pentecostal preacher, neither one had been saved. McPherson recounted, "[W]e heard the melodic refrain of a song, and recognizing it to be religious in nature, stopped to listen for a moment. This time, I heard more then [*sic*] just a melody, I listened to the words of the preacher."[1] Despite his wife's dismay, McPherson knelt down on the street and prayed the sinner's prayer. At that moment, a realization washed over him. "All my life I had labored under the stigma of being born an Indian. I had always been made to feel I wasn't quite as good as people with white skin. I was amazed after laboring under that stigma all my life to find the One who so loved me that He died upon the cross for me. He wasn't ashamed of me or my copper skin. He wasn't ashamed of my humble beginnings or ancestry."[2]

From that moment on, John McPherson became Brother McPherson and, after the end of World War II, embarked on a long career as a traveling evangelist and AG missionary. As it did for many of his other Pentecostal Indian brothers and sisters, conversion and the baptism of the Holy Spirit changed Brother McPherson's life. He had grown up as an Indian in the white man's world because his mother had sold her allotment; they did not live on the reservation. Born and reared in Drumright, Oklahoma, during the Depression, Brother McPherson experienced not only racial prejudice but also grinding poverty. In his autobiography, he jokingly described his house as being so rickety that "if the termites had stopped holding hands it probably would have fallen on top of us."[3] He went on to note, "our furniture, instead of 'Early American,' I think was 'Early Orange Crate.'"[4] Despite poverty, he grew up in a happy home, well loved by his parents. Their love, however, could not shield him from the realities of American life. He recalled that he "was reminded daily that I was an Indian growing up in a white man's world. When I started to school, I can remember coming home in tears, crying because of the cruelty of the other children as they mocked and called me names because of my dark skin."[5] Hatred inflicted deep wounds. But once Brother McPherson became a Pentecostal and an AG missionary, he found theological and spiritual ways to address his pain—and the pain of his Indian brothers and sisters.

In June 1955, Brother and Sister Rehwinkel, home missionaries to the Menominee in Wisconsin, published an article in the *PE*. While the article served mainly as a report on their mission in order to raise more funds, it also contained language that indicated the ethnocentrism that prevailed among white missionaries of the era. In talking about a group of traditional Indians, the Rehwinkels described their "pagan" customs. "At their ceremonies they beat drums and dance all night. Hours are spent in feasting and sitting in a circle while they pass out a drug called 'peyote.' Strange to say this ritual is called 'prayer.' These Indians, in bondage to dope, drink, and tobacco, desperately need the message of Christ, the Deliverer."[6] By today's standards, this language is troubling, but we need to consider the context. The article revealed the Pentecostal worldview: traditional Indian religion, along with newer traditions such as peyote, were of the Devil, and American Indians needed Christ to keep them from such sin. The Pentecostal audience that the Rehwinkels addressed expected this sort of insider language because they viewed themselves as spiritual warriors for Christ. In Pentecostals' minds, there was only one way to God—their way.

Brother McPherson's conversion narrative reveals a deep undercurrent of cultural pain—he had been stung by racism and ethnocentrism his whole life and had suffered because of it. Part of this has been caused by how outsiders perceived Native peoples and Native religion—a perception highlighted by the Rehwinkels' observation of a peyote ceremony. Their words reveal entrenched views of Native peoples in American society and among Christian missionaries—that they were "noble, wretched, and redeemable."[7] Therefore, they echoed nineteenth-century attitudes about

American Indians, as in need of the Gospel because of their inherently inferior, pagan, savage culture, an idea that even in the early twentieth century, still remained in American society. Their description also showed the typical Pentecostal reaction to Native religion and culture—one that stigmatized their particularly "heathen" aspects and that warned of the "darkness" that missionaries were sent to combat.

This chapter wades into the messy and at times ugly undercurrents that took place in Pentecostal missionary work to American Indians. White missionaries viewed Native religion and culture as suspect at best, and some (although not all) loaded their articles in the *PE* regarding traditional religions with ethnocentric and racist language. Meanwhile, Native Pentecostal converts were trying to find new ways to heal from the general racism and ethnocentrism that they had encountered before conversion and turned to Jesus and Pentecostal belief for this task and, in the process, redefined Pentecostal healing. Yet their own ministries were often tainted by the ethnocentrism of their colleagues, as evidenced by how Brother McPherson, a Cherokee, came to preach in a Plains Indian warrior suit. Through these examples we can see that Pentecostalism was both hurtful and healing, that it encouraged Native leadership while also subtly undermining it.

Throughout this innovation and pain, the indigenous principle began to emerge as the steady practice of Native Pentecostalism that helped Pentecostal Indians survive some of the stormier weather surrounding complex questions of tradition, religion, identity, and Native culture. In the previous chapter, the indigenous principle was described as something that white missionaries tried to embrace but only "halfway." Native missionaries, on the other hand, wholeheartedly championed it because it allowed them to build successful ministries. In this chapter, the practice of the indigenous principle becomes more complex—it goes beyond simply building churches and setting up ministries and instead becomes something that Natives wielded to gain authority, autonomy, and the beginnings of power within the AG. As Natives discovered these small pockets of power, they used them to subtly critique the AG. The indigenous principle gave them the authority to grapple with problems of culture versus religion, and how they were to preserve Native culture while removing traditional religions and replacing them with Pentecostalism. The indigenous principle allowed them to redefine Pentecostal healing in Native terms and to challenge how white missionaries conceived of healing. Finally, the indigenous principle helped them to define their own Indian identity in creative ways, even in instances when ethnocentrism and racism were always present.

This chapter is divided into three major sections. It focuses on how white missionaries viewed traditional native religions and how Native missionaries responded to this view; how Indian Pentecostals come to redefine Pentecostal healing and reconciliation in new ways; and raises the issue of John McPherson's Indian suit—how did a Cherokee evangelist come to be decked out in an inaccurate Plains warrior suit that mirrored the Hollywood idea of how an Indian should dress? In this last section I explore some of the complicated issues that arise in how Native evangelists portray themselves in their evangelistic work. These examples show that for Native Pentecostals the indigenous principle was much more than a theology that emphasized local leadership; it became a dynamic tool to criticize, innovate, and find a new way to be a Pentecostal and an American Indian.

The Devil and His Darkness

White Pentecostal missionaries to American Indians saw themselves as battling three different incarnations of the Devil: Catholicism, traditional religion, and peyote religion. All Pentecostals, white and Indian, believed in the Devil. In fact, they saw the Devil as constantly testing one's faith. Such language in Pentecostal periodicals was not uncommon—American Indian religion was not the only native religion to be viewed as demonic—all forms of non-Christian faith (and some forms of Christian faith) emerged as problematic in Pentecostal periodicals. If anything, white missionaries' sense of the demonic displayed a mix of their Pentecostal belief with their own ethnocentrism and biases against "heathen" belief. In this section, an examination of white missionaries and their perception of the demonic displays how white Pentecostals viewed their Catholic competition, along with traditional believers and members of the Native American Church.

In the 1950s, white AG missionaries were the latest in a long series of white missionaries who had worked among the Indians. By this time, however, most other Protestant missionaries had left the Native American mission field for a variety of reasons.[8] Sometimes the only non-Pentecostal missionaries still on the reservation were Catholic, usually priests who remained in areas that retained some adherents. However, the local AG missionaries regarded Catholicism as only slightly better than traditional religion or peyote. Pentecostals retained anti-Catholic feelings well into the twentieth century; they also saw Catholic missionaries as competition.[9] Some Catholic mission stations, particularly in the Southwest or in the Great Lakes area, had prospered among the local Native Americans for centuries and wielded strong influence. According to Brother George Bolt, a missionary to the Chippewa in Wisconsin, "The predominance of Catholicism made it very difficult to gain a foothold in the area."[10] Ruth Lyon, AG missionary to the Chippewa and former *PE* editor, echoed this sentiment. She agreed that Catholicism was "a major problem" among the Indian tribes of the Great Lakes regions.[11] In a dispatch to the *PE* in 1958, Sister Lyon showed her distaste: "There are other forms of heathenism on the reservation as well. For instance, in the little village of Guadalupi [*sic*] in Arizona at Easter time, the usual festivities, which are a mixture of Catholicism and paganism, took place. If you could have accompanied the missionaries and observed the activities you would have felt as they did: *Can a thing like this take place here in America?*"[12] AG missionaries and most other Pentecostals viewed Catholicism as barely Christian. Because Catholic missionaries had long allowed a certain amount of syncretism in their work among Native Americans, AG missionaries viewed Catholicism as "tainted" by traditionalist practices.

AG missionaries also believed that Catholic missionaries did not properly emphasize the Gospel. Pentecostals did not agree with the importance that Catholics placed on devotional objects like rosaries and holy water or on one's relationship with the saints or the Virgin Mary. According to Pentecostal missionaries, those beliefs tainted the Gospel and turned it to heathenism. One *PE* reporter commented, "Once the Catholic Church goes in and indoctrinates the people, exchanging their feather fetish prayer sticks for rosary beads and their yellow powder for statues of Mary, they are far harder to win to the Lord than from their pagan ways."[13] According to AG missionaries, the Catholics confused the impressionable Indians with their rituals and beliefs, thus making it harder for AG missionaries to clarify the true meaning of the Gospel.

While most Pentecostals saw Catholicism as a significant impediment in the mission field, traditional religion loomed larger. The *PE* continually demonized it. Missionaries were horrified to discover the "Devil dances" that took place on the reservations. In one such case, Sister Kaufmann sent the *PE* a sensationalistic account of traditional dance:

> To the Apache, many illnesses are demon possession, especially a stroke, or lightening [*sic*] striking an individual. That person is then

bound with cords of yucca plant and placed beside a bonfire. Four
cedar trees are put upright in the ground pointing toward north, east,
south, and west. Tom-toms beat and chants fill the air. Then four
black-hooded men emerge from the darkness. They wear long tails
and twirl whips that sing eerily in the night. Making owl-like sounds
they dance about the fire, disappear into the darkness to the west
and emerge again from the north, doing this until every direction
has been covered.[14]

Sister Kaufmann closed her description of the Apache sing by noting that
the sick person was "pronounced cured, and there ensues a wild drinking party with yells and screams that fill the canyon until dawn."[15] Sister
Kaufmann clearly viewed the sing as the work of demonic forces—to her
it signified the "darkness" that she was battling on the reservation. Sister Kaufmann's description of the Apache sing also shows her own ethnocentric outlook. She speaks of "darkness," "whips that sing eerily," and
"black-hooded men," and she ends with references to heavy drinking. Her
description clearly played on white Pentecostal fears about traditional
religion, with its images of the "wild savage" dancing before the fire. All
of the descriptions of traditional religion in the *PE* conform to the same
fear-stirring type as the one given by Sister Kaufmann. The word "tom-
toms" was almost always used, not "drums," because "tom-toms" evoked
the "savage."[16] *PE* authors depicted sings or dances as always taking place
in "darkness" and usually ending in alcoholic celebration. The missionaries never described the colorful and beautiful dances that marked certain
stages of Indian life or the dances and ceremonies that took place during
the daytime for the public. They never mentioned that at many dances and
ceremonies, alcohol was banned.

Sister Kaufmann was not the only missionary who reported sensationalistic "heathen" rituals. A similar account of traditional religion also
came from Sister Naomi Johnson who worked on the Papago reservation,
about sixty miles from Tucson. After traveling to the AG's General Council,
Sister Johnson returned to her mission station to discover that some of the
Papago had turned to the traditional medicine men in order to cope with
an ongoing drought.

The medicine men are having a hard task trying to appease "Etoy"
(their god) and the people. The rain dances have been going on
day and night for weeks. All night long, we can hear the beat of the

tomtoms and the drunken shrieks of the people. They make a very potent liquor from the fruit and sap of the Saguar [*sic*] cactus and everyone drinks until he cannot walk anymore. Their plea is that their god "Etoy" will saturate the ground with water as they have their bodies with the fruit of the desert in his honor. Entire villages become completely intoxicated, from the very old to the young ones who are old enough to walk.[17]

Again, as in Sister Kaufmann's account, traditional religion was tied to drinking, superstition, and alcoholism. Again, notice the use of "savage" language markers, such as "shrieks" and "tomtoms" in this account. They are evidence that Natives need salvation in the eyes of Sister Naomi Johnson, and she notes, "As I see their pitiful efforts and hear their frenzied cries in the night, I think and pray 'Oh Lord, make me as fervent and determined to bring them the light of Thy way as they are in serving their god.'"[18] She knows that the Papagos' traditions are deeply rooted in their culture and recognizes them for what they were: religious competition.

Sister Kaufmann and Sister Naomi Johnson did not understand traditional religion—to them it was the work of the Devil, because that was their only frame of reference for processing what they were seeing. For Pentecostals, spiritual matters were black and white; religion was either of Jesus and the Holy Spirit or of the Devil. They allowed no shades of gray. In Native cultures, religion contained nuances and contradictions that defied black-and-white categorization. In one example, the Apache traditional religion included healing and the belief in good and evil. Both were important concepts. An Apache "witch" (or *inlgashn*) could make a person ill, mentally or physically, and a sick person would undertake a "sing" to be healed. Witchcraft, however, was not the only reason for illness. People could bring illness upon themselves by behaving "without respect" and not following the multitude of taboos that Apaches accepted.[19] In the majority of Native traditional religions, the key was achieving balance. Sin was not a part of the traditional Native worldview, and Natives defined morality by the customs of each particular tribe. Those customs were often more liberal in matters regarding sex and marriage than those of the Christian missionaries. Thus, missionaries did more than confront the problem of belief—in trying to convince Indians to accept Christianity, they also confronted deep-seated aspects of Native culture.

Traditional religion was often portrayed by missionaries as something exotic, which Native people needed to move on from, and some missionaries were careful to report the facts about traditional religion in a detached way in order to avoid the inflammatory rhetoric of their peers. In an article by Sister Elva Johnson, who worked among the Navajo, she described the Navajo traditional beliefs surrounding ghosts of the dead.

> One sad day a member of the family, sick unto death, will be carried through the door that opens towards the rising sun, to die nearby, perhaps under a juniper bush. He must not die inside the hogan, or it cannot be used any more for habitation as it will become a "chindee" Hogan (possessed by an evil spirit). But if he does die there, his family will pull some logs from the back of the Hogan as a sign that it is "chindee," gather their few belongings, and go somewhere else to live. Strange customs to us, perhaps, but the Navajos have lived in this fashion for generations on the vast reservation lands in the Southwest.[20]

Sister Johnson strikes an even tone in her observations, which are not exaggerated lies or half-truths—what she describes is what happens when a Navajo dies because of the traditional fear of "ghosts" or spirits of the dead becoming entrapped in a structure. Initially her observations do not come across as offensive in regards to traditional practices but rather as matter-of-fact. But later in the article, Sister Johnson revealed her real feelings about Native religion. "But there are still many, many Navajos in the spirit of superstition and fear of evil spirits,"[21] she begins, and then goes on to describe a traditional healing ceremony as set up by a medicine man. Again, her description is factually correct and not as sensationalistic as other missionary observations printed in the *PE*, but she does close out her description by noting "It is to these people who, 'wait for the light, but behold obscurity' that our missionaries have gone."[22] Sister Johnson is far more careful and much less inflammatory than other missionary observers when it came to traditional religion, but in the end, she believed that traditional belief led only to "darkness."

Missionaries also, at times, pointed out the divide between traditionalist and Christian Indians on the reservation. Aside from a few mentions in the *PE*, missionaries tended not to talk about the rifts that surely occurred between the Indians who embraced Pentecostalism and those who remained steadfast in their old beliefs. One report came from Brother and Sister Robert Wheeler on the Gila River reservation. They noted that "there is so much fear in the hearts of many of our Indians that they are afraid to come to our church. It is not fear of the evil spirits but it is fear of the elders of their formal [sic] church who make threats."[23] The missionaries are unclear if the elders came from another church or if they came from a traditionalist movement, but reports like this give the readers of the *PE* some hints that there were rifts among Indian communities over religion. Pentecostals certainly had competition for souls.

Missionaries also had to contend with the growing use of peyote among North American Indians. White AG missionaries believed peyote, like traditional dances, to be of the Devil. Peyote is a small cactus. When consumed in its dried form, its detractors said it brought about hallucinations and visions. Members of the Native American Church countered that the cactus brought about clarity of mind and closeness to the divine when taken properly and with respect for its powers. The peyote ceremony was both communal and nocturnal and often conducted because a member sought healing. Many Natives turned to peyote in order to be cured of alcoholism, or familial troubles. Some peyote users who incorporated Christianity into the use of peyote regarded peyote as a form of communion that could bring on an experience of God.[24] Missionaries reported to the *PE* about peyote in the same negative tones that they used for traditional religion. According to one, "Peyote is a far greater menace than is often recognized. Some Indians believe the use of peyote induces dreams that will guide one's future steps and make him rich. Recently an Indian woman was given peyote instead of being taken to the hospital—and she died from it. . . . One of our men here in the church lost his sister in death because she ate it. Peyote acts like acid and eats away until the user finally dies."[25] The account is clearly a gross and ethnocentric exaggeration of peyote's power, written in order to inflame readers about the usage of peyote on reservations. Although most Catholic missionaries were just as likely to frown on peyote as Pentecostals, AG missionaries also linked peyote to Catholic and Episcopal missionaries in order to support their anti-Catholic rhetoric. One missionary wrote: "It is unthinkable that any denomination claiming to be Christian could ever be sympathetic to the Native American Church, when the drug employed in the rituals of this church will eventually paralyze and possibly kill the users. Christ could never be glorified in such a practice. To its slaves *Father Peyote* is god."[26]

Missionaries found peyote suspect because they viewed it as a drug and viewed anything that was not explicitly Christian as a "false God." Those opposed to peyote saw it as no different from LSD or acid, and they often conflated its use with the use of other drugs. Even some Native missionaries took this view of peyote—indeed, Indian missionaries tended to be more sympathetic toward traditional belief than peyote, which could be because peyote displaced many traditional practices in the twentieth century; therefore it was more likely to compete with Pentecostals for souls. Cherokee evangelist Luther Cayton stated, "The Indian himself has had a social gospel for fifty years or more, along with his customs, witchcraft, traditions, and Peyote worship. . . . The drug [peyote] eventually paralyzes its victims and it is a slow but sure death to all who use it. It is sometimes used along with marijuana."[27] This is a mischaracterization of peyote (which does not cause paralysis), and the ritual is also conflated with other drugs. What is so fascinating about Brother Cayton's observation is how complicated this sentence is. He notes that Indians have long had a "social gospel" as he puts it, along with customs, traditions, "witchcraft," and Peyote. So he acknowledges that not all of Native culture is inherently evil, but that parts of it can be separated out from what is evil (the witchcraft and the peyote.) This approach that Native missionaries take toward their own customs hints at the trends that are discussed later in this chapter.[28]

Most white Pentecostal missionaries did not recognize the likelihood that some of their converts moved between Pentecostal belief and traditional practices, including the use of peyote. Of course, the *PE* never provided any evidence of such "backsliding," but anthropologists encountered Native people who retained dual religious identities. One example is that of an elderly Paiute woman who told the anthropologist Omar Call Stewart: "I'm a Christian lady. I go to the Assembly of God church all the time. I prayed to God, worshipped God, worshipped Jesus in the peyote meeting. The Christian church and the peyote meetings are the same."[29] Such an admission would likely make an AG missionary cringe, but many Native people did not see traditional beliefs or peyote usage as incompatible with Christianity. Some Indians viewed Christianity and traditional beliefs as complementary.

In the minds of most white Pentecostal missionaries, Catholicism, traditional dancing, and peyote all represented the Devil. In addition, they stood as impediments in the competition for souls. AG missionaries felt that they had to fight these evils, because if they did not, the souls of the Indian people would be lost forever. However, their categorization of these practices as evil reveals the ethnocentrism that pervaded the worldview of the white missionaries in the 1940s through the 1960s. White missionaries had no way to come to terms with the Native religions that they encountered, so they framed its practice in terms of the demonic, which they did understand. Despite their restorationist views on missionary work, white Pentecostal missionaries fell into the same trap that bedeviled their nineteenth-century counterparts—the denigration of traditional religion, Catholics, and some aspects of American Indian culture. Their views on the demonic reveal their Pentecostal mindset but also their idea that anything but (Protestant) Christianity impeded Native "progress." The *PE* gives the reader no information on how Native traditionalists, peyote practitioners, and Catholics viewed the white Pentecostal missionary mindset, but it suffices to say that their impression of white Pentecostal missionaries was probably not positive. By demonizing traditionalism and peyote, white missionaries displayed their own ethnocentric attitude toward Native culture, creating a barrier between them and important aspects of Native culture and religion—a problem never rectified despite the best efforts of their Native counterparts.

Native Pentecostals and Traditional Religion

Indian missionaries deeply believed that the Gospel answered all their problems, but they still had to contend with traditional believers on the reservation. While some Indian missionaries regarded traditional religion as demonic, as did their white counterparts, Brother Lee and Brother Cree articulated a more telling argument against traditional religion. Both believed that traditional religion could not help their people because it was not true Indian religion. They contended that because traditionalist religion was not actually "traditional," it no longer contained the power that it once held and lacked answers to Indians' modern-day problems. Because of their authority and particular practice of the indigenous principle, these two men managed to find a way to criticize traditional Native religions without echoing the offensive and ethnocentric language of their white (and some Native counterparts.) This section explores their particular arguments against traditional religion and then considers why it is that so many other Native evangelists remained silent on this topic.

According to Brother Charlie Lee, the problem with Indian religion was that its believers were not exactly sure what they believed. Brother Lee placed great emphasis on how the elders were no longer respected in Navajo society, and he obviously thought that this lack of respect was a problem. "In the days of old, the people listened to the medicine man. They respected what he taught concerning spiritual things and upheld the moral standard, but now he was no longer a leader. The old folks were no longer respected because they were thought to be old fashioned."[30] Lee directly correlated the lack of respect toward one's elders with what he called a "low moral standard."[31] In his view, many young Navajos had turned away from the strictness of the old ways and found themselves adrift in a sea of alcoholism, hatred, and misunderstanding. But Lee also felt that those who wanted to resurrect the "old ways" were misguided. "If you bring back Indian religion and pick out that part that appeals to you emotionally, that's not Indian religion. . . . If you really want to go back to the old Indian ways, it's a strict life, a disciplined life. The old ways were definitely strict and demanded conformity to certain standards of behavior, and you don't want that."[32] Lee argued that the true "old ways" were no longer remembered by Native people; the way of life that had supported them had disappeared. Many of the people were no longer on their traditional lands, and without traditional lands and traditional family structures, how could you have traditional religion? Brother Lee believed that those who were claiming to return to traditional religion were eclectically choosing from past traditions, not totally participating in all the traditional practices.

Brother Lee was not the only one who viewed Indian religion in this light. When asked about traditional religion on his reservation, Brother Rodger Cree replied that it is only in "recent times that people have gravitated to this pan-American Indianism. They have adopted a lot of things they saw in the movies. Usually they are Sioux—they are going to wear a headdress, they are going to do this, they are going do that. It has nothing to do with who we are."[33] According to Cree, each tribe had its own distinct identity and its own traditionally held religious beliefs. These no longer existed in their original form; the modern versions were simply "deceptions." Brother Lee and Brother Cree thought their fellow Indians could move beyond the problems of reservation life by accepting Pentecostalism and establishing a truly "indigenous, self-perpetuating church."[34] Cree's critique is likely also a critique of the rebirth of some traditional practices in the 1970s, after the American Indian Movement, a rebirth that was often conflated with Plains Indian practice, sometimes to the detriment of individual tribal practices.

Brother Lee clearly believed that Christianity could be successful on the reservation only if the church advocating for it was indigenous. He argued that Indians mistrusted white people with good reason because white missionaries had mistreated Indians. Therefore, the only way that Indians would wholly embrace Christianity was if it were fully indigenous and responsive to their needs.[35] Only in this way could Christianity gain authority and authenticity for Native people. In his defense of Christianity against traditional religion, Brother Lee was clearly calling for an embodied and lived indigenous principle for Native Pentecostals.

Brothers Cree and Lee understood that progress for Indian society lay in a religion's ability to address the problems of both the past and the present. They did not think that traditional religion could address those problems, but Christianity could. Moreover, both were adamant that by becoming Christians they were not forfeiting what made them Indians. Instead, they overturned the traditionalist argument that one repudiated one's Indian identity by becoming a Christian. They affirmed that the only way one could be a moral and righteous Indian was to become a Christian. For them, conversion strengthened one's Indian identity.[36] In doing this, they turned Christianity from the "white man's religion" into a religion that distinctly addressed Native problems and began to untangle Christianity from its colonizing roots. Brothers Cree and Lee saw traditional religion as not explicitly evil but as something that was in the past, something that was unable to be maintained now because the social structures that framed it no longer existed.

Yet Brothers Lee and Cree are the only two examples that I know of who address Native religion or traditions in this manner. What is most telling in regard to this particular issue is the silence of Native leaders. The documentary evidence offers very few glimpses into how Native missionaries viewed traditional religion beyond the general consensus that traditional beliefs just no longer work (see the testimonies of Brothers Dann and Maracle from chapter 2). This may have been strategic, along with the attitude of some Native missionaries against traditional religions, such as Luther Cayton's stance against peyote. In her study on modern Native evangelicals, Andrea Smith points out that "some Native evangelical writings that critique syncretism are strategic. That is, they are written to be persuasive to evangelicals who might reject the inclusion of all Native cultural practices within Christianity."[37] Arguing strongly against one aspect of Native religion—Luther Cayton's diatribe against peyote, for example—may actually allow room to include aspects of Native culture that are not seen as so problematic. Smith expounds on this: "In fact, some Native evangelicals do not separate Native spirituality and Native culture and do not see the practice of traditional Native spirituality as a contradiction to Christianity."[38] But they do not advertise this fact because to do so would undermine the underlying reason for their critiques.

Within the AG's Native leadership there is mostly silence as to what aspects of Native culture would be okay to include within Pentecostal practice. Few Native leaders voiced how they would draw boundaries around Native culture that would not include Native religion, or if one could even separate Native culture and religion (many traditionalist Native Americans argue that one cannot separate the two). For this reason, it is difficult to see where any lines might actually be drawn. From the documentary evidence, Native leaders seem to include Native language, food, and dress as aspects of Native culture that were compatible with Native Pentecostalism, with language being the most useful in terms of winning souls—but beyond that there are no explicit mentions of whether drums were ever allowed in the services, or if smudging was still considered permissible for a Native person once he or she converted to Pentecostalism. While I know that preachers such as Brothers Lee, Cree, Andrew, and later John Maracle preached in their native languages, I do not know how they utilized the languages to do so—how did they explain concepts like the Holy Spirit or speaking in tongues? Are these done solely in Native terms, or are they converted into Pentecostal terms, and if so, what does that mean for the translation of Christian ideas into Native forms? The answers to those questions are beyond the scope of this book, but are important to keep in mind when trying to understand how Native evangelists navigated both white and Native worlds.

Much later in the twentieth century, beyond the time period covered in this book, Native evangelicals and charismatics tried to define what amount of Native culture was acceptable within Christian practices, including within the AG.[39] This also included other groups who evangelized Native peoples in the late twentieth century—the Church of God (Cleveland, Tennessee) and the Vineyard Fellowship. Many also spoke out directly against syncretism. There is also a faction within the AG and among both white and Native missionaries that stridently combats Native traditionalism, especially in the modern era.[40] My main point here is to show that from reading the archival sources from the middle decades of the twentieth century, the Native AG view on traditional religion and practices was hazy at best or, at worst, completely absent from the sources.

Even though Native leaders within the AG did not leave behind an explanation of how they strategically used their Native languages to preach the Gospel, one recent study has explained some of the complexities in utilizing Native languages to spread Pentecostalism. Clinton Westman, a Canadian anthropologist, undertook field research among late twentieth-century, early twenty-first-century First Nations Pentecostals in Canada, chiefly the Cree people (whom, early in his career, Rodger Cree evangelized before the effects of rheumatic fever forced him to move south into the United States). Westman's study explicitly examines the Cree language and how Cree Pentecostals utilized Native and Pentecostal forms within their language. He notes that the Cree notion of *acimonwin* (a telling), which retains an importance in everyday modern Cree life, can be "both an elder's teaching and a salvation narrative."[41] Westman goes on to point out that Pentecostalism is a highly oral tradition, which mirrors traditional Cree culture, and that Cree Pentecostals, "including unilingual Cree-speaking elders, have been able to adapt these Pentecostal discursive practices within spoken Cree."[42] Westman's use of language as a tool for understanding Native Pentecostalism is groundbreaking and shows that Native languages are not incompatible with the Pentecostal uses of language in preaching, testimony, speaking in tongues, and shouting.

Although Westman's study focused on modern Canadian Cree Pentecostalism, it does raise a few important points in regards to the United States–based AG Native experience. Native Pentecostal leaders in the AG did preach in native languages (those who could speak them), so it is likely that they probably adapted some of the Native forms of their traditional languages in their manner of preaching, although that is hard to know for sure without any outside confirmation. Pentecostalism and traditional Native cultures in the United Sates are both highly oral traditions, with knowledge passed down orally and with status granted to those who are orally gifted. One can see that the Pentecostal testimonial, as discussed in the previous chapter, gave authority to both white and Native evangelists and was also a way for Natives to prove that they were equally blessed by the Holy Spirit. Therefore, although the documentary sources are silent on the complexities of how Native leaders preached Pentecostalism in their native tongues in mid-twentieth-century America, the usage of traditional languages within a Pentecostal context was probably the most powerful way that Native AG leaders merged their new Pentecostal beliefs with their own tribal cultures.

Although the AG leaders on whom this book focuses for the most part kept silent on the thorny issue of traditional religion and culture (aside from their strategic critique of it), certain Native forms have made their way into some Pentecostal services—and have even been championed by white missionaries. In the Church of God (Cleveland, Tennessee), a smaller Pentecostal denomination than the AG, the Native American ministries have, in the latter part of the twentieth century, created a new movement known as the Native American Contextual Movement, which allows for certain aspects of Native culture that are usually associated with Native traditionalism to be incorporated into Native Pentecostal services. The specific practices included language, smudging, the use of drums and rattles, dance, and talking circles. This is documented in a small but fascinating study written by Corky Alexander, a white minister and scholar within the Church of God who makes the argument that encouraging these practices (which take place in five Native Pentecostal communities associated with the Church of God that he studied) will mean that Christianity will become more in tune with the needs of Native people and therefore more appealing to them. His book also ties each practice to Christianity, therefore justifying how they can be separated from Native traditional belief, and makes the argument that they are cultural, and also humanly universal practices, rather than traditional Native religious practices. He concludes by arguing that the inclusion of these practices will actually guard against syncretism, thereby inverting the critique that the inclusion of Native practices into Christianity actually is syncretism.[43]

Alexander's study confirms that some Pentecostal Native Americans do indeed incorporate aspects of their culture that many white missionaries would consider problematic into Pentecostal services. It is striking, however, that a book calling for contextualization of aspects of Native traditional practice into Pentecostalism was written by a white Pentecostal minister—Alexander is surely not immune to critique by white Pentecostals who do not agree with him, but he does enjoy a certain distance, in that his ministry or leadership within the Church of God is not affected as much as it would be if he had instead been a Native Pentecostal authoring such a book. In light of continuing paternalism and ethnocentrism that still marks Native ministries, even in the modern era, it is easier for a white man to make this sort of argument. Alexander's work is also based on much more recent ethnographic scholarship, and he does not address the first generation of Native Pentecostals, for whom it was even more perilous to speak out in favor of anything that seemed too close to traditional Native religion. Yet what this work does show is that, as Pentecostalism continues to grow and change over time, some forms of the religion (in this case, the Church of God) are open to accepting some aspects of Native culture.

Only extensive ethnographic study could explain how AG Pentecostals deal with the issue of incorporation of traditional religion and culture into their Pentecostal Indian identity, and even that would not reveal what the first generation of Native leaders thought about traditional religions and possible religious syncretism. Without the discovery of personal journals or extensive reflective writings from these leaders, their thoughts about Native religions and culture will remain unknown. The silence is likely strategic, and other scholars, such as Smith, Westman, and Alexander, have pointed out that in the modern era Native Pentecostals have a complicated relationship with traditional Native beliefs and practices. Yet the two opinions that are public, those of Brother Lee and Brother Cree, show that they believe that only an indigenous form of Christianity could help address American Indians' spiritual needs—thus solidifying the utmost importance of the practice of the indigenous principle for these two men.

White Missionaries and Miraculous Healings

Healings were essential to Pentecostal evangelization because they functioned as dramatic and tangible evidence of God's imminence. For Natives, healing helped fill the void that surrendering their old beliefs had left, but white missionaries put much emphasis on dramatic and miraculous healings—more, in fact, than their Native counterparts. They felt that they had to prove the miraculous power of Jesus and the Holy Spirit in order to convert Indians to the "Jesus Way." This emphasis on dramatic healings also paralleled the American Pentecostal healing revivals of the 1940s and 1950s.[44] Spurred by reports of miraculous healings and revivals among the non-Indian population, white missionaries fanned out across the reservations and reported their own miracles. One must keep in mind that the *PE*, in which most of healings were reported, followed a stylized sequence for healing narratives that always ended in success. For white missionaries, healings were an essential part of classical Pentecostal evangelization, whereas for Native missionaries healings were transformed into a form of racial reconciliation and part of how they lived out the indigenous principle.

Publicized miracles and resurrections point to the strong primitivistic impulses within American Pentecostalism. They believed that the era of miracles had not ended with the apostolic age but that true believers could perform miracles as vessels of the Holy Spirit. The beginning of Sister Washburn's mission work coincided with the "great revival" within American Pentecostalism. Historian David Harrell notes that "the great revival that launched the careers of the independent ministers lasted roughly from 1947 to 1958 and was predominantly a healing revival."[45] In Harrell's memorable words, "the common heartbeat of every service was the miracle—the hypnotic moment when the Spirit moved to heal the sick and raise the dead."[46] In the greater American Pentecostal culture, believers flocked to these revivals and witnessed miraculous healings. AG missionaries read of these events and prayed that the Holy Spirit would send great acts of healing to the reservations.

White missionaries often wrote of miraculous transformations that led skeptics into the Pentecostal fold. Early in her initial missionary posting on the Apache reservation in White River, Sister Washburn experienced her first "great miracle" as a Pentecostal missionary. In the middle of a sermon on God's miraculous nature, an Apache woman ran in carrying a baby.

> She literally threw the baby into my arms. The baby's little body was cold and stiff in death. She had just taken it from the hospital morgue and was on her way to the cemetery for its burial. Reckless faith, however, directed her to the church. She wanted us to pray her baby would live again! There I stood holding that little corpse. This had to be possibly the greatest challenge of my ministry. . . . As I prayed, I began to feel warmth return to that little body and the rigid little limbs became limp and moveable, I handed that baby restored to life into its mother's arms. All of us in that Sunday service were overcome with the knowledge that we had actually beheld the resurrection power of the Lord.[47]

According to Sister Washburn, her congregants were awed, and she was unable to finish her sermon. After word spread among the Apaches, her ministry began to grow. Eighteen years later a young man and his mother visited Sister Washburn's parsonage in Phoenix, where she was serving the All-Tribes Church. He asked for her blessing before his departure for Vietnam. The young man identified himself as the Apache baby whom she had healed, and Sister Washburn prayed over him that he might come back from Vietnam alive. A few years later, she heard that he had returned safely to the reservation without any battle injuries.[48] Sister Washburn's autobiography brims with reported miracles and the blessings of the Holy Spirit that she witnessed in her many years in the ministry. From her commentary on each incident, it appears that the miracles not only affirmed God's power but also reminded Sister Washburn of God's call in her own life. They affirmed the importance of her work.

Most of the reported miracles from this era were not as extreme as Sister Washburn's "resurrection" and usually involved accidents and physical infirmities. For example, in one such report, boiling water badly burned a Navajo infant. The *PE* reported, "The skin had slipped several places and water was running from her body where there was no skin. Little Marian was in great pain."[49] According to the doctors, the child would be in the hospital for four weeks for skin grafting, but instead of waiting for modern medicine to work, the missionaries implored their congregation to pray for the healing of the child. According to a report in the *PE*, within two weeks she experienced healing.[50] In another case, missionaries prayed over a young, crippled Apache woman. A week later, they returned to visit her and found that "Ardella had not had to use her crutches since the last time we prayed for her. She had been cutting wood and even had walked about one-half mile to a friend's home."[51] The missionaries concluded, "God definitely healed this young lady and she has been able to remain true to the Lord."[52]

According to the reports from the *PE*, many of those who were healed "stayed true to the church," as might be expected since they had received tangible experience of God's power.[53] In one case reported to the *PE*, a group of Christ's Ambassadors, teenage evangelists from the All-Tribes Mission in Phoenix, visited with a young Indian couple expecting a child who doctors believed would not survive. "The CA's told them of God's power to heal and prayed for the lady with her permission . . . at the same time that the Christians were praying for the woman, a fine, healthy baby was born to her."[54] The father of the child was reportedly amazed at the miracle and realized that it was "God who gave us our child."[55]

Healings proved crucial for successful missionary work, because the act of healing spoke of God's power in a manner understood by both missionaries and those to whom they preached. Often, white missionaries did not speak the language of the people on the reservation, which led to heavy reliance on Indian interpreters. But miraculous healing stepped beyond the language barrier. Miraculous healings also boosted the restorationist version of the Gospel that white missionaries were seeking to spread among American Indians. Healings were just one of the signs and wonders that God sent down to reaffirm Pentecostal progress—at least in white missionaries' eyes. Healings also meant to white missionaries that God blessed their work and showed the readers of the *PE* tangible evidence of this. Still, white missionaries and the white-run *PE* regarded healing differently from many of the Indian missionaries who came after them. For white missionaries, healing focused on actual bodily healing. Indian missionaries expanded that idea to include healing that encompassed righting not only physical and spiritual wrongs but also mental and cultural ones.

Native Missionaries and the Great Physician

Indian missionaries, like their white contemporaries, emphasized the Gospel and the death and resurrection of Jesus. But they interpreted the Gospel according to their needs as Indians. They reshaped it as a Gospel of healing—not just from illness and alcoholism, but also from the bitterness of past wrongs and hatred of white people. Through published articles and pamphlets distributed to the greater AG public, Indian missionaries attempted to alleviate stereotypes and misconceptions of Indians. By interpreting the Gospel for their own purposes and disseminating to white Pentecostals information about their history and culture, Indian missionaries used their autonomy to fight paternalism and ethnocentrism. They presented a "performance of reconciliation" to their white counterparts and, in doing so, "offer[ed] striking critiques of both past and present-day colonial practices."[56] Thus, they defined themselves as Pentecostal Indians who embraced reconciliation and wielded the authority of the indigenous principle to reimagine Pentecostal healing.

Indian missionaries knew that most white Americans, including their own AG brothers and sisters, held misconceptions about Indians, and they sought to address them. Their main venue was the *PE*, which Indian missionaries used to their advantage. First, they educated the greater Pentecostal public on the wrongs done to American Indians, particularly by the government. With the exception of a handful of outspoken early white missionaries, white Pentecostals rarely criticized the American government for its Indian policies. Most white Americans did not know what life was like on the reservations and did not really understand the intricacies of Indian policy, so it was left to Indian missionaries to explain how badly the American government had treated them.

The two events that Indian missionaries used to gain the public's attention were the Cherokee's Trail of Tears and the Navajo's Long Walk, episodes that showed the cruelty and indifference of the American government. Notably, the two men who were responsible for the articles in the *PE* and subsequent tracts not only were significant Indian evangelists but also came from the Cherokee and the Navajo tribes.

John McPherson, a Cherokee, developed the "Trail of Tears" article and tract from a popular sermon he often used while evangelizing. The tract contains both a creative retelling of life on the trail and the historical facts of the forced march. Brother McPherson boldly asserted that many Christian Cherokees were among those removed from their homelands in North Carolina and Georgia. He also noted that the tribe aided the U.S. government in its battles against the Creek Indians.[57] Brother McPherson described the removal as especially brutal: "Men were seized in the fields; women were taken from their hearths; children were taken from their play and always if they looked back, the victims saw their homes in flames."[58] He continued by vividly describing the forced march, undertaken in harsh winter weather, with an emphasis on the large numbers of women and children who died in the ordeal. His creative retelling parallels the eyewitness accounts written by the Baptist missionaries who witnessed the violence.[59]

Brother McPherson hoped to arouse the sympathy of his white readers with a vivid account of government injustice and to inspire them to become missionaries to Indians. But the most informative part of the article is the closing paragraph, where Brother McPherson offered the Gospel as a means of reconciliation.

> But I, as a descendant of one who walked the death march, can hold no malice against my fellow man. For what has happened to my people I can harbor no ill in my heart because I have been born again and washed in Calvary's flow. God, the perfect Judge, in His own hour will settle the account and His judgment will be swift and sure and just. The "Trail of Tears" of the Cherokee is history. It has been duly recorded in eternity's archives awaiting the position of the Almighty. Let the judge of all the world weigh the action and the actors who must explain more than four thousand silent graves.[60]

Brother McPherson stated that by becoming a Christian, he could move forward and leave behind his anger at those who inflicted so much pain. In essence, Pentecostal Christianity healed him from the wrongs of the past and allowed him to overcome his hate. Note that Brother McPherson strongly emphasized judgment: while it may seem that the government and President Andrew Jackson escaped punishment for their misdeeds, he believed they would have to face God and answer for their actions. Brother McPherson's tract offers an example not only of an accessible account of the cruelty of the government toward American Indians but also of how he as a missionary reshaped the Gospel.

Sister Coralie Lee, the white wife of Navajo missionary Charlie Lee, wrote "The Long Walk" tract. Like "The Trail of Tears," it saw publication as both a *PE* article and a pamphlet for fellow Pentecostals. Also like "The Trail of Tears," "The Long Walk" emphasized the injustices of the federal government toward Indians (in this case, the Navajos), a piece of history that the American public largely ignored. The tract describes how the government, through its agent Kit Carson, starved Navajos who resisted removal from their homeland. Sister Lee painted a vivid picture of Carson and his men slaughtering Navajo sheep herds and cutting down fruit trees in order to break the spirit of the Navajos. Most Navajos surrendered and gathered at Fort Defiance. Next, they found themselves forced to walk to Fort Sumner, where the government imposed an experiment on them.[61] The government forced the Navajos to become farmers and live in settled towns like the Pueblos, but the experiment failed. The government sent them back to their homeland to herd sheep.[62]

Sister Lee's purpose in writing this article was twofold. First, she hoped to educate Pentecostal readers about a major event in Navajo history. Second, she addressed the need for educated, indigenous missionaries and the money to support them. She states, "The great need is for the Indians themselves to go to Bible schools and come back as missionaries, especially to those who are unreached as yet due to the language barrier. But most Navajos are not wealthy enough to pay for schooling and families are large."[63] Sister Lee understood that the most effective way to reach other Indians was by training Christian Indians to become missionaries. Like her husband, she had fully embraced the indigenous principle and was willing to take the risk of asking *PE* readers for support and money to implement an idea that the white AG leadership did not completely accept.

Besides educating the general Pentecostal readers on Indian history, Indian evangelists used their writings to make their fellow Indians seem less exotic and alien and to clarify the special difficulties of reservation life. One article, written by Brother McPherson and Brother Paul Kienel, tried to dispel long-held stereotypes regarding Indians. "Often the published material about Indians is either sentimentally unrealistic or brutally untrue. Indians were and are neither ignorant and blood-thirsty savages, nor misunderstood heroes. Indians are human beings, living interesting lives in accordance with customs and beliefs which though ancient in origin, are greatly modified by several hundred years of contact with white people."[64] Unlike their white missionary colleagues, who generally emphasized the exotic or savage nature of the people, Indian missionaries wrote about the essential humanity of the people they served. Brothers McPherson and Kienel pointed out the diversity of Indians in North America, including the differences of language and customs.[65] They underscored the difficulty of evangelizing Indians without skilled missionaries who could speak the Native languages. In addition, they emphasized the terrible condition of the infrastructure of the reservations. Money for repairs and building would aid in the spread of the Gospel. Unemployment and poverty were hard to overcome without help.[66] Although the article ended with a plea for donations to the AG's Indian home missions, it also quietly promoted the indigenous principle, and Brothers McPherson and Kienel challenged stereotypes—stereotypes upon which their white counterparts played in the very same pages of the *PE*.

At the very heart of Pentecostalism lay its restorationist impulse, which allowed believers to frame the Gospel in terms of healing, miraculous events, and prophecy. For Indian missionaries, however, the focus on healing proved more internal and more collective. They framed healing in terms of release from the pains of racism and the injustices of history. This emphasis contrasted with that of white missionaries who tended to report specific physical healings. This is not to say that Native missionaries did not also experience direct physical healing. Many did. But those same men also reported a kind of spiritual healing, one that they felt gave them the power to navigate a new path in becoming a Pentecostal Indian. As previously noted, both Brother McPherson and Brother Cree felt that the Holy Spirit freed them from their personal hatred toward the white man. This idea of healing was not an anomaly, but rather the norm among Indian Pentecostals. For them, the most important sort of healing was one of the heart as well as spirit.

Indian missionaries often gave hints of their own view of healing in the articles they wrote for the *PE*. Brother Effman, a Klamath Indian, elegantly summed up Indian missionaries' approach. "When Christ enters the life He gives a new heart. This removes from the Indian all the former hatred and mistrust for the white man. Christ is the Great Physician and He can meet both the physical and spiritual needs of the heartsick Indian."[67] Even though Christ can "give a new heart," as the majority of Indian evangelists believed, giving up old prejudices still proved hard. Brother Cree was careful to make this point.[68] Although he credited the Holy Spirit with helping him overcome his hatred of the French, it was at times painful and difficult, especially when the French did little to convince him that they deserved his forgiveness.[69]

Native evangelists acknowledged the pain of the past and the atrocities their people had suffered. Even though most embraced the rhetoric of reconciliation, they held those who sinned against their people to account. Brother McPherson made this point strongly in his "Trail of Tears" sermon, stressing both judgment and the power of Christ to turn the deep anger of his fellow Indians into more productive feelings. "In recounting the migration into exile of the Cherokee in 1838, with its atrocities, its blood and death, we are appalled and rise up to protest the way the Cherokee were treated by fellow men. But I ask you, how have you treated the Christ, who left heaven and adorned in the robes of flesh, was born in a manger and later suffered and died that you might have life and have life more abundantly? He too walked a trail of tears, a journey of sorrows."[70]

At the end of his sermon, Brother McPherson challenged his fellow Indians to understand that Christ was someone like themselves. Jesus was a poor man, despised by many and eventually beaten and killed by his detractors. In other words, since Christ bore similarities to their fellow Indians, he could truly understand and address the difficulties of their lives and history. Brother McPherson believed that accepting Christ would change the harshness of Indian life and give his people hope, something he felt many lacked. In advocating forgiveness and reconciliation, evangelists like Brother Cree and Brother McPherson were attempting to live a true Christian life, one in which they forgave those who had committed wrongs against their people. Their interpretation of the Gospel moved beyond the idea of salvation. For Indian evangelists, salvation and the gifts of the Holy Spirit were not enough to solve the ongoing problem of being an Indian in a country that over the centuries had stolen their land and destroyed their way of life. Brothers Cree and McPherson understood that their fellow Indians had to move beyond the wrongs of the past. Becoming a Pentecostal and embracing a Gospel of healing and reconciliation was one way for American Indians to do just that.

Healing and reconciliation also proved to be important in the practice of the indigenous principle. By reinterpreting Pentecostal healing, Native Pentecostals put the power of reconciliation in their own hands and on their own terms. They framed it as a part of their experience, their identity, and their own struggle. Therefore, their understanding of healing gave an American Indian flavor to Pentecostal restorationism; it was not just signs and wonders but a form of healing that could be shaped by a particular ethnic group's own experience of colonization and abuse. This Pentecostal healing stepped beyond the physical and even the spiritual to

embrace circumstances that were particular to the American Indian psyche—thereby subtly changing Pentecostalism in profound yet often unac-
knowledged ways.

Dressing Up Like an Indian

American Indian leaders faced a problem that their white missionary
contemporaries rarely thought about: how should they dress in public?
As Indians, the different evangelists held distinct tribal identities, but as
members of the AG, they had to contend with a white bureaucracy that saw
them as all the same. Though many *PE* pictures show Indian evangelists
dressed just like their white counterparts in the dark, formal suit of the
era, by the mid-1950s pictures also appear showing Indian leaders in Indian regalia. Native Pentecostals had to deal with the issue of how to present themselves, and a deeper exploration of this issue shows that choosing
to "dress like an Indian" was complicated and unearthed issues surrounding how Native people were perceived in the mid-twentieth century. The
evidence from the period is sketchy in the documentary sources; in most
cases, it is unclear why some Indians wore tribal regalia while others did
not. But one evangelist did give an explanation.

Brother John McPherson wore his famous Plains headdress, although
he was a Cherokee.[71] He donned the headdress on the advice of a white
minister. Early in Brother McPherson's evangelization career in California, he met a genial white AG pastor, Brother C. E. Pershing.[72] The latter
took an interest in Brother McPherson's early work and helped him attend
the local AG Bible college. When Brother McPherson entered the ministry,
Brother Pershing advised him to define himself as an Indian. "He told me
he felt impressed by the Lord that I should buy an Indian suit and use it
when I preached. He felt it would draw needed attention to the plight of
my Indian brothers and sisters, and it would also be something different
and novel that would draw the unsaved to the services. . . . I had no reason to buy the suit and no money with which to make such a purchase,
but I felt Bro. Pershing had truly heard from the Lord."[73] Brother Pershing
lent Brother McPherson $350 to buy the Indian suit, but this left Brother
McPherson with a problem: "I had no idea where to go buy a suit like
Brother Pershing had in mind. All right, I was an Indian, but I had never
worn the leather costume and full bonnet he was talking about."[74] Shortly
thereafter, on a trip to Phoenix, he encountered a man at a trading post
who sold Indian clothing, but not the type he wanted. The dealer told him

to look up Pawnee Bill's Trading Post, which carried the full Plains warrior suit.[75] Brother McPherson wrote to Pawnee Bill's for a catalog and picked out his costume, noting that it was "a complete Indian costume: a full leather suit, beautiful feather bonnet, leather breachclout, etc."[76] Brother McPherson purchased the Indian clothing although it did not match his tribal affiliation—Cherokees did not wear the kind of war bonnet that was so popular among Plains tribes.

Once outfitted in his Indian costume, Brother McPherson wore it for most of his public appearances. The pictures in his autobiography—including the one on the cover—show him resplendent in a full Plains war bonnet and leather suit. *PE* pictures also usually showed the same. Brother McPherson acquired a variety of war bonnets: the AG still owns not only the large one on display in its archive museum but also two other smaller versions locked in the archives vault.[77] McPherson claimed that when he purchased his first suit, "I had no idea that I was entering into a relationship with the good people at Pawnee Bill's that would stretch for over 40 years of ministry."[78] But the relationship proved to be a crucial one, indeed.

Although Brother McPherson consistently wore his Indian suit in his public appearances, he recognized it played into white stereotypes of what a "real" Indian looked like. In his autobiography, Brother McPherson noted that Western movies flourished in the 1950s and 1960s. Consequently, the publicity photos of him in the suit helped draw curiosity seekers who wanted to see a "real" Indian.[79] Brother McPherson also acknowledged that his suit was especially useful for children's ministry because its bright colors and exotic appearance piqued their curiosity.[80] He created an entire "Indian skit" as a way to draw children into his work, prominently featuring the suit and a teepee that he built from a design in a book.[81] The tepee, like the suit, was not a part of Cherokee culture, yet Brother McPherson felt that these objects proved effective for his ministry and helped him save souls, so he was justified in using them.[82]

Saving souls came with a cultural price. The suit not only played into typical white stereotypes of Indians but also trivialized the traditional culture and tribal ties of Brother McPherson. He was a Cherokee wearing a generic Hollywood rendition of a Plains Indian warrior suit. Most ordinary Indians retained some traditional dress that was not as garish as the Indian suit and proved more functional—velvet skirts for Navajo women, elaborate hairstyles for Hopi women, and traditional jewelry that graced the bodies of both men and women from any number of tribes. As a rule, Indians did not wear traditional dress every day. They tended to dress like working-class Americans—especially the men, whose standard uniform was that of the day laborer: jeans, t-shirt, flannel overshirt, and heavy boots. Ordinary Indian dress would not draw the white American public, however, and Brother McPherson understood that he would garner more attention if he wore Indian costume rather than the standard three-piece suit of a Pentecostal evangelist.

Encouraging local Natives to dress up in costume, however, proved common among white missionaries to a variety of native peoples, as historian Susan Billington Harper pointed out in her work on white Anglican missionaries to India. In India, white mentors and leaders pressured the first native Anglican bishop to "dress like an Indian," which deeply bothered the bishop; he rejected their ideas outright.[83] Brother McPherson, in contrast, embraced the Indian suit and developed his ministry around it. The reactions of his fellow Indian missionaries and evangelists to his colorful costume remain unknown, but Brother McPherson turned up in photographs at Indian conventions and meetings wearing the suit while standing next to his fellow evangelists.

Brother McPherson's costume also relates to the "Hobby Indians" cultural phenomenon of the 1950s. At the time that Brother Pershing encouraged Brother McPherson to wear the Plains Indian suit, white "Hobby Indians" had begun to emerge. These were white people who traveled the "hobby powwow" circuit in order to dance and sing with real Indians and promote Indian culture and arts and crafts.[84] They paid "real Indians" to sing and dance with them, they wore elaborate costumes, and they constructed their own "white Indian" identity. These "hobby powwows" grew popular with white Americans, and although we do not know for sure, they might have given Brother Pershing the idea to encourage Brother McPherson to dress up in a Plains suit. As Philip Deloria states, "Racially different and temporally separate, Indians were objects of desire, but only as they existed outside of American society and modernity itself."[85] Dressed in his Plains suit, Brother McPherson transformed himself into a powerful conception of what an Indian was: different, "other," and exotic. By taking advantage of those white conceptions of "Indian-ness," Brother McPherson drew large crowds, expanding his opportunities for evangelization. In some ways, Brother McPherson bested a white leadership that encouraged a Cherokee to "play Indian" by dressing up as a Sioux: by willingly showing himself off as "other" and agreeing to wear the costume so as not to offend his white superiors, Brother McPherson gained authority that eventually led him to a leadership role as the first national Indian representative. Because he appeared amenable to the input of white leadership, the AG chose him as Indian representative, likely believing that he would continue to comply with their requests. In this position, however, he would go on to challenge subtly the very white leadership that had "otherized" him in the first place.

Whether or not he was influenced by the popular "hobby Indians" of the era, Brother McPherson was at the very least, "playing Indian" in order to fit white expectations of what an Indian should look like. There is a long, complex history of "playing Indian" within American culture that spans from the original Boston Tea Party, to hippie "Indians," to the modern Tea Partiers who protest the government by reenacting how the original Boston Tea Partiers "played Indian."[86] In the end, the fact that Brother McPherson "played Indian" says as much about white AG culture as Native AG culture. White AG members expected their Native counterparts to look a certain way, and in order to fill those expectations, Brother McPherson, a Cherokee, dressed up in a Hollywood-style Plains suit and war bonnet.

While a few other Indian evangelists chose to wear an Indian suit during their public ministry, many did not. Pictures from the PE demonstrate that Brother Andrew Maracle, a Mohawk, and Brother James F. Pepper, another Cherokee evangelist, occasionally were photographed in a traditional Plains war bonnet.[87] But the pictures in the PE indicate that most Indian evangelists wore the dark suits of the 1950s and 1960s. Most men in the AG dressed in this manner, especially evangelists and pastors, and from the pictures in the PE, Indian evangelists literally followed suit. Doing so did not mean they were rejecting their Indian culture; rather, they were adhering to the norms of Pentecostal evangelists and pastors. One of the most militantly indigenous evangelists of the 1950s and 1960s, Brother Charlie Lee, was rarely shown in a costume in Pentecostal publications. The PE always photographed him in a dark suit, even in pictures that showed him in action around his church. Even the self-portrait that now hangs at the American Indian College is of him in a blue suit. There is one picture of him in traditional Navajo garb from his youth, but it was not until the late 1970s, after his church had become the first indigenous church in the AG, that more pictures appeared in the PE showing Brother Lee in everyday, Navajo dress: a dark velveteen shirt and Navajo silver jewelry.[88] Brother Lee's use of Indian clothing differed from Brother McPherson's. Brother Lee wore everyday dress that accurately reflected his tribal affiliation, not a spectacular costume like Brother McPherson's. Moreover, Lee's pattern of dress endured. To this day, most Indian evangelists prefer to wear a business suit when appearing in public, like the rest of their AG contemporaries. When I met and interviewed Mohawk evangelists Brother Rodger Cree and current AG Indian Representative Brother John Maracle, nephew of Andrew Maracle, they both wore formal lightweight summer suits, accessorized with touches of traditional Indian jewelry.

Brother McPherson's Indian outfit points to some problems, most of which the sources do not explain. On one hand, that a white AG pastor suggested that Brother McPherson wear an Indian suit highlights the paternalism and ethnocentrism so common in white AG missions to Indians. On the other hand, perhaps Brother McPherson's acceptance of the Indian suit can be seen as a way of developing his own particular Pentecostal Indian identity. Although of Cherokee ancestry, Brother McPherson was fair-skinned. Perhaps he felt that the Indian suit helped to legitimize him as an Indian in the eyes of his audience. Brother Lee, however, was a dark-skinned Navajo who spoke Navajo. Perhaps he felt that he had to wear a "white man's suit" in order to legitimize himself as an AG evangelist. The motivations of these two men, as well as of their contemporaries, are lost to us. Almost all of them are dead, and they left behind no written record on the issue. But the dress of Indian missionaries is important to consider, because it shows that some Indian missionaries sought to define their own Pentecostal-Native identity in ways that were both creative and sometimes puzzling.[89]

Conclusion

Native missionaries found themselves having to navigate the tricky issues of Native culture and identity once they converted to Pentecostalism. At the same time they began to find themselves as leaders and champions of the indigenous principle. For the Indian missionaries who were willing to speak out, Pentecostalism became the only truly indigenous option for their people, because they believed that traditional religion no longer spoke to their people's needs. As a group, they reworked the Gospel to emphasize not only the redemptive power of Christ's death and resurrection but also his healing power over an ugly past, hatred, and racism. They struggled with how they should physically portray themselves in dress; whatever their answer they established public personae as missionaries who were both Indian and Pentecostal.

Detractors of Pentecostalism might charge that Pentecostal Indians "sold out" their traditional beliefs to become Christians, that conversion erased converts' tribal cultures, or that Indian missionaries were simply witless tools of the white AG establishment. The history I have described shows how such assumptions lack nuance, for Native people have been shaping their own religious identities since contact. When Indians converted to Pentecostalism, they did not just decide to fall into place behind the white leaders of the AG. Instead, they actively engaged the denomination to build their own churches, beliefs, and leadership. At times, they maintained a strategic silence. In other moments, they subtly critiqued the AG by using its own Pentecostal principles and were outspoken proponents of a Native understanding of judgment and reconciliation. They adapted their Native languages to Pentecostalism and learned to preach in it, and all along they consistently championed the indigenous principle. They *chose* their Pentecostal Indian identity and created something new and innovative within the AG.

By making that choice, and living it, Indian missionaries began to define the practice of the indigenous principle. By fighting to include their own voice and their own experiences into Pentecostalism, they subtly shaped Pentecostalism's trajectory. By showing white missionaries that they could indeed run their own churches and be responsible for their own religious lives, they embodied the indigenous principle and showed that it could be realized. By using it to create their own understanding of Pentecostalism, it became more than theory, and it could be lived out in new ways that spoke to the American Indian experience.

Yet the elephant in the room in the mid-twentieth-century AG remained white Pentecostals who were not as quick as Native missionaries to embrace the indigenous principle. Some white missionaries, however, acknowledged their biases and rose above them, as well as the need for indigenous churches. During Sister Washburn's ministry at the All-Tribes Mission in Phoenix, she was troubled because there were not enough trained Indian evangelists. The comment of a young Indian evangelist, a student having adjustment problems at a regular AG Bible school, addressed the problem directly: "'Sister Washburn,' he questioned, 'Why can't we Indians have our own Bible school? We can preach in our language but we need a place where we can study the Word together; a place where we can have more in common than in a school where most of the students are Anglos.'"[90] Sister Washburn acknowledged that they needed such a place. She knew that white missionaries faced multiple hurdles in their ministry, hurdles that would not stand in the way for Indian missionaries. She knew that an indigenous church required indigenous pastors and missionaries. She also knew that her idea would be opposed by those who believed that the Indian converts did not need special treatment and could never take on full leadership roles in the AG. Sister Washburn knew that many difficulties had to be overcome before the founding of her Indian Bible college, yet she willingly faced the opposition of fellow white missionaries and AG personnel. She assumed her especially heavy "burden" for an all-Indian Bible school because, in her mind, the power of the Holy Spirit was behind her, and nothing would stop her from what God wanted to be her life's work. In doing so, she not only founded the first all-Indian Bible college in the country, the All-Tribes Bible School, in September 1957, but also laid the major cornerstone on which an AG indigenous church would eventually be constructed. Sister Washburn, through her strength and faith, moved beyond the paternalism and ethnocentrism of most white AG missionaries and showed the AG as a whole the steps necessary for an indigenous church and, in the process, helped Indian Pentecostals begin to institutionalize the practice of the indigenous principle.

*Native evangelist
Charlie Lee, drawing a
picture, 1978 (FPHC)*

*Native evangelist
Andrew Maracle
speaking (FPHC)*

Founder of the American Indian College Alta Washburn and her husband Clarence Washburn (FPHC)

Native evangelists John McPherson (left) and George Effman (FPHC)

Native evangelist John McPherson in full Indian regalia (FPHC)

Native evangelist Rodger Cree (FPHC)

*Students and staff with banner in front of dormitory at the American Indian
Bible College (FPHC)*

Administration Building and Dormitory at the American Indian Bible College (FPHC)

Summer American Indian camp meeting in Arizona, 1988 (FPHC)

Institutionalizing the Indigenous Principle *The American Indian College and Mesa View Assembly of God*

Sister Alta Washburn had a problem. After many years on the mission field in Arizona, she faced competition from an independent Christian evangelist for the souls of the Phoenix area Indians.[1] The evangelist's emotional preaching style horrified Sister Washburn; in her opinion, he exploited people.[2] She believed that she was losing Indian converts to him because they did not possess a solid biblical education. In her mind, the AG, though not perfect, represented firm, biblically based, evangelical teaching. This experience convinced Sister Washburn that the only way she could encourage the conversion of Indians and loyalty to the AG was through well-educated Indian missionaries and evangelists. Unsure of where to turn, Sister Washburn prayed. A few days later, she received her answer.

> Plainly the Lord spoke to me, "There came a bear and a lion, and there came Goliath who roared against the camp of Israel. What did David do? He arose in the name of the Lord God of Israel. He laid hold of the bear, the lion and Goliath. He did more then [*sic*] pray. He attacked them and prevailed." As I left the meeting I was more assured than ever that God would help us build a Bible school for American Indians. There they could learn to fight the good fight of faith with sound Bible doctrine against the bears, the lions and the Goliaths who might come against them.[3]

A white, female missionary who had completed only middle school, Sister Washburn identified closely with the young David, who had battled

Goliath. In this case, Goliath proved to be not only the ministerial competition but also the AG hierarchy.

Initially Sister Washburn had a hard time convincing white AG missionaries to support her idea for an all-Indian Bible school. Her fellow missionaries feared that if they sent converts to the Bible school, they would never return to the reservation. Others questioned the need for a Bible school and wondered how she would find the money to build it.[4] But Sister Washburn clung to her vision, bolstered by letters of support from like-minded missionaries. She wrote to Brother C. M. Ward of California for guidance. Ward, a rapidly rising star in AG circles, responded with encouragement. "'Sister Washburn,' he wrote back, 'keep yelling about that Bible school. Someone will hear you.'"[5] Sister Washburn followed his advice. She spoke so loudly and clearly that no one, even the AG hierarchy in Springfield, could ignore her. In September 1957, against significant odds, Sister Washburn's all-Indian Bible school opened. By holding to her convictions, she changed the face of AG Bible school education and forced the AG to recognize the needs of its Indian converts.

Sister Washburn's sincerity was noted by the indigenous leadership within the AG. As Mohawk evangelist Rodger Cree remembered, "In the conversation that followed with Sister Washburn, Esther and I both sensed that she was indeed a visionary pioneer in uncharted and even controversial territory—that of 'raising up' indigenous Native pastors."[6] Cree first met Washburn in the late 1950s and stressed the importance of her work to Native Pentecostals. "Her vision was not only to reach Native Americans with the gospel, but also to equip them to reach their own people—an integral component of the indigenous principle propagated throughout the apostolic era, especially by the great apostle Paul."[7] Note that Brother Cree not only invoked the importance of the indigenous principle to Native Pentecostalism but also claimed both his Native and Pentecostal identities. He affirmed that Native people could indeed be leaders within the church, and he also traced their own authority as Native leaders back to the apostle Paul, thus making their Christian identity inarguable.

Sister Washburn was not the only missionary who made the AG grapple with the indigenous principle. When Brother Charlie Lee arrived on the Navajo reservation in the 1940s and began preaching in Navajo, fellow missionaries, white and Indian, took notice. He asked his congregation to negotiate the transition from being a supported mission to a fully indigenous, self-supporting, district-affiliated church. Lee's work took place well under the AG radar and was not as well documented as Sister Washburn's

Bible school, but there is no doubt that he was pivotal among the Native Pentecostal leadership in showing how the indigenous principle could be realized. In 1976, his Navajo church became the first AG home mission on a federally recognized reservation to give up its mission status in favor of a district-affiliated church.[8] Lee's work among the Navajos set off a national push for AG Native-run churches and forced the AG to acknowledge it was possible to build indigenous churches.

During the 1960s and 1970s, the implementation of the indigenous principle in the AG home missions program proved painful and slow for both white and Native missionaries. Native evangelists and their sympathetic white counterparts launched a two-pronged movement toward realizing the indigenous principle. This chapter explores the first part: the development of the American Indian College of the Assemblies of God and the creation of indigenous churches led by Charlie Lee.[9] The following chapter considers the long struggle for a national American Indian representative to the AG's General Council and for tangible power within the AG. For Indian leaders and their supporters, their struggle to make the AG acknowledge their need for tangible power and leadership within the denomination came to define their practice as Pentecostals.

The leaders of the indigenous church movement and the founder of the American Indian College (AIC) were quintessential Pentecostal outsiders: an uneducated white female missionary and a famous Navajo artist-turned-evangelist. Sister Washburn's position as a woman and as an appointed home missionary (an area traditionally seen as not having much institutional power) allowed her to defy her white male superiors and stand by her Native brothers and sisters, because she had the authority of the Holy Spirit and an unshakable sense of mission. Brother Lee's ministry took part in one of the more remote sections of the Navajo reservation, which gave him the latitude and autonomy to put into place his indigenous church ideals. Moreover, Sister Washburn and Brother Lee embodied the pragmatic and restorationist impulses that characterized the Pentecostal experience.[10] Sister Washburn and Brother Lee believed in their ability, through the power of the Holy Spirit, to transform the AG so it would meet the needs of their flocks. They hoped to shape the Pentecostal vision of the church and to integrate a population regarded by most white Pentecostals as outsiders.

This chapter argues that the individual work of Sister Washburn and her vision for an all-Native Bible college and Brother Lee's dogged pursuit of building the first indigenous church were the first large-scale actions that took the practice of the indigenous principle and catapulted it on a national level that the AG could no longer ignore. Their work, and the support that came from the Pentecostal Indian community, prodded the AG to recognize the importance of the indigenous principle on a national scale. Sister Washburn's Bible college gave Pentecostal Indians a place where they could hone their own distinct Pentecostal and Native religious practices, develop their identities as Natives and Christians, and be taught and embrace the practice of the indigenous principle. Therefore, the American Indian College was integral to the institutional realization of the indigenous principle, the propagation of the idea and its practice, and it helped to pave the way for later institutional recognition of American Indian leadership. At the same time Brother Lee's push for indigenous churches was the culmination of Melvin Hodges's indigenous principle and showed that it was indeed possible for Native Pentecostals to run their own churches and, in doing so, to subtly redefine Pentecostalism. Lee's closeness to the Bible college also meant that he provided an example to the students on how to plant an indigenous church. Brother Lee and Sister Washburn's histories were parallel, personally intertwined, and made more powerful in how they supported each other's endeavors. Together they were the one-two punch that made the AG sit up and realize that Native people were serious about the practice of the indigenous principle.

The Role of the Bible School in the Assemblies of God

As the AG began to grow rapidly in the 1920s and 1930s it looked to the Bible school as a place where believers and future evangelists could gain what they considered a practical, biblically sound education. The earliest Pentecostal Bible schools tended to be short-term schools. They focused on issues of faith and introductory interpretations of the Bible.[11] They typically lacked proper facilities, textbooks, or standardized curricula.[12] Consequently, the skills of the teachers mainly shaped the schools. What the schools lacked in academic quality, they made up for in zeal. Students often punctuated classes with spontaneous prayer and speaking in tongues. Because most of these schools had a relatively brief existence, they usually trained only a small number of students.[13]

More formal Bible schools and missionary institutes sprang out of the need to make sure that evangelists and missionaries were at least properly trained in doctrine and biblical interpretation. Early Pentecostal leaders who received training at these schools encouraged the AG's General

Council to consider the educational opportunities the denomination should offer its people.[14] According to historian Edith Blumhofer, the AG was suspicious of education in its secular form and grounded its approach in typical Pentecostal pragmatism. "The Council did not define education; the nature of the training that they wanted to provide was essentially indoctrination in fixed truth as perceived by the Fellowship. . . . From one perspective, the Bible school training endorsed by early Assemblies of God leaders fit into the model contemporary fundamentalists were establishing: It set out to proclaim fixed truth and to locate where those who differed were in error. Its concerns were more practical that theoretical."[15] The AG concerned itself with Bible schools to ensure sound doctrine and to control what their evangelists and ministers were preaching. From the outset, Pentecostal education was deeply practical and tied to the spreading of the Gospel. The mission of Pentecostal Bible schools resembled that of their conservative Protestant counterparts, but the education level of the students was lower and the schools were poorer, especially during their early years.[16]

The AG began to build a Bible school network starting in the early 1920s. Initially, supporters of Pentecostal education found themselves opposed by those who "disdained formal education as potentially 'quenching' the Spirit."[17] Supporters persevered, particularly those on the West Coast who in 1920 founded both the California Bible College in San Francisco and the Berean Bible Institute in San Diego. Although linked to the AG, these schools were not the first General Council–approved Bible schools. The first such institution came into being in 1922 when the AG launched the Central Bible Institute (CBI) in Springfield, Missouri.[18] Initially, the school was run by faithful instructors who received little or no pay, but as it grew, it added larger facilities and more staff.[19] Admissions requirements and academic standards remained low, as CBI's mission was to train missionaries and evangelists rather than to provide a college- or university-level education. Because many students arrived at CBI ill-prepared, it launched a one-year preparatory program in order to enable those with little education to enroll.[20]

With CBI as its flagship school, the AG tried to standardize the curricula of its Bible institutions. In 1925 the General Council voted that if a school could demonstrate that it met the same educational standards as CBI, then it was an AG Bible school and would enjoy the same standing as CBI. The members of the General Council also agreed that they should have representation on the boards of all AG-recognized Bible schools.[21]

By the 1930s, CBI established a correspondence school to support members of the laity who worked in churches, especially those responsible for Sunday school programs.[22] As the Bible school network grew, local Bible schools and AG-affiliated regional Bible schools began to spread, with their chief emphasis always on practical training for the ministry. In fact, Pentecostals remained suspicious of liberal arts and university education until 1955, when the AG founded Evangel College as its first liberal arts college.[23] The AG recognized the need for advanced seminary education but moved slowly because of concerns that establishing a seminary would distract from Bible college education. Finally, in 1973, the AG founded the Assemblies of God Theological Seminary as a graduate school specifically for Bible college graduates.[24] The AG had finally completed its educational system with a network of local Bible schools, accredited regional Bible colleges, a liberal arts college, and a graduate seminary.

Contrary to the convention that early Pentecostals opposed all forms of higher education, the history of the AG Bible school network demonstrates that Alta Washburn's wish for a Bible school for Indians was rooted in the Pentecostal mindset. The start of the All-Tribes Bible School (later AIC) followed a pattern established by the AG and the pioneers of the Bible school movement. At first, founders of Bible schools acted on a perceived need for a basic Pentecostal education geared toward the ministry and the development of one's Pentecostal faith. Schools, especially those that started without full AG backing, typically began as local Bible schools and expanded from there.[25]

The Birth of the All-Tribes Bible School

Once Sister Washburn decided to go forward with her plans for her all-Indian Bible school, the project preoccupied her. She wrote, "I began to dream, talk, write and pray about the Bible school. The burden consumed me. The very thought of it excited my spirit because I knew I was moving in the center of God's will."[26] She spoke to all who would listen and sent letters to fellow missionaries. The Arizona district superintendent, J. K. Gressett, decided to meet with Sister Washburn and her supporters in Phoenix. The meeting took place on June 2, 1956, and along with the Washburns and Brother Gressett, Brothers Shores, Russell, Gribling, and Bruhn and Sister Elva Johnson all attended.[27] Sister Johnson was a local home missions colleague and a supporter of Sister Washburn's idea. The men were all AG ministers who supported Sister Washburn, albeit with some reservations. No American Indian missionaries or leaders attended the meeting, probably because at the time there were so few of them. It is also possible that no one thought to invite them.

It quickly became apparent that the men held reservations about Sister Washburn's idea. The minutes of the meeting indicate that she arrived with negative feelings created by the language the men had employed in their letters to her. Both the denominational leaders in Springfield and the men at the meeting believed that Sister Washburn's school should be called not a "Bible school" but a "Bible training school." The ministers also emphasized that the school would be a "local" institution, in no way linked to the AG's national Bible school network.[28] If Sister Washburn did not like this, the minutes do not show that she fought it, although she might have raised objections.[29] Sister Washburn probably knew she could not succeed without the help of Brother Gressett and other local support-ers. She seemed to choose her battles wisely.

The biggest objection to Sister Washburn's Bible school related to its financing. According to the minutes:

> Brother Gressett said that they are already putting about 80% of
> their home mission funds into the Indian work. He also said that the
> financial angle of the Bible school was their biggest objection, and he
> mentioned the problem of support. Brother Gressett said that since
> the Indian work had been put into the hands of the district, they have
> tried to help both white and Indian works. But they are hindered by
> lack of sufficient funds. . . . The district attitude is precautionary about
> the Bible school, but they recognize the need. They just don't want to
> get into something they can't financially handle later on.[30]

Despite the financial obstacles, Brother Gressett and the other men as-sured Sister Washburn that she "did not have any grounds for discour-agement."[31] What is clear from the minutes is that Sister Washburn was not able to depend on the Arizona district for support; rather, she would have to raise money from supporters elsewhere through her own ingenu-ity and faith.

The curriculum also loomed during the planning meeting. Once the ministers made it clear that the AG was treating the Bible school as a "local" institution and a "Bible training school" rather than a Bible col-lege, the question of the mission of the school had to be decided.[32] Brother

Gressett raised another concern: "Indians' minds are limited from lack of education and other handicaps."[33] He believed that the early curriculum should follow the model of a Sunday school course with an emphasis on basic biblical literacy and interpretation. The other ministers, in agreement, suggested the Workers Training Courses from the AG's Sunday School Department as a model for the early curriculum.[34]

At the end of the discussion, the purpose of the Bible school was set forth: "Not to be a regular Bible School, not a reciprocal school with other Bible Schools; not to accumulate credits to be transferred to other schools; there is no ambition to make it a full-fledged Bible School. Many missionaries need Sunday school teachers, deacons, and helpers. The purpose of the school would be to train these people to go back and help their own missionaries and they would strongly be urged to do so."[35] The language in this statement is striking. Sister Washburn had originally envisioned a Bible school that resembled any other Bible school, yet the ministers she consulted and the AG wanted it to create helpers for the AG's current missionaries, not to create indigenous missionaries.[36] If American Indians wanted a full Bible college or ministerial institute certificate, they would still have to attend one of the larger AG Bible schools, such as Central Bible Institute. The kind of Bible school suggested by the white AG leadership would defeat what Sister Washburn had hoped for, that is, a place to train Indians for leadership positions. Yet Sister Washburn probably knew that the only way to further her idea with the AG was to comply with the white, male hierarchy. Her hope rested on the potential success of her Bible school. If it could build on its initial success, it might someday become what she had originally intended. Officially, however, her Bible school was to be a local institution, run as part of her All-Tribes Mission.

Sister Washburn hinted at her difficulties with the district officials in her autobiography, but the record is sparse on how she really felt about the way that she was treated by the white male leadership in her district. Sister Alma Thomas, a longtime instructor at the school, who came to Phoenix to work with Sister Washburn in the early 1960s, gave this description of Sister Washburn during this time period:

> She was very deliberate. She was business. There was nothing about her that was not connected together. She knew what she wanted, what she wanted to do, and she, if you read the book, you remember, she did write something about her break, not her break, but her situation with the district leaders. They didn't think she could do it, or that she

should do it. But she was determined. To start that school. And she did. And she was my leader, my teacher, my mentor, and my husband also had great respect for her.[37]

Because of Sister Washburn's eventual success with the Bible school, few within the AG are willing to publicly acknowledge that initially the district was slow to support her. Sister Thomas, who at the time of her interview was a feisty eighty-nine-year-old retired missionary, was one of the few white leaders within the AG I could find who was willing to even acknowledge the difficulty that Sister Washburn faced. The fact is that Sister Washburn defied the AG hierarchy to carry out what she believed to be God's plan and made the district officials uncomfortable in doing so.

Once the purpose was defined and Sister Washburn promised that students of the Bible school would be encouraged to return to the reservations, the discussion turned to the school's financial needs. Five thousand dollars was required to start, and Sister Washburn had about one thousand dollars pledged from supporters.[38] The group charged Sister Washburn with finding the rest of the money and other resources. She also identified eight interested students who were willing to enroll as the first class. One of the ministers, Brother Bruhn, expressed concern that the students would not be able to obtain sponsorship to cover their expenses.[39] Sister Washburn replied, "The girls could easily get housework to support themselves, and the boys, work in cotton. They would go to school in the afternoon or evening, but not in the mornings. They would eat mainly beans and potatoes."[40] Sister Washburn and other local AG pastors who were willing to donate their time would serve as staff. The meeting adjourned with the committee drawing up a letter of appeal and approval to be considered by the AG's national office.[41]

The end of the planning meeting marked the beginning of the true challenge for Sister Washburn: how to solicit contributions. Her initial financing came from an AG congregation in Houston. Brother Gressett found that it was looking for a project to sponsor and directed it to Sister Washburn.[42] The congregation contributed an initial thousand dollars even before the meeting, enough to pay for the concrete floor, plumbing, and a portion of the masonry blocks.[43] With that money in hand, Sister Washburn and members of her All-Tribes congregation in Phoenix broke ground.

Sister Washburn prepared the plans for a main school building, "consist[ing] of dormitory rooms, reception room, classrooms, dining room, kitchen and utility rooms."[44] Her husband, an expert in construction, drew the plans to scale. The men from her All-Tribes congregation, with the help of local AG pastors and parishioners, donated much of the labor.[45] When they had exhausted the initial funds, Sister Washburn began traveling, speaking to any congregation that invited her. The second significant donation to the Bible school came from the First Assembly of God in Covina, California. It raised and sent sixteen hundred dollars.[46]

Donations then flowed from a variety of places. The Southern California District of the Assemblies of God gave linens, beds, and bedding for the dormitory. The Weatherford family arrived with a truckload of supplies, including food and a freezer. The Southern California District's Women's Ministries sent classroom equipment. An unnamed California church donated a central heating and cooling system, and a refrigerator came from the Orange County, California, Women's Ministries. A Brother Bryant donated ovens, and the Scio and Clutter pottery companies of Ohio contributed dishes and cookware. As word of Sister Washburn's Bible school spread through the various AG networks, believers in her cause sent whatever they could to support her.[47] The Indian congregants of All-Tribes contributed traditional handicrafts, including rugs, in order to give the buildings a colorful touch, and "Chief" John McPherson painted a mural on the walls of the reception room.[48]

The outpouring of support strengthened Sister Washburn's resolve. "Each day as we saw the building moving towards completion, and every needed item supplied, any doubts about the project being in God's will were erased. We beheld the hand of God hovering over all the activities, and we knew He was honoring our faith. My burden to see Indians taught sound Bible doctrine was coming to fruition."[49] During the summer of 1957, Sister Washburn traveled to Indian camp meetings in Arizona, New Mexico, Nevada, and northern California to speak about her Bible school and to find potential students. She also employed four teachers for the first semester: all were Bible college graduates and all were willing to work for free. Those included Brother and Sister Carruthers, Sister Virginia Kridler, and Sister Ruth Gardiner.[50] The All-Tribes Bible School (ATBS) opened on 28 September 1957, with thirty-two students.[51]

While Sister Washburn's work for the Bible school was extraordinary, she was also following a well-established path among female Pentecostal missionaries. From the very beginning, large numbers of female Pentecostal missionaries sought to build institutions such as schools that would serve their converts. The most famous of these early missionaries was Minnie Abrams, who constructed a school and a Pentecostal missiology based on her experiences. According to missionary historian Dana Robert, "In Abrams's missiology, seeking the Holy Ghost and fire was not for the faint-hearted or unconsecrated, but for those truly and completely at God's disposal. . . . Abrams thus interpreted Pentecostal phenomena as signs of the Spirit and empowerment for mission, within the broader context of Christian love."[52] Robert concluded that Abrams's missiology was the most influential for Pentecostal women missionaries because of the emphasis on self-sacrificing love.[53]

Sister Washburn exemplified the early Pentecostal female missionary figure whom Abrams described. She devoted herself to her dream of an all-Indian Bible school in a manner that emphasized self-sacrifice and God's love, and she actively sought signs and wonders and understood that she was completely at God's disposal. Robert underlines how common it was, during the early years of Pentecostalism, for women to found Bible schools or training institutes in order to spread the faith: "From the [beginning], women have founded and taught at many Bible institutes founded by Pentecostals to train indigenous evangelists."[54] Sister Washburn, then, was following in a long tradition of women's leadership within Pentecostal education.[55]

Sister Washburn, however, differed in one major way from her Pentecostal sisters. This kind of leadership among Pentecostal women was mainly limited to the first decades of the movement, in generations before male leaders tightened their control.[56] But Sister Washburn operated her Bible school from 1954 to 1965. She was not an early female evangelist, yet she exhibited many of the characteristics that marked the previous generation. She did have to contend with the male power structure, but she also managed to navigate around that power structure to achieve her goals. Not only did she display self-sacrifice and emphasize divine love as the previous generation had espoused, but she also showed typical Pentecostal pragmatism. She was, in fact, a pioneer in her field, much like the earlier generation of female foreign missionaries. Because home missions to American Indians took root several decades after Pentecostals had embraced foreign missions, it was still a young movement when Sister Washburn founded her Bible school. She was also in a region that at the time was still considered geographically remote within the United States. This may explain why Sister Washburn enjoyed more freedom than those in the more established, male-dominated wings of the AG.[57]

Sister Washburn opened her Bible school with little more than force of will, charisma, and faith. Although it boasted financial supporters, she found herself left to do all of the major planning. She barnstormed from church to church, from camp meeting to camp meeting, throughout the American West to raise funds and to find recruits. Such work was no small task for a woman in 1950s America. Her conviction led others to believe in her. Indeed, they were even willing to work for free, whether in the construction of the building or as teachers and maintenance staff. Fellow Pentecostals felt that Sister Washburn was truly doing God's work, and her belief in the power of the Holy Spirit gave her unshakable conviction as well as authority.

The Miracle of the Fishes and the Fry Bread: Student Life at All-Tribes

Life for students at the All-Tribes Bible School, although governed by faith, proved financially difficult, even though the school charged only a dollar a day, a fee that did not cover operating costs.[58] Most students came from poverty-stricken families that could not support them, and all of the students had to work while attending the Bible school.[59] Sister Washburn regarded the hardship as a test from God. The first students came from nearby southwestern tribes, but as word of All-Tribes spread, Pentecostal Indians from around the country began to arrive. Once at the Bible school, they developed a shared experience, one that centered on the miraculous and the mundane, faith and trust, cultural similarities and differences. This was the beginning of their training in living life as Pentecostals. As much as the indigenous principle figured into the mission, education, and ideas behind the All-Tribes Bible School, so did the classic markers of Pentecostal identity, such as speaking in tongues and the miraculous nature of God. By focusing on both developing the typical markers of Pentecostal faith and priming the students for the practice of the indigenous principle, All-Tribes asserted its unique identity as a training ground for Pentecostal Indians and encouraged a pan-Indian Pentecostal identity.

Most of the early Indian students at All-Tribes traded reservation poverty for Pentecostal urban poverty. The quest for support began immediately. Male students worked in the fields outside the city or as day laborers, while female students labored as cooks or housekeepers. Some lived in the dormitory, while married students, who often had children, had to find a place to live as well as a way to support their families. In order to accommodate their needs, Sister Washburn set up night classes so that the majority of her students could work during the day and study at night.[60]

Sister Washburn said she believed that if God wanted something to happen, he would make it happen, and that the Lord would always take care of those who followed him. In the face of pervasive personal hardship and the poverty of the school, the students struggled to accept Sister Washburn's teachings, she said. In her autobiography she recounted a story of two such students, a married Indian couple named Juanita and Alvin. Juanita needed dental work, but they did not have enough money for the procedure. Alvin asked Sister Washburn for help, and she instructed him to pray and have faith.[61] The day of the appointment came, and Alvin had not yet found the money. Dejected, he went to Sister Washburn and began to speak of his despair, when a stranger walked through the entrance of the All-Tribe's building. Sister Washburn recalled: "'I just came from Canada,' the man said as he introduced himself. 'I felt the Lord would have me come visit your school and give a contribution to help one of your students.'"[62] Sister Washburn herself was surprised at the good fortune. "Alvin and I looked at each other, remembering how we discussed that God works on His own schedule and is never late."[63] The money covered the dental bills as well as groceries and a badly needed new tire for Alvin's car.[64]

Because Sister Washburn was a believer in the miraculous, stories like that of Alvin and Juanita pepper her autobiography. While they function as simple Pentecostal testimonials, they can also be interpreted as parables with deeper meaning.[65] Pentecostal Indians had to learn to trust that the Holy Spirit (often in the guise of other believers) would provide for their needs. This proved especially true for young converts who left the reservation and its traditional forms of familial and tribal support. Once converted, their family circle widened to include fellow Pentecostals, white and Indian.[66]

Alvin and Juanita were not the only ones whose faith was tested—Sister Washburn's was too. In one newsletter to supporters, she wrote: "A cold winter in Phoenix, most unusual. Students have a siege of the mumps and flu. Hardest month to pay bills. Fewest contributions for the work. The Washer broke down. The refrigerator. The car. The record player. Had a leak in the roof and I lost my Scofield Bible. We turned the sheets and patched the blankets and added pinto beans for breakfast."[67] Poverty was a way of life for Sister Washburn's Indian students; it was also the way of life for a Pentecostal missionary. This poverty equipped the All-Tribes students for the faith-based ministry work of the AG. The students and faculty experienced scarcity daily, but they also learned how to fight against desperation, have faith, and lean on each other, skills they would need in future ministry.

The interpretation of poverty as a positive force, something beneficial to the students, was very common within the Bible school experience, creating what historian Virginia Brereton calls "a culture of scarcity."[68] Indeed, students at All-Tribes were poor not only because they were Indians but also because they were Bible school students. The emphasis on a lack of material goods alleviated by miraculous gifts of money and support was not limited to Pentecostal Bible schools but was a constant in the conservative Protestant Bible school experience.[69] Although Sister Washburn frequently noted in her autobiography that a lack of money plagued her, she did so with a certain amount of pride that she could run a Bible school with very limited resources. Such an attitude permeated virtually all American Bible schools: the school leaders, like Sister Washburn, were proud that they could do so much with so little.[70]

Although many Native students came from working-class or poor backgrounds, most—especially those from reservations—enjoyed an extended kinship network that supported family livelihoods. So, while many Native students might have been cash poor, most lived well within traditional subsistence economies on the reservations: they often had plenty of food from gardens, flocks of animals, and traditional methods of gathering and trading. Those who left their families to go to Bible school, however, were forced to adapt to a cash economy. Although no evidence exists from the period, adaptation to an urban cash-based lifestyle was probably hardest for those who came from reservations that had extensive barter and subsistence systems.

Although Pentecostals preferred to frame the gifts of money, food, and support as works of the Holy Spirit, the truth is they heavily leaned upon a network of believers. The students at All-Tribes had to learn how to trust each other, work together, and depend on each other as fellow Pentecostal Indians. But these students came from a society that trusted few outsiders. Trust was usually located in the family unit and extended to the tribal unit. Sister Washburn's emphasis on faith prodded Pentecostal Indians to move past their distrust, not only of each other but also of non-Indians, including Sister Washburn and her faculty. By doing so, they entered the greater AG network of believers, as well as the network of fellow Pentecostal Indians. By learning to identify with communities wider than family and tribe, they deepened not only their beliefs but also their identities as Pentecostals and Indians.

In the early years of All-Tribes, miraculous stories abounded in regard to the students and their faith, therefore marking the school as being blessed by God's favor. These occurrences, however, were not limited to the earliest years of the school. According to recollections from faculty, staff, and students, spontaneous outpourings of the Spirit were regular occurrences at the school, even after it became an accredited college in the 1980s. As one faculty member, Belinda Lopez, stated, "Over the years we've heard reports of people being filled with the Holy Spirit even in the classrooms. Students took time to pray with one another to be filled in chapel, in classes (such as the late Don Keeter's book of Acts class), and even back in the dormitories."[71] The constant outpouring of the Spirit affirmed the students' faith and strengthened their own sense of classical Pentecostal practice: the Spirit flowed freely at the school. Sandra Ticeahkie, a Kiowa/Comanche alumni and later staff member at the college, echoed Lopez's observation. "I recall that once during a five-week period we had people laid out on the ground because they had been profoundly touched by the Lord's hand—it was like a bomb had gone off!" What Sister Ticeahkie was describing was the Pentecostal practice of being "slain in the spirit," which was in a sense, an extended outpouring of the Holy Spirit that often resulted in visions or signs and wonders from God (not unlike a traditional Native vision quest.) Such occurrences emphasized the Pentecostal nature of the school and developed the students' Pentecostal faiths.

All-Tribes Bible School was more than a place of faith transformation and education; it also served as a matchmaker.[72] Because the Pentecostal community on the reservation and among urban Indians was small, Pentecostal converts often experienced trouble finding suitable mates. Pentecostal Indians preferred to marry fellow Pentecostals, ideally an Indian of the same tribe. However, many male Indian Pentecostal converts intermarried with white Pentecostal women whom they met through Bible college or church functions, including Brothers Charlie Lee, John McPherson, and Andrew Maracle.[73] All-Tribes gave Pentecostal Indians not only a place of community and fellowship but also a place where they could meet like-minded potential mates. In doing so, it helped cement the Pentecostal Indian identity as paramount, even perhaps to the detriment of tribal identity.

Sister Washburn had anticipated that the young, single people of ATBS would become interested in each other: "The 'love factor' and Cupid would be permanent residents at ATBS."[74] Because of this, she studied the catalogs of other AG Bible schools to find precedents for rules and regulations about dating and marriage. Rules regarding dating were strict at AG Bible schools in general, and Sister Washburn's were no exception. Students could go off campus to date only in chaperoned student groups, and couples were not allowed to be alone together on campus.[75] According to Sister Washburn, the students did not find the rules onerous: "They were glad for any opportunity to spend some time together, even if that time was controlled."[76]

Sister Washburn took a pragmatic approach to dating. On one hand, it was often good to have a spouse who would accompany an AG missionary or evangelist, but on the other hand, it had to be the right kind of spouse. ATBS did not allow its single students to marry until after graduation. Sister Washburn and the faculty advised those who did marry as follows: "After couples became engaged, faculty members and I counseled them about the importance of placing God as the highest priority in their lives. We did not discourage them about marriage. But we tried to show them that God always has a right person and time for marriage."[77] In her autobiography, Sister Washburn listed many of the single students who married each other, a list that grew as the school became bigger and gained reputation.

Marriage played a crucial role in strengthening Pentecostal Indian identity, as Sister Washburn's willing acknowledgment of her school's matchmaking function indicates. Students wanted to wed fellow Pentecostals because of shared beliefs and values. Marriage to a fellow Pentecostal Indian was even better, because even if the students came from different tribes, they shared an understanding and experience as Indians. Finally, the school's matchmaking allowed Pentecostal Indians to make alliances with others from their own and different tribes, thus expanding their circle within Pentecostalism. A wider familial alliance meant that one could gain more financial support as a missionary or easier entrance to a reservation that was not one's own. The other side of this argument, however, is that Pentecostal identity became more important than tribal identity. Pentecostalism encouraged marriage outside of one's tribe simply because it was often hard to find a suitable person within the tribe. Intertribal marriage often meant that one spouse would have to abandon age-old customs in order to accommodate the other person's tribal culture.

The mission of the All-Tribes Bible School faced difficulties during the first decade. Apart from economic issues, the student body became aware of deep divisions that threatened to overwhelm the similarities among them. As Indians, they shared a culture, yet their tribal differences impinged more and more. Sister Washburn, in planning an all-Indian Bible school, did not anticipate the problems that tribal differences would cause. Although no student memoirs or recollections exist from the earliest years, one issue stands out in Sister Washburn's autobiography: food. Sister Washburn's presentation of the problem of feeding her students emphasized the miraculous power of God and the Holy Spirit for her Pentecostal readership. The nuances of the autobiography, however, make clear that it was really about how Pentecostal Indians had to confront their tribal differences while also learning how to trust each other and construct their own unique Pentecostal identity.

The first students at the Bible school easily adjusted to the standard culinary fare: pinto beans, tortillas or fry bread, and chilies.[78] The Pimas and Papagos who made up the initial classes typically ate this food. So, at first, the evidence does not reveal any complaints.[79] Not only was this food local, but it was also cheap. Beans were inexpensive, chilies could be easily bought or grown, and fry bread and tortillas were easy to make with little effort and few ingredients. For these reasons, Sister Washburn believed that she had found a way to feed her students while keeping expenses to a minimum.

Once word of All-Tribes Bible School began to spread, students came from well beyond the Southwest. The first out-of-state contingent included Mohawk converts, and they disliked the school's food. Sister Washburn recalled, "However, when the Canadian Mohawk students came and were faced with pinto beans every day, they were not happy. 'Please, Sister Washburn, we are not sorry we came to school,' they said, 'but this desert wind, it is so dry. This food—there is no fish to eat.'"[80] Sister Washburn faced a problem—how to find fish for her Mohawk students in the middle of the Arizona desert.

This request was not Sister Washburn's only dietary dilemma. When a large group of Navajo students arrived at her Bible school, the students begged Sister Washburn for their traditional food. Sister Washburn now had another problem. "The Navajos were asking for mutton. How were we going to come up with a ewe or lamb? Mutton was much too expensive to buy in the market."[81] Students from a variety of Plains tribes were also unhappy over the food: they wanted wild game, while the Apache students longed for beef.[82] Sister Washburn wanted her students to be content and remain at the Bible school, so she struggled with the dilemma of how to provide their preferred foods when the budget could afford only beans and tortillas.

Sister Washburn approached the problem in a typical Pentecostal manner: she prayed to God to send them the desired provisions, and she solicited her supporters, telling them that the school needed fish, mutton, wild game, and beef. Predictably, her supporters sent the needed food. A local minister donated lambs, too large now to keep as pets, for mutton stew; a local man donated a freezer full of fish; somebody sent forty live chickens; a beekeeper donated a truckload of honey; local hunters donated the extra deer and elk that they had shot; and another local minister brought home a deer that she had accidentally hit while driving on the highway.[83] The flow of donations helped satisfy students' craving for a change from beans and tortillas. The different foods also allowed them to share some of their tribal cultures.

Sister Washburn placed her recollections regarding the need for a variety of food at the beginning of her history of the All-Tribes Bible School. She told the story in order to give a testimony about how God answers prayers. The described need for food evoked the story of Jesus and the loaves and fishes from the Gospels. She asked, and God provided. Not only did he provide, but he also sent food that would make life easier for her Indian students. For Sister Washburn, the appearance of the needed sustenance was a miracle, an answer to her prayers and those of her students, and she presented it as such.

Yet, the stories that surround the food at All-Tribes are important not only because of their miraculous content but also because they exemplify the complexity of Sister Washburn's Bible college. This college was an all-Indian college, where Pentecostal Indians could train for the ministry in a comfortable setting. They would grow to be stronger Christians through a shared identity, both Indian and Pentecostal, even though distinct tribal differences divided them. They were not all the same; while they had a shared background as Indians in the United States, their cultures, languages, dress, and food were all diverse. The Pentecostal literature about early days at All-Tribes rarely explored the Indian students' differences, yet the story surrounding the miracle of the food clearly shows that conflicts appeared. Sister Washburn had not counted on problems with the food, but as usual, she rose to the occasion, found a way to accommodate her students, and defused the issue.

For all these differences, however, All-Tribes emerged as a place that encouraged a sort of pan-Indian Pentecostalism. Once students enrolled in the school, they met other Pentecostal Indians, often intermarried, and then would set off on missionary work—sometimes to their own people, sometimes to other tribes or to urban areas. At All-Tribes they participated in the classic aspects of Pentecostalism, such as Bible study, speaking in tongues, and seeking the miraculous. What emerged from All-Tribes was a class of Native leaders who understood themselves as Indians from particular tribal backgrounds, but who also belonged to a greater Native Pentecostal community. Because there are so few recorded student voices from the first decade of the school, it is hard to know how much an overall Pentecostal Indian identity might have trumped individual tribal identities among the student body, but there were certainly tensions that existed at the school. The indigenous principle, however, is the one idea that did hold enormous sway over All-Tribes. Sister Washburn and her supporters' belief in it spurred the creation of the school, and the practice of it defined the very existence of All-Tribes.

From All-Tribes to the American Indian College

For the first ten years of its operation, Sister Washburn oversaw every aspect of life at the All-Tribes Bible School. But in 1964, she suffered a broken arm in an automobile accident, followed by a freak accident in 1965 that damaged her lungs.[84] Weak and unable to continue running her Bible school with the same vigor, Sister Washburn began to look toward the future of ATBS. She had proved that Indians could be evangelists. She commented on this cherished belief: "They were taking initiative in leadership and responsibilities in the church. I was beginning to see the indigenous principle develop among them."[85] Believing that the success of her Bible school would lead the AG to embrace the program, Sister Washburn began to arrange for what would happen on her departure and resigned. With her resignation in 1965, ATBS began the transformation from a local school run by a local church into a full-fledged AG Bible college. The AG's willingness to commit its money to support this change shows that Sister Washburn's work at ATBS had finally led the AG to realize that it needed an all-Indian Bible college.

After her resignation, Sister Washburn felt called to go back into more practical missionary service. Meanwhile, the AG began to take steps toward bringing ATBS under its official auspices, redesigning its original operating plan so that it could become a Bible training institute. Sister Washburn was thrilled: "The vision that God gave me in 1954 for the Bible school had never dimmed, nor had I ever doubted the far-reaching potential of the Native American."[86] She officially turned the school over to the Department of Home Missions, which set up a board composed of Arizona and Southern California District leaders to appoint a new head of ATBS. It chose Don Ramsey, a former Bureau of Indian Affairs (BIA) schoolteacher on the Navajo reservation and a missionary.[87] In 1966–67, the AG's Southwestern Districts (composed of Arizona, New Mexico, West Texas, Rocky Mountain, Northern California–Nevada, and Southern California) formed a new board, and, with the Department of Home Missions, reorganized ATBS as a ministerial institute of the AG. The AG changed the curriculum to adhere to the standards for Bible institutes, and Brother Ramsey found a site for the newly renamed American Indian Bible Institute (AIBI). With a major expansion in the works, the original building would no longer suffice.[88]

Brother Ramsey and his wife came from Oklahoma. Unlike Sister Washburn, he was a well-educated man, having earned both a bachelor's and master's degree from Oklahoma East Central State College. Whereas Sister Washburn had run ATBS with neither training nor experience, Brother Ramsey was a career educator with plans to put AIBI on par with the AG's other Bible institutes. He set about raising money.[89]

Before AIBI became an official AG regional Bible institute, the *PE* mentioned it only once. After it gained regional status and official recognition in 1965, the *PE* took notice by covering the fundraising campaign. Although Brother Ramsey was able to sell the original site and building of the old ATBS, that move did not yield enough money to fund the new campus. As they broke ground and began construction of the new buildings in February 1968, supporters of AIBI had raised only $45,000—just one-fifth of the projected cost of $225,000.[90] During construction, AIBI bore the additional financial burden of renting a building for its displaced students. The AG planned to build two dormitories, a dining hall, and a classroom building, and to expand the campus further as the money came in.[91] The *PE*, meanwhile, appealed to the greater Pentecostal public for funds, equipment, and books for a desperately needed library.[92] Money and help poured into AIBI from individuals and entire congregations, just as when Sister Washburn founded ATBS.

On 1 October 1971, with the first phase of the construction completed on the new campus located on the north side of Phoenix, the supporters of AIBI dedicated the first building. Reflecting the change from Bible school to ministerial institute, the mission of the school officially changed from educating Indians to be missionary helpers to providing "a foundation for an indigenous Indian church program."[93] No longer would AIBI focus on training future Sunday school teachers and church workers. Now, its graduates would be missionaries and AG Indian leaders. Since its inception as ATBS, 173 students had attended the school in some capacity: 41 completed the three-year certificate program, 7 of the graduates were heading Indian churches, 2 received appointments as home missionaries, and the rest were church workers.[94] With the new focus on the indigenous principle, the school intensified its efforts to train more Indian pastors and missionaries. Now, finally, the AG could begin to turn its Indian ministry into a program headed and run by Indians.

After presiding over a growing school for thirteen years,[95] Brother Ramsey stepped down, making way for AIBI's first Indian president. In 1978, Simon Peter, a member of the Choctaw Nation and a World War II veteran, was appointed the new president of AIBI. Brother Peter grew up in Oklahoma and attended Chilocco Indian School and Oklahoma Presbyterian College. Like his Navajo contemporary Brother Lee, Brother Peter was well educated for his time and place, having earned a B.A. at Oklahoma State University. He served as pastor in Indian and non-Indian churches in Oklahoma, Arkansas, Texas, and Colorado.[96] When he took over the presidency of AIBI, the school was burdened with $60,000 in debt as well as an urgent need for continued growth. Yet the students of AIBI were jubilant that they had an Indian president, and revival broke out.[97] Students and Indian leaders believed that great changes lay ahead for AIBI now that it was in the hands of one of their own. Unfortunately, their jubilation was short-lived. Soon after installation as president, Brother Peter fell ill with cancer. The entire Pentecostal Indian community joined the students in prayer for his healing, but Brother Peter worsened. Sensing that the end was near, he resigned in 1979, only one year after his appointment. On 5 November 1979, Brother Peter passed away, much to the grief of his many Indian and white supporters in the AG.[98]

AIBI's vice president, Eugene Herd, took over the administration of the school until late in 1979 when Carl Collins, a white professor at AIBI, was selected to be president. Brother Collins was an experienced educator, missionary, and pastor who, compared to most AG pastors and leaders, was exceptionally well educated. He had earned a B.A. in Bible from Bob Jones University and an M.A. in Higher Education Administration from North Carolina's Appalachian State. He served as a pastor at AG churches in Georgia and South Carolina and taught at the University of South Carolina, Clemson University, and Spartanburg Technical College. He had moved to Phoenix initially to take over the student employment program and to teach at AIBI.[99]

Brother Collins inherited not only the rising debt of the school's ambitious construction project but also factionalism and distrust. Many students lamented that the school would not stay under Indian leadership; some had also become radicalized, influenced by the racial politics of the era.[100] As AIBI grew, so did student factionalism. Some students had difficulty getting along with each other. One former AIBI student recalled: "I remember my friend saying 'I don't like my roommate. She's always longing for the ocean and the green forests. She even eats fish! I don't think she really likes Navajos either. Why doesn't she just go back to her North Country anyway?'"[101] Other students harbored anger toward non-Indians. In one incident in the dining hall, an angry young Indian man erupted: "I hate white people! They have always mistreated our people. Every treaty they ever made with us, they broke. How can I study under such teachers?"[102] Faced with simmering tensions, Brother Collins reemphasized that the school's mission was not to remove the students from their Indian culture, but to provide them with a place to define themselves as Christian Indians. The faculty urged the students to retain and develop their individual tribal cultures. Brother Collins made major changes by hiring a dean of students and counselors. He helped the staff become more sensitive in dealing with the various Indian cultures and encouraged the students to meet with counselors and faculty to air their frustrations and worries. Modern psychology and cross-cultural communication had finally come to the AG.[103]

In the early years of the 1980s, AIBI underwent one final transformation. The governing board voted to change its status again, this time from a ministerial training institute to a four-year Bible college. This change meant that AIBI became the American Indian Bible College (AIBC) and would offer two-year associate's degrees in business management, secretarial science, and social work and four-year bachelor's degrees in Christian education and ministerial studies, as well as the three-year ministerial certificate already offered. In 1982, after scrutiny by the North Central Association, the AIBC became an accredited Bible college of the AG. Later that year, rising enrollment forced Brother Collins to construct more buildings, both dormitories and classroom spaces. The AG finally renamed the school the American Indian College of the Assemblies of God.[104]

That the AIC was of primary importance in the gradual institutionalization of the indigenous principle and the formation of Indian Pentecostal identity cannot be emphasized enough. Before its founding by Sister Washburn, no such place existed for the training of Pentecostal Indians.

Academically gifted students could attend other AG Bible colleges, and many did, but the AIC gave them a place of their own, a place where they could form friendships with other Indian Pentecostals. Many of the alumni of the college went on to pastor missions to other Native people, and understood themselves as being part of a moment that was bigger than just Pentecostalism—they were ambassadors of the indigenous principle. AIC alumnus Marco Burnette put it succinctly in his recollection of time as a student at AIC: "Truly, AIC is a place where Native leadership is trained and the consistency of the vision that was given from the beginning continues fifty years later. That was always the vision and dream, and AIC has stuck to that vision and dream—continuing to equip a new generation of quality Native leaders."[105] Without trained Indian missionaries, the AG would not be able to turn its missions into indigenous churches, and without indigenous churches, the AG would likely not appeal to American Indians. Once the AG fully embraced the AIC, it used its power and influence to transform what had been a small local Bible school into an accredited Bible college in only seventeen years. But it was Sister Washburn who, back in the 1950s, prodded the AG into action. She and her supporters worked hard to make the AG face reality: without educated indigenous leadership, there would be no indigenous church. Without an indigenous church, there would be no way to proclaim the Gospel with authority in Indian communities. In the end, Pentecostal pragmatism won out—the AG wanted to find the most effective way to proclaim the Gospel. By the late 1970s, all agreed that indigenous missionaries were essential for gaining converts among the Indian tribes. Although AG officials initially opposed Sister Washburn's vision, in the end she proved victorious.

Mesa View Assembly of God and the Indigenous Church Movement

One of Sister Washburn's strongest Native supporters was Brother Charlie Lee, who shared with her a deep commitment to developing Indian leadership within the AG. In his mission to the Navajos, Brother Lee had immediately impressed the AG with his innovative ideas. Resolute about applying the indigenous principle, he toiled for decades to show that Indian missions could be transformed into self-sustaining Indian churches. By the late 1970s, Brother Lee's mission had progressed to the point where it was almost fully indigenous and was ready to become the first indigenous district-affiliated church. With this success, Brother Lee delivered an important message to his fellow Pentecostals, both white and

Indian: the indigenous principle worked, and the AG must consider how using it could change the home missions program.

In 1953, Brother Lee returned to the Navajo reservation after graduating from the Central Bible Institute in Springfield, Missouri. Once there, he reached out to Navajos in the far northwestern corner of the state while successfully battling the Navajo Tribal Council for the land he needed to build a church. His church was not the only Christian mission in the region. A quick scan of the church directory in the local newspaper, the *Farmington Times-Hustler*, shows that Lee competed with Baptist, Methodist, Christian Reformed, Mormon, and Roman Catholic missions in the Shiprock-Farmington area.[106]

We should attribute Brother Lee's enthusiasm for the indigenous principle and his strong stance against paternalism within missions in part to his Navajo background. Brother Lee grew up during a tumultuous time in Navajo history. During his 1930s childhood, the Navajo people suffered severely because of the federal government's policy of stock reduction. That is, in order to curb the overgrazing of Navajo lands, the government proposed a total reduction of all "extra" goats and horses, and a 10 percent reduction of sheep. Such measures hurt small subsistence sheep-holders more than families with large flocks raised for marketable wool and meat. Because Brother Lee came from a subsistence-level sheep-herding family, it suffered.

Meanwhile, the government's attempt to dissolve the Navajo Tribal Council in favor of the Wheeler-Howard Act, a new federally backed version of tribal government, also created deep fissures between the Navajo people and the federal government.[107] During this period, the first Navajo Tribal Council chairman, and Christian Reformed missionary, Jacob C. Morgan, publicly sparred with BIA commissioner John Collier.[108] On the reservation, the sentiment was that the federal government could not be trusted, especially in light of stock reduction. The Navajo had their own form of government in the Navajo Tribal Council and did not want the government to dictate a new form of tribal government.[109] Parts of the Wheeler-Howard Act were progressive—it reversed allotment and allowed tribes to manage their own assets.[110] But the Navajos opposed it because they tied it to stock reduction, which destroyed not only their livelihood but also the old communal way of caring for each other, in which wealthy families often kept extra animals around for their poorer neighbors. The stock reduction caused many poor Navajos to go hungry during the harsh

New Mexico winters, since they depended on the extra goats and horses that the government destroyed for food.[111] This grim situation was compounded by the eradication of their last-ditch food source, prairie dogs, which the government also destroyed as part of a New Deal public works project in the desert.[112] Although Brother Lee never mentions his childhood in any of the Pentecostal literature, because he came from a sheep-owning family, the events of the 1930s no doubt touched him in some form. The stock reduction campaign remains seared into the collective Navajo psyche, together with a distrust of outsiders and a special hatred for the federal government.

Lee was not the only Navajo leading a mission during this period. Former Navajo tribal chairman Jacob. C. Morgan (the Navajo leader who railed against stock reduction) led a Christian Indian congregation in the Farmington area with a satellite church in Shiprock.[113] Although Morgan had a long affiliation with the Christian Reformed Church, it appears that he had grown disenchanted with the denomination by the 1940s and had broken away to form an independent Navajo mission.[114] Though he was no longer tribal chairman, Morgan remained involved in fighting the federal government for proper healthcare and schools for his people. In 1946, the National American Indian Defense Association elected him vice president, in which position he continued his work as a progressive voice for Navajo rights.[115] A foe of peyote and traditional religion,[116] Morgan stands as a non-Pentecostal example of a Navajo who had begun to build a church for his own people. The evidence does not reveal if Lee personally knew Morgan, but since Shiprock and Farmington were small towns, separated by only thirty-five miles, he surely knew of him. Morgan seems to have been a confrontational character who gathered some detractors. Brother Lee, on the other hand, either was a gentler soul or realized that an outsized personality could create problems for missionary work. This irenic posture could explain why Brother Lee flew under the AG General Council's radar for most of his career, despite his own controversial stand on indigenous churches.

The late 1940s and the 1950s proved to be a time of change for the Navajo people. The *Farmington Times-Hustler* argued that the lack of an on-reservation school system was the reason that the Navajos suffered from poverty and inequality.[117] The newspaper also kept the spotlight on the New Mexico legislature's attempts to disenfranchise reservation Navajos.[118] The editors of the newspaper publicly opposed the legislature's actions, stating, "The *Times-Hustler* has for years advocated granting full citizenship to our Navajo Indian friends and neighbors as a matter of simple American justice."[119] Thanks to Morgan, the Farmington-Shiprock area remained a hotbed of Native leadership, both politically and within the church. The Navajo people still smarted from the pain of stock reduction and the destruction of their traditional lifestyles. As the Navajos wrestled with issues of citizenship, equal education, and the need for healthcare, Brother Lee emerged as a leader who exemplified how Navajos could engage white bureaucracies successfully.

Religiously, the Navajos remained a mixed bag in the mid-twentieth century. Catholic, Mormon, and Methodist missions thrived in the area. The use of peyote exploded exponentially in the 1940s and 1950s. Christian and traditionalist Navajos opposed peyote religion because they saw it as "non-Navajo" and as a vector for drug abuse. Although the Tribal Council made the use of peyote illegal by 1940, the peyote movement began to spread and take root among the Navajo at the same time that Lee built his indigenous church.[120] By the year 2000, the peyote movement encompassed approximately 40,000 out of 244,000 tribal members.[121] Approximately 9 percent of Navajos solely practiced traditional Navajo religion; the rest of the tribe was a mix of Christian groups (Catholic, Mormon, evangelical Christians, and Pentecostals) and those who retained a dual religious identity (e.g., peyote believers who also belonged to a Christian church).[122]

Toiling for decades on the remote reservation, Brother Lee and his wife built a solid reputation among their fellow Indian evangelists and missionaries. Once Sister Washburn founded her Bible College, Brother Lee sent promising Navajo converts to be trained for mission work. A staunch supporter of the AIC, he felt that an all-Indian Bible school was necessary in order for the AG to successfully adopt the indigenous principle. He retained close ties with the AIC for the rest of his life, serving as the graduation speaker in 1968, as a featured speaker at the dedication of the new campus in 1971, and as a faculty member after his retirement from the pastorate in the 1980s.[123] At AIC he found a willing audience for his ideas and methods, theories that would influence many young Pentecostal Indian leaders of the next generation, including AG Indian representative and member of the Executive Presbytery Brother John Maracle, who trained under Brother Lee.

In September 1978, the *PE* printed a four-page story on Brother Lee and his indigenous church in Shiprock, New Mexico, with Brother Lee featured on the cover of the magazine.[124] It took the denomination's magazine of record nearly two years to report on the church's indigenous status; in 1976, the year it was accepted by the General Council, the *PE* made no public announcement. We do not know why, but it is possible that the idea of a fully indigenous Indian church was an uncomfortable one for the AG—or at least for the editors of the *PE* at the time. In addition, the content of the article might have caused discomfort, for it gingerly addressed the problem of white missionary paternalism.

The article began with negative comments about two historic foes of American Indians, white missionaries and the BIA, and then proceeded to a statement of how an indigenous missionary could do better. The author, unnamed, faulted white missionaries for not allowing Indians to play any meaningful role in the building of their missions. "When mission work began on the various reservations, missionaries came to bring the gospel thinking in terms of "poor and illiterate" Indians. The practice that prevails with the BIA became common among most non-Indian missionaries of all denominations. They provided for both the material and spiritual needs of the Indians. . . . Paternalism developed which reduced many Indians to charity cases. Some attended missions partly because of the material benefits they received."[125] Such a statement represented a radical move by the editors of the *PE*, because they were acknowledging the problem of paternalism within missions programs, including (although indirectly) in their own. The editors of the *PE* also acknowledged that by the 1970s the indigenous principle had gained a foothold beyond the Indian missionaries who had always supported it.

Brother Lee's formula for successful evangelization, as described in the article, no longer called for building a mission and acting as an example. Instead, he engaged his potential converts. He stated, "Any missionary should acquire a thorough knowledge of the culture of the tribe that he is to serve. Through this he can gain a better understanding of the thinking and practices of the people."[126] In a dramatic departure from the AG's historic outlook, he also urged missionaries to avoid denigrating traditional religion or traditional practices and stated that a strong connection to tribal culture could coexist with being a Christian. Brother Lee recommended education: "Missionaries who use correct grammar and understand Indian culture will make a better impression on better educated Navajos."[127] Many young Indians were now educated, Brother Lee argued, and missionaries had to stay relevant with current Indian thought, including the writings of those whom the AG saw as "radical" Indian writers, historians, and philosophers. Do not ignore them, he warned, because the young people of the tribe were interested in what they were saying. In other words, a truly astute missionary had to stay current on all aspects of Indian culture.[128]

Brother Lee also offered a model of how an indigenous missionary should actively involve converts in the building of the mission. The Lees encouraged tithing, and in order to show how it worked and to be accountable, they made the mission's financial records public. They trained Indians with potential to become teachers in the Sunday school or to administer other aspects of the mission. Some they sent to the AIC for training as potential pastors and evangelists. They filled every church leadership position with a Navajo. As the church grew and expanded, the people decided that they wanted more control over the mission. So, in 1973, Brother Lee surrendered his missionary appointment. Influential members of the church came together and formed a board of directors, drafted a constitution and bylaws, and decided on the pastor's salary and the operation of the church.[129]

By the mid-1970s, Mesa View Assembly of God was entirely self-supporting. It no longer received donations as a mission and had even begun to give donations to further the Pentecostal Indian cause. Brother Lee showed his trust in the people of his church by turning over all of the financial decisions and paperwork to the treasurer and secretary of the church. On 1 October 1976, the Mesa View Assembly of God became the first district-affiliated indigenous church located on a federal reservation to be approved by the General Council.[130] Brother Lee saw his vision realized—his Shiprock mission was no longer a mission but a fully indigenous church with a Navajo pastor, a Navajo board of directors, and Navajo staff. The church proudly exemplified the indigenous principle.[131]

In 1979, Mesa View Assembly of God expanded its ministry by erecting several buildings, including classrooms, a nursery, and a fellowship hall.[132] Lee's congregation constructed the buildings as finances allowed, so that the church could avoid any indebtedness. The men and women of the church donated the labor.[133] As Brother Lee's church grew, he continued to champion the indigenous principle among his own people, to the greater Pentecostal public, and to the AG that had yet to accept it fully. Usually in the *PE*, articles on American Indians ended with a plea for funds to help the missionaries in the home missions program. Brother Lee's example changed that. The article on his church ended as follows: "The Division of Home Missions encourages the establishing of indigenous churches as an effective means of reaching the American Indians with the gospel."[134] Such a statement signaled a major change of view by the AG and the editors of the *PE*. Thirty years after Melvin Hodges at CBI had taught Brother Lee about the indigenous principle, the AG had finally embraced it within its home missions program.

Brother Lee's drive for the indigenous principle stemmed from reasons more complicated than his classes with Melvin Hodges at CBI, his work in the missionary field, and the AG's Pauline ideal. His experiences as a Navajo were the most important factor. The evidence suggests that Brother Lee felt so strongly about the indigenous principle not only because its realization benefited the church but also because it protected Pentecostal Indians. If the people took control of the church, they could be shielded from white AG paternalism and develop their own religious identity. Brother Lee knew the power that white people had and how they could exert it over American Indians—he had witnessed such abuses of power when he was a boy. He also knew that indigenous leaders could seize control of their own destinies as the Navajos had done when they protested the Wheeler-Howard Act. This lesson applied even though the entity he was battling now was not the federal government but rather the AG white hierarchy. The development of indigenous churches neutralized the power of the AG, empowering Pentecostal Indians.

Although Brother Lee did not leave behind an autobiography or extensive writings as his contemporary Sister Washburn had, his influence on Native leaders among the AG remains profound. A hogan-shaped building on the modern campus of the AIC is named after him, and his presence is still felt at the school, and no doubt at his old church. Brother Jim Dempsey told me how in faculty meetings Brother Lee would draw funny comics with captions on the margins of his notes in order to while away the time. Another staff member told me the story of his self-portrait, which sits in the entrance of the building named after him. Apparently the original painting depicted Brother Lee in a tan suit, which he often wore, but after displaying the portrait publicly, Brother Lee was not satisfied with it, so he secretly took the painting from its place of honor at AIC, and when it returned, the color of the suit had been change to a more complementary blue. His colleagues described him as a gentle man with a great sense of humor and a love for animals, art, and the landscape of his homeland. His unwavering belief in the indigenous principle was also well known. He was a visionary man in a changing Pentecostal landscape.

Conclusion

Sister Alta Washburn and Brother Charlie Lee proved unorthodox missionaries who clearly perceived the flaws in the institution they served. They responded by acting first to meet the needs of the people, even if the AG hierarchy might not approve. Sister Washburn thought that in order to further the AG's missionary program to Indians, the AG needed more Indian missionaries and leaders. She believed that these future leaders had to be trained in the fundamentals of Pentecostalism, such as interpretation of the Bible, leadership, and preaching. She also believed that Indian Pentecostals should be trained in their own Bible school. Despite initial opposition from fellow Pentecostal ministers, a lack of adequate funds, and the reluctance of the AG to support the project, she persevered and built her Bible school with the dogged determination of a woman with a vision. She ran the school on hope and prayer for years, until the AG finally realized that her idea was important for successfully building its home missions program among Indians and officially took over the school. Without Sister Washburn's determination to do what she believed was right, the American Indian College of the Assemblies of God would never have existed.

When Charlie Lee returned to the Shiprock region of his youth, he was determined to build an indigenous church among his own people. Influenced by Latin American missiologist Melvin Hodges and by his own experiences as a Navajo, Brother Lee set out to change how the AG approached Christian missions among Indians. Aware of the injustices of the past and the mistakes of other Christian missionaries, Brother Lee took a different approach. He involved the people of the church in every decision and gave them responsibility for and pride in their church—literally building a church of the people. At the time that Brother Lee was transforming his mission into a church, the AG still had not made the move toward making the indigenous principle an official part of its home missions program for Indians. Leading by example, Brother Lee persuaded the AG to see that Indian Pentecostals could indeed run their own church and run it successfully. The indigenous principle could be applied to home missions for Indians, and this change empowered Pentecostal Indians and made them more secure in their dual identities.

Although their work appeared similar, Sister Washburn and Brother Lee drew inspiration from very different personal histories. Sister Washburn's restorationist beliefs and pragmatic orientation motivated her work—God told her to build a Bible college, but God left the particulars to her. Her work was rooted in the accomplishments of the Pentecostal female missionaries of the past: innovation in the face of stasis and leadership in empowering indigenous converts. Brother Lee's experience as a Navajo convinced him that Indians must lead their own churches so that they could control their own religious fate. Knowing from his own experience that non-Indians abused power when dealing with Indians, Brother Lee sought to wrest control from the white AG leadership and give it back to his fellow Pentecostal Indians. By establishing indigenous churches, he hoped that Pentecostal Indians would find a way to embrace their new, hybrid identity.

The efforts of Sister Washburn and Brother Lee ultimately encouraged the AG to change. Sister Washburn and Brother Lee showed there was a better way to approach home missions, a way that helped neutralize the problems of paternalism and ethnocentrism. With empowerment and education came Pentecostal Indian pride and a deeper sense of identity. With a sense of identity and pride came leadership and willingness to confront the system. With the indigenous principle in place, and with their own Bible College established, Pentecostal Indians were lacking only one thing: institutional recognition within the General Council. They still did not possess a leader, someone who could speak for them as Pentecostal Indians in the AG bureaucracy. As the 1970s drew to an end, the demand for representation on the General Council and on a national scale was the last major fight that the first generation of Indian missionaries, leaders, and supporters would wage.

The Fight for National Power and the Indigenous Principle *The Development of the Indian Representative Position and the Native American Fellowship*

On 2 December 1977, T. E. Gannon, the national director of Home Missions, sent Cherokee evangelist Brother John McPherson an important letter. It read in part:

> You will recall that the General Council in session in Oklahoma City adopted a resolution authorizing the Executive Presbytery to appoint one to serve as an Indian representative. Unfortunately the resolution was so brief that little or no guidelines were given as to area of responsibility and no provision was made to fund this office. It was the unanimous decision of both the Home Missions Board and the Executive Presbytery that we should appoint someone to assume this position on a part-time basis. . . . I am indeed happy, Brother McPherson, that the Executive Presbytery in session unanimously selected you to serve in this capacity.[1]

Brother Gannon ended by asking for Brother McPherson's prayerful consideration of the offer of the position of Indian representative. Shortly after receiving the letter, Brother McPherson responded to Brother Gannon, writing, "I am overwhelmed and deeply grateful to the Executive brethren for the confidence they have placed in me in regard to my serving in this capacity."[2] He closed by indicating that he would visit Springfield, Missouri, after the Christmas season to discuss the position with Brother Gannon and the personnel of the Home Missions Department.[3] Brother

McPherson's appointment to serve as the first national Indian represen-tative for the AG gave him and other American Indian Pentecostal leaders hope that the AG was finally embracing its Pentecostal Indian constitu-ency. But at the beginning, the position lacked tangible power and did not bring immediate changes to the AG's approach to home missions.

Indian missionaries and evangelists worked for decades to achieve greater influence over the AG's home missions program to American In-dians. During the 1950s and 1960s, the small circle of Pentecostal Indian leaders began to expand and exert more power within Home Missions.[4] Sister Alta Washburn and the AIC, along with Brother Charlie Lee's work for the indigenization of Native churches, were major factors in chang-ing how the AG perceived evangelism among American Indians. By build-ing their own Bible school and cultivating a distinct Native leadership among AG missionaries and evangelists, Indian Pentecostals challenged white leaders to realize the indigenous principle. They next focused on achieving institutional leadership in the appointment of a national Indian representative. Native leaders wanted the appointee to work with the De-partment of Home Missions in order to deal directly with the needs of Indian congregations. In 1977 the General Council approved the position at its annual meeting, and the Home Missions Board and Executive Pres-bytery sent John McPherson that letter.

Problems plagued the position from the outset. As the letter Brother McPherson received clearly stated, the position of Indian representative had no clear responsibilities or funding, and it called for a part-time ap-pointment. When Brother McPherson accepted the position, he had to contend with these problems as he attempted to make the job of Indian representative address the needs of Indian believers. The struggle over the definition of the position of Indian representative indicated Indian Pentecostals' efforts to gain more control over their place within the AG. The decades of the 1950s to the 1970s had been a time of hard work that brought quiet change for Indian Pentecostals and their white supporters within the Home Missions Department. But from the late 1970s to the end of the twentieth century, Indian leaders and congregations struggled more overtly against the white leadership in Springfield to carve out their own space.

This chapter concentrates on the final decades of the twentieth century and how the Native leadership within the AG tried to define itself and gain more autonomy. While the Home Missions Department and the power structure of the AG greatly hindered Indian efforts to expand official leadership roles, Indian leaders stuck to the ideals of the indigenous principle and continued to demand a fair hearing. When the national Indian representative idea did not work out, they innovated. The result was the creation of ethnic fellowships, in which Native leaders carved out their own autonomous space within the AG. The decades-long battle that Indian leaders waged for more say in the running of Home Missions might have disillusioned others who were less sure of their identities, but Indian Pentecostals never wavered in their faith. They refused to give up on the indigenous principle and, as this final chapter shows, made the fight for its realization the very core of their Pentecostal Indian identity and practice. They were both Pentecostals and Indians, and they were determined to make changes in the denomination they called their spiritual home.

This chapter first examines the creation of the position of Indian representative and the ways in which its first holder, Brother John McPherson, fought to define and give power to the job through an exploration of the letters that he left behind—showing an uphill fight to give the position meaningful power. The section also includes comparisons with contemporary examples of minority representation within religious bodies: Indian activist Vine Deloria Jr.'s work for indigenous leadership within the Episcopal Church and the development of Latino and African American ministries within the AG. Then the chapter looks at the Indian struggle in 1989–2006 for more power in the Home Missions Department and the failed attempt to create a separate Native American Department under the Home Missions/Special Ministries umbrella. Finally, this chapter explores the recent Native American Fellowship within the AG and how its composition, both democratic and separate from Home Missions and Special Ministries, has given Native leaders hope for change.

The Early Fight for Leadership

The December 1977 appointment of McPherson resulted from a resolution that American Indian leaders had drawn up in March of that year for consideration by the General Council. But long before that, in 1955, Indian leaders had requested that the General Council select a national Indian representative to speak for their interests and continued to do so as missions to American Indians expanded.[5] By 1977, bolstered by the success of the AIC and Lee's church, Indian leaders believed the time was right to demand representation. The resolution, signed by thirty-three Indian leaders and white supporters, pointed out that the American Indian field held the largest number of missionaries in the Special Ministries Division of Home Missions.[6] It also noted that the Indian field was larger than some AG districts and supported 199 Indian missionary posts, but that evangelization occurred among only a fraction of the American Indian population. The letter emphasized the need for Native leadership and indigenous churches.[7] Finally, the resolution ended by stating: "Whereas, All of the Special Ministries in the Division of Home Missions have representation and promotion on the national level, be it therefore, Resolved that a person with Indian Ministries experience, and preferably one who is an American Indian, according to Federal definition, be appointed by the Executive Presbytery to serve as a Field Representative to the American Indian Field by January 1978."[8] All of the other sections within AG Special Ministries (Deaf, Gypsies, Jews, and Latino) enjoyed national representation, while the American Indians did not, despite having the largest number of appointed missionaries and their own thriving Bible College.

The Home Missions Board reviewed the resolution. The main problem, it noted in its records, was that the resolution had no provision for funding. Home Missions calculated that it would take $35,000 to $40,000 to pay for the Indian representative position, yet the AG was not willing to divert money from other projects.[9] The Home Missions Board also stated that the Indian representative needed to be someone who would work well not only with the missionaries in the field but also with the AG administration.[10] After some consideration, the Home Missions Board decided it would recommend the following to the Executive Board: "A field representative for the Indian missionary work [who will] not be a full-time person but one who would serve as a liaison in Indian Ministries and maintain an Indian mission station as a basis of his work."[11] In other words, the job became a part-time position with no funding, held in conjunction with a regular home mission appointment.

According to its records, the Home Missions Committee expected the Indian representative to care for his own mission station or parish, as well as spend up to one-fourth of his time in Springfield on administrative duties, while continuing to evangelize and raise money to cover the expenses of the office.[12] The amount of work was tremendous and made the job problematic because it did not allow the Indian representative to concentrate on any one aspect of the position. Besides those requirements, the

Home Missions Board left the job description vague and offered no statement regarding the Indian representative's duties.

The Home Missions Board faced another problem—it had to determine the guidelines for appointment. The board decided to adopt a resolution that the Indian representative be "Indian according to the Government definition of an Indian."[13] This statement removed from it the responsibility of defining what "Indian" meant, but it also excluded prominent leaders from the Lumbee tribe of North Carolina, where the AG was especially active, because the federal government did not recognize Lumbees as a tribe. The board suggested several prominent Indian leaders, among them John McPherson, Rodger Cree, Charlie Lee, John Maracle, and Simon Peter.[14] The committee settled on Brother McPherson.

Some members of the AG leadership expressed doubts about having an Indian serve as Indian representative. Brother Tommy Crider, the presbyter of the northwest section of New Mexico, was one of the most vocal critics. In a letter to T. E. Gannon, Brother Crider voiced strong reservations about the Indian representative position. He argued that more thought should have gone into the resolution. He highlighted some of his concerns, which he said were shared by white pastors and missionaries in his region: "The feeling from them seems to be, that this is needed but that it was aimed against the white missionary. Some of the Indian pastors and missionaries have indicated that the white missionaries are not making the Indian churches indigenous as soon as they can. However most of the white missionaries have this as their goal. It is taking time."[15] Brother Crider was probably talking about Brother Charlie Lee and his vocal support for the indigenization of the Indian churches. Brother Lee's church, Mesa View Assembly of God, was located in Brother Crider's region. Brother Crider also stated that he did not believe that the Indians in his area (and, by implication, other Indian mission stations within the AG) showed enough responsibility to run their own churches, adding, "Sure it works in foreign lands, but they don't have some of the legal hassle we have in the States."[16] What exactly the legal hassle was, Brother Crider never explained.

Brother Crider ended his letter by stating, "My feeling is that it would be much better for this man to be Anglo. There seems to be more competition, rivalry, and mistrust among tribes than against the Anglo."[17] He illustrated this point by explaining how Navajos attended only the local Indian camp meetings, while Indians from other tribes often attended the white camp meetings because they did not want to be associated with Navajos.[18] While Brother Crider based his reasoning on the divisions that he observed among the American Indian Pentecostals in his region, he also clearly suspected Native pastors' power and ability. He was probably correct in pointing out that some tribes harbored animosities toward each other that ran deeper than their Pentecostal commonalities, but Charlie Lee's work with the Navajos refuted his views that Natives were incapable of running their own churches. In Brother Crider's own district, Brother Lee had managed to create what so many white missionaries had believed was impossible: an indigenous church. It is also likely that Brother Crider viewed Brother Lee and his flock as somewhat radical, especially because Lee had gained a reputation for preaching in Navajo and championing Indian self-determination.[19] In short, Brother Lee's desire for indigenous churches and an American Indian leadership within the AG threatened the roles of the white missionaries. Brother Crider's attempt to make the Indian representative an Anglo shows that he believed that white AG leaders still knew what was best for their Indian flock. In other words, Brother Crider championed a continuation of a paternalistic power structure that seemed to keep the home missions movement safe from "radicals" such as Charlie Lee.

While the Home Missions Board noted Brother Crider's letter and mentioned it in the memorandum, the committee maintained that it would be best to appoint a representative who was Indian by federal definition and also amenable to the white AG leadership.[20] John McPherson, the Cherokee evangelist known for wearing a magnificent Plains Indian headdress and for his folksy style of evangelism, seemed to fit the bill.

McPherson's Early Years as Indian Representative, 1979–1980

Brother McPherson accepted the position in 1978 and immediately discovered that its vague description meant that he had to create a position out of nothing. Correspondence between T. E. Gannon and Brother McPherson shows that the Home Missions Committee and General Council left it to them to define the job with little guidance. The correspondence also reveals that the position lacked power or influence—in other words, it appears that white leaders in Springfield created it to quiet the demands of Indian leaders. The evidence suggests that in Brother McPherson, the white leadership in Springfield hoped to have a cooperative Indian leader who would not fight them. From the outset of his work however, the AG's lack of institutional support trapped Brother McPherson between the white hierarchy and the wants and needs of Indian Pentecostals. Brother McPherson strove to serve amid conflicting demands, yet he quickly found himself in an impossible situation.

In a letter to Brother Gannon dated 21 March 1978, Brother McPherson asked a series of basic questions, including why the position was only part-time.[21] That fact had drawn the ire of some of the Indian leaders, and Brother McPherson wanted the official explanation. Brother Gannon replied that the appointment was part-time because of a lack of funding and because the Indians' resolution had not called for a full-time appointment.[22] Even more revealing, he stated, "Since the bylaws places [sic] the full responsibility of administration and supervision of all special ministries work upon the district wherein it resides, this dictates to the program a certain degree of limitation."[23] In other words, the Indian ministries within Home Missions remained under the jurisdiction of each district, so though the Indian representative could mediate and influence the home missions, he exercised no real power over how those programs would be run. Brother McPherson could act as a mediator between the Indian leadership and Home Missions, but in reality he had no direct control over Indian ministries. Brother Gannon tried to make this arrangement more palatable by pointing out that the Gypsy ministries had only a part-time representative, much in the manner of the new Indian representative, and that the Jewish ministry did not have a representative at all. In other words, the Indian ministries should accept what they were given.[24]

The lack of funding became an immediate problem for Brother McPherson.[25] In his first report of the national Indian representative to Home Missions, he emphasized his frustration with the structure of the position, particularly because he was already committed to a full revival schedule before he accepted the job. Brother McPherson argued that he could not cancel his planned appearances: "It would be a breach of ministerial ethics and violate a practice I have endeavored to follow for many years."[26] He also noted that "there were difficult obstacles in the way that would hinder in the realization of the objectives that our Indian brethren no doubt had in mind when they submitted the resolution that gave birth to the mentioned portfolio."[27] Besides the lack of funding, he pointed out that some of the "difficult obstacles" included the job description, which was "vague and nebulous at best,"[28] and the job's part-time status. Brother McPherson told the committee, "Of course it would be an exercise in futility to think that one person could visit a great number of stations in thirteen weeks especially with their geography being what it is and my attempt at staying on the field."[29] From the information in Brother McPherson's memo, it was clear that he already knew what it would take to make the Indian representative into a functional position. The job as currently constructed was hopelessly untenable. But to his credit, Brother McPherson seemed optimistic; indeed, his generally sunny and willing personality probably explains why the AG initially selected him. Brother McPherson gamely attempted to make the best of a difficult situation.

Brother McPherson began his labors with a letter-writing campaign, which he hoped would raise funds.[30] He did this with the encouragement of Brother Gannon, but the letter-writing campaign provoked a new problem. Many of his potential supporters pledged funds, but they also wanted him to preach at a Sunday service.[31] Brother McPherson did not have time to preach Sunday sermons in addition to his preexisting evangelistic campaign commitments. He implored Brother Gannon to think prayerfully about a way to help him with this problem.[32]

Traveling among Indian Pentecostals, Brother McPherson encountered a multitude of questions. American Indian missionaries pointed out that they did not have enough input on AG policies and that they needed better vehicles and financial support. The leadership at the AIC asked Brother McPherson what to do about Pentecostal students who, after graduating, established independent, non-AG churches on the reservations.[33] With so nebulous a job description, Brother McPherson struggled to be of service to his constituency.

Brother McPherson asked Brother Gannon for help in defining the job while he formulated a plan for dealing with the rigors of his new position. His plan, he informed Brother Gannon, was to write notes of support to all appointed Indian missionaries, contact all AG Bible colleges to let them know of his availability as a speaker, and start a small newsletter in which he hoped to publish news that pertained to Indian Pentecostals and those who lived and worked among them.[34] Although overwhelmed, Brother McPherson understood that he needed to continue to be out listening to the people, too. In the closing sentences, he wrote: "I trust that soon certain obstacles can be removed or modified that will facilitate the office of national Rep and that it will contribute to the advancement of the kingdom and that our effort together will find its expression in many new works being established and many Indians being saved."[35] This statement forced Brother Gannon to confront the real reason that the AG needed to clarify and support the position of Indian representative: the white establishment's weakening of the Indian representative position did more than keep Indians out of power—it kept souls from being saved.

Brother McPherson's guarded warning at the end of his letter to Brother Gannon was not the only indication of his feelings about the job. While he was dealing with an uncooperative leadership in Springfield, Indian leaders and constituents were complaining about Brother McPherson's ability. In a copy of a speech, apparently prepared for a mostly Indian audience,[36] Brother McPherson tried to clarify his views about his appointment. "I refuse to participate in a program that would make the job of Indian Rep. a placebo or a straw man, I have been a Revivalist and Children's Evangelist for 25 years and it is not unprecedented for a new job or portfolio to go to waste in a ministry or reduce him to 'a null and void' status. . . . If I am going to serve in this capacity I want to be of help. If not, then I'm gone."[37] The wording suggests that Brother McPherson must have faced harsh criticism that he was nothing but a puppet for the white leadership in Springfield. Brother McPherson also identified the greatest obstacle to his work as Indian representative: "It is an exercise in futility to think that one man or person could cover so vast a field of U.S.A. where dwells the Indian population."[38] Apparently criticized by some for his inability to travel freely for the job, Brother McPherson added, "I know that you would like to have a visit from your Rep. and that's a justifiable and legitimate desire and I am apologizing for my 'no show.' However I appeal to you beloved friends to show patience in this regard."[39] He went on to reassure the audience that he would work out some way to travel more freely; he also told them of his plans to be in contact with Indian leaders as he worked on defining the responsibilities of the job. Brother McPherson ended this short talk with a plea for cooperation among the Indian leaders and laity, using colloquialisms to express charges that likely were leveled against him. "I am not an apple (red on the outside and white on the inside). Neither am I an Uncle Tomahawk."[40] He wanted to state clearly that he stood in solidarity with the Indian leadership as well as with the laity.

The AG structured Brother McPherson's position in a manner that made it nearly impossible for him to initiate change. With no funding and only part-time status, Brother McPherson could not even begin to address the needs of Pentecostal American Indians. And, unfairly, these Pentecostal Indians began to criticize Brother McPherson as not being willing to initiate the changes they wanted. Some Indian leaders believed that Springfield was deliberately putting obstacles in the way of Brother McPherson; others saw Brother McPherson as too sympathetic to the white AG leadership.

The structure of the job as well as the power struggles between whites and Indians left Brother McPherson in an unenviable position: caught between two different factions.

The criticism regarding the vague job description for the Indian representative forced the Home Missions office in 1979 to create a formal job description. This description amended the existing resolution concerning the Indian representative. While the nature of the job did not change and funding was still not forthcoming, the amendment did clarify the duties of the position. These included encouraging the growth of indigenous churches, acting as a resource for special ministries, developing promotional material for Indian missions, assessing the needs of Indian missionaries, developing missionary curricula, traveling on the Indian camp-meeting circuit, and raising additional funds for special projects.[41] The amendment concluded by stating a specific goal: "It is envisioned that the main responsibility is to assess and strengthen each district Indian missions program, thus developing a strong, viable ministry under the supervision of the district."[42] Brother McPherson finally possessed a detailed job description given to him by the members of the General Council.

Soon after this clarification, Brother McPherson set off for the Indian Institute, a colloquy of leaders and missionaries in the Indian field.[43] Afterward, he reported to T. E. Gannon with a list of "critical issues," some of which had been problems in AG missionary work among Indians for decades. The AG had tightened the education standards for missionaries, demanding that all missionaries have at least a three-year Bible institute degree. Brother McPherson pointed out that the stricter rules concerning the education and training of appointed home missionaries meant that some Indian evangelists were having a hard time securing appointments.[44] He also stressed that many Indian churches, while thriving, were not yet ready to become indigenous and that some of the reservations "may soon be closed."[45] Although he did not elaborate on this, he probably meant that tribal governing bodies on certain reservations were making it harder for missionaries to set up new missions. Brother McPherson also suggested that the AG put more emphasis on using the AIC to funnel pastors and missionaries toward Indian work.[46] The AIC not only would serve the AG best as a training ground for more indigenous clergy but, if utilized properly, would "interject the stimulus that will cause the student to desire a ministry among their own people."[47]

While all the aforementioned problems contributed to the small number of Indians going into the ministry, Brother McPherson pointed to lack of support from the general AG constituency as the number one problem facing Indian home missionaries.[48] Without enough funding, Native ministries remained undeveloped. It was the same problem that Brother McPherson faced in his own job: if forced to travel around seeking money, how could missionaries focus on their evangelistic work? AG missionaries prided themselves on their willingness to go out on faith missions, sacrificing their own financial security in order to do missionary work. Yet raising funds was harder for Indian missionaries and evangelists, since their constituency was poorer than the average American.[49] This forced them to turn to the *PE* as well as to the generosity of white supporters, but with their Native parishioners unable to donate money to their cause, Native missionaries were at a distinct disadvantage.

Finally, Brother McPherson added, "Some concern was voiced about the age-old rift that has existed between Anglo missionaries and Indian workers. We all know it exists—we know what causes it, but we desire to see it end so that all of us with one mighty voice be unified in this great effort."[50] Although reports in *PE* had long hinted that a rift had existed between white missionaries and their Indian colleagues, this was the first and only direct acknowledgment of the problem. Brother McPherson mentioned it only briefly, but that he brought it up at all is telling. Because Pentecostal missionaries came from the lower- and working-class segments of American society (like many American Indians) the "rift" probably stemmed mostly from ethnicity rather than class. One might think that someone had directly addressed this problem by 1979, yet it seems that both white and Indian missionaries had chosen to ignore it. Resentment of white missionaries on the reservation had long festered in the Indian community, and that resentment could have come about in several ways. Some Indian missionaries saw their white counterparts as paternalistic, while others saw them as having good intentions but not enough knowledge of Indian culture to be effective evangelists. Other Indian leaders wondered why they did not receive more power over their own affairs on the missionary field and chafed at being under a white district superintendent's gaze. The sources do not reveal the actual feelings of Indian missionaries. They did not make their views public (with the exception of Charlie Lee, and even he mentioned the problem only in passing).[51] They did, after all, have to get along with their white colleagues, and Pentecostal culture did not encourage confrontational tactics.

Brother Gannon's response to Brother McPherson's letter was swift and circumspect. He did not directly address Brother McPherson's comment on the "rift" but noted that "In some ways, I find myself a bit frustrated, and the frustration is not altogether bad. . . . I have a great sense of joy in the progress we have made in the last few years. Not all of our Indian missionaries are continuing to be defensive and many of them have upgraded their own ministry, for which they should be commended."[52] Again, like Brother McPherson, T. E. Gannon is vague about what he means by "defensive" and does not elaborate on the problems between white and Indian missionaries. He implies that working with certain Indian missionaries is difficult, but again, he is unspecific. Yet this letter, like that of Brother McPherson's, confirms that even as late as the 1970s, white and Indian missionaries to American Indians experienced some tensions.

Brother Gannon defended the new requirements for home missionaries, arguing that they "have automatically brought into existence far better qualified personnel than we had for a long time."[53] He amended that statement by noting, "This is not to belittle nor to reflect upon those faithful workers who have served so diligently for many years. In fact, I do not know how much of Indian work we would have had if it has not been for many of the 'less qualified' workers who blazed the trail."[54] Brother Gannon recognized that early white evangelists, many of whom did not possess a Bible college education, carried out substantial missionary work to American Indians. He defended the AG's change to the stricter standards for appointment, arguing that the new standards would address some of the problems that Brother McPherson had mentioned.

In other respects, Brother Gannon proved sympathetic to Brother McPherson's overwhelming problems as Indian representative. In order to facilitate the "continuity" and "unification" that Indian missions lacked, he proposed an Indian committee so that they could contribute "a broad field of wisdom and understanding which can give balance to any program."[55] He went on, "I could envision such a committee consisting of Indian ministers, Indian missionaries, and perhaps one or two district officials who have outstanding Indian works within their districts. . . . These, together with our Indian Representative, the national director of Home Missions and our special ministries representative could sit down together and review the things you have spoken of in your letter."[56] Such a committee, as envisioned by Brother Gannon, would ease Brother McPherson's burden and counsel him on important decisions concerning the Indian Pentecostal community. The letter closes with an offer to propose the idea of an Indian committee to the Executive Presbytery via the Home Missions Board, if Brother McPherson agreed.[57]

Brother McPherson's response is lost, but it must have been positive. On 29 January 1980, Paul Markstrom, a white missionary, sent a memo to Brother Gannon with a list of Indian and white missionaries recommended for the National Indian Committee. The AG approved the committee to "serve in a consultative capacity" by 10 March 1980. Correspondence between Brother Gannon and Brother Lee hints at Brother Lee's approval to serve on the committee in an advisory manner.[58]

The AG's refusal to provide funding and tangible power for Indian leaders was not the first instance of a major denomination downplaying its Indian congregants' calls to be included in the running of their own churches. About a decade before the creation of the AG's Indian representative position, a similar drama played out in a Protestant mainline denomination. As the 1960s came to a close and the Red Power movement began to gain momentum in Indian country, Native activist and writer Vine Deloria Jr. laid out his idea for the creation of a national Indian Christian Church. Deloria believed that the mainline Protestant denominations should join to foster this national Indian church, which would be run wholly by Indian people themselves.[59] While Deloria did not include Pentecostal Christianity in his vision of a national Indian church, it is informative to look at how the mostly white mainline denominations (chiefly the Protestant Episcopal Church) dealt with Deloria's call to arms.

According to historian David Daily, during this period the Episcopal Church was trying to find meaningful ways to engage the urban poor and began to pour millions into urban ministries.[60] This development gave Deloria hope. In 1968 the Episcopal leadership elected him to the Executive Council of the Episcopal Church.[61] There, Deloria proposed that the Episcopal Church establish an "Indian Desk," a national advisory committee consisting of Indian leaders, and called for the recruitment of Native clergy as well as increased Indian representation on major Episcopal committees.[62] At first, it seemed that the Episcopal leadership reacted positively to Deloria's request by establishing and funding a National Committee on Indian Work and by offering development grants to Indian churches.[63] But Episcopal leaders quickly sabotaged Deloria's ideas. They sent a mole to Deloria's meetings who dispatched secret reports expressing doubts that Indians could run their own churches and warned that Indians did not have enough training or knowledge to move beyond the missions level.[64] With that, support for Deloria's ideas began to wane. The church fired white supporters of Deloria and seasoned missionary personnel to make room for new "ideas" people, and Deloria, aware that his proposal was in trouble, grew bitterly disillusioned. He resigned from the Executive Council and stated, "At any rate I can't see staying in the church and struggling for years to get the church to act while the rest of the Indian world marches on beyond Christianity."[65] Between 1969 and 1974, the Episcopal Church quietly phased out its National Council of Indian Workers by refusing to fund it.[66] It stalled out, and the Episcopal Church tried to forget that the incident ever took place. Deloria never directly engaged Christianity again, except to write scathing critiques of it.[67]

Deloria's attempted engagement with the Episcopal Church is important to this study for several reasons. First, it shows that the AG was not alone in its reluctance to hand over power to Indians. In the case of the AG, however, the Indian leadership was large and well organized, which allowed it to continue to seek different avenues to national representation. Second, Deloria's work with the Episcopal Church shows the climate of the time. By the end of the 1970s, when AG Indians made a concerted bid for national power and leadership, the Red Power movement had imploded, but the ideals that drove it lingered on many reservations. While I have found no hard evidence that the Red Power movement included any AG Indian leaders, there is no doubt that they were aware of it. Stationed mainly on the remote western reservations, AG Indian leaders likely witnessed how Red Power militancy swept up their young people. While no AG Indian leader referred to the American Indian Movement (AIM) in any published AG record (such as the *PE*), Brother Lee did advise missionaries to "be aware of current Indian thinkers" in order to be in tune with the young people of the tribe.[68] This comment suggests that Lee probably read Deloria during this period, as well as the works of other Indian activists. In fact, in Deloria's hugely successful bestseller, *Custer Died for Your Sins*, he proposed a national, Indian-run Christian church. AG Indian leaders had watched how AIM and other activists on the reservations demanded their rights throughout the early 1970s, and while Native Pentecostals did not embrace the violence and outward anger of the Red Power Movement, they did move to channel some of their own grievances into a call for action.

While a comparison to Deloria's work with the Episcopal Church is useful in understanding how other denominations dealt with Indians, it is also important to compare the Indian struggle to that of other ethnic minorities within the AG. The AG targeted Latinos for evangelization shortly after its formation in the early twentieth century. The ministry to Latinos shared some similarities with the ministry to American Indians. A sympathetic female white missionary founded an ethnically specific Bible college for Latinos, which fostered the development of a distinct Latino Pentecostal identity.[69] More important than the similarities between the two groups, however, were the differences. Unlike the missions program to American Indians, the missions program to Latinos grew rapidly, developed a Latino leadership early, and eventually became powerful enough to have its own autonomous districts.[70] Meanwhile, American Indians remained under the home missions designation and general white district control. While Latinos, like American Indians, waged long battles against the perils of paternalism, they fit more comfortably into the Assemblies of God and developed innovative ministries such as the Victory Outreach movement that was inspired by the AG's Teen Challenge ministry.[71]

Three reasons for these differences present themselves: the size of the ethnic group, the social location and mobility of the group, and the "cultural baggage" of the group in terms of integrating into white America. Latinos are the fastest-growing ethnic group in the United States in the twenty-first century; American Indians, in contrast, make up only 2 percent of the overall American population. Latinos often start out as poor immigrants, but they usually find their way into the working class and in many cases the American middle class. While poverty and prejudice are factors inhibiting Latino economic growth, Latinos do not face the daunting obstacles that American Indians did on reservations, where economic and social struggle are institutionalized, the products of years of federal Indian policy. Finally, although Latinos certainly encounter racism and prejudice as well as anti-immigrant sentiment from white Americans, at least their presence is well acknowledged.[72] Most Americans remain largely unaware of the modern American Indian struggle and even forget that Indians live among them. Modern American Indians remain in the shadows of the collective American imagination, which view them as a vanishing race.

The habit of freezing Native peoples out of leadership roles in Native ministries continued into the twenty-first century. In her work on Native evangelicals, Andrea Smith discovered that "it is important to understand how Native ministries replicate the colonial structures of the United States and Canada. That is, much more than any other racial or ethnic minority church or parachurch organizations, Native ministries are controlled by non-Indians."[73] This pattern also proved to be the case for the AG's missions to American Indians, especially when compared to the Latino ministry. Unlike Latinos, American Indians were not a group large enough and geographically concentrated enough to demand their own district organization, so they worked to gain control of the missions program through other types of organizations and leadership. And while the indigenous church ideal was more fruitful numerically for Latinos than for American Indians, the Indian leadership within the AG was not willing to give up on its goal.[74] That American Indians continued working with the AG to define themselves as Pentecostal Indians was extraordinary, given that the AG had given them a national leadership position in name only.

Yet the conflicts of both groups also show the inherent flexibility of Pentecostalism, a religion embraced by many different ethnic identities while its core beliefs remained the same. Historian Arlene Sánchez-Walsh comments on this fact in her analysis of Victory Outreach, a movement that grew out of the Latino community to address problems of violence, gang membership, and drug abuse. "Pentecostal worship fulfills certain needs: its orality, music, intercessory prayer, testimony, informality and relaxing of class signifiers such as dress and occupation. There is an invitation in Pentecostal churches to imbibe in the ritual life of Christianity available to the marginalized and the outsider that many do not find in mainstream Protestant churches."[75] Sánchez-Walsh's explanation for why Pentecostalism proved so popular among the dispossessed holds true not only for the former inner-city gang members that she studied but also for American Indians. Despite everything that the Indian leadership went through in its effort to gain national recognition within the AG, it remained within the denomination because Pentecostalism gave them something that they could not find in mainline Protestant Christianity. Sánchez-Walsh describes it as "Pentecostalism's transcendent value: an offering of a ritual life to groups who do not feel welcome in other surroundings."[76] American Indians found this "transcendent value" in the AG and pushed the denomination to live up to its own Pentecostal values.

In the case of African Americans in the AG, their history is much more troubling than that of Latinos. After the earliest days of the Pentecostal movement, the races separated, and the AG became known as the "white" Pentecostal denomination, while the Church of God in Christ (COGIC) became known as the "black" Pentecostal denomination. The reasons for the separation stemmed from both racial and theological factors. Theologically, COGIC was rooted in the Holiness movement, whereas the AG's roots were in the Keswick movement. Racially, the AG decided in 1939 that it would not ordain African American pastors, and instead urged them to seek ordination in COGIC.[77] During the pre–civil rights era, the AG did not support integrated churches and often depicted African Americans in the *PE* as simple, uneducated people who all spoke in the same "colored" dialect.[78] It was not until after the civil rights movement that the AG began to move toward integrating churches. In the 1970s, the denomination began to address how to reach out to African Americans and develop an African American ministry.[79] The AG did not face its past with African Americans until 1994, when, at the Memphis Colloquy of the Pentecostal Fellowship of America, the AG finally repented of its racism.[80] Like American Indians, African Americans carved out autonomy in their own ethnic fellowships in the 1990s. In 2004 the AG claimed only 269 preponderantly African American churches.[81] Compare this with the 1989 statistic on Indian churches—the AG had 189 Indian churches and missions.[82]

The history of African Americans within the AG tells us that the AG was often loath to challenge the perceived American status quo. While segregation was the norm in the United States, the AG quietly retained segregated churches. The AG changed after the civil rights movement, but it did not join the movement and often discouraged its members from seeking social change. Native peoples, however, did find more autonomy early on in the AG, and unlike African Americans, they gained appointments as missionaries and pastors in the pre–civil rights era. This difference stemmed from a different approach to the two ethnic groups—Indians, because of their perceived "heathenness," became objects of missionary work, whereas African Americans, who already had deep ties to Protestant Christianity and who were members of the Pentecostal movement from the outset, were relegated to their own separate denomination. Also, institutionalized and personal racism made it very hard for the AG to step beyond stereotypes toward African Americans. In this way, Native peoples and African Americans within the denomination both suffered from ethnocentrism and paternalism. The white leadership in Springfield assumed that it knew what was best for its minority constituents. Native Pentecostals, however, were able to use the indigenous principle as the driving force of change within the denomination. African Americans, not viewed as a missionary target like Indians, could not marshal this theology of missions in quite the same way. Also, Native peoples did not possess a denominational alternative to the AG, unlike African Americans, who already had a long history of their own churches.

Although the last letters in the Indian representative archival file are dated 1981, other sources reveal that over the next two decades the Indian leadership continued to fight. Brother McPherson remained the Indian representative until the early 1990s, when William Lee (called Bill Lee, a Navajo and Charlie Lee's nephew) assumed the post. In 2000, Brother John Maracle, nephew of the early Mohawk evangelist Andrew Maracle, became the Indian representative. In 2008, he remained in the post.[83] From the last letters in the file, we know that Brother McPherson continued to struggle with the demands of his job as Indian representative. The same problems surface repeatedly. Notably, Brother McPherson left out of his public autobiography the story of his tenure as Indian representative—his frustrations appeared only in the private letters. The AG created the position to appease Indians and to quell dissention, but Native leaders wanted Brother McPherson to be an instrument of change, something the very nature of the job and lack of funding kept him from accomplishing. The Indian leaders within the AG, realizing Brother McPherson was not personally responsible for the stasis brought on by the problems with the position, fought even harder for change. For the next two decades, the 1980s and 1990s, they endeavored to find a new way to achieve leadership positions within the AG.

The Role of the Indian Representative and the Formation of the Native American Fellowship at the Dawn of the Twenty-First Century

The main concerns of Native leaders in the 1980s and 1990s were addressing the shortcomings in the Indian representative position and finding a better way to make Native voices heard. This determination resulted in the creation of an American Indian Fellowship within the AG—a move that gave them an autonomous space within the AG and the possibility of voting rights in the Executive Presbytery.

Lack of funding for the Indian representative remained the most important problem. Instead of focusing on his duties as Indian representative, Brother McPherson spent much of his time itinerating for funds. Indian leaders were not the only ones who recognized that a lack of money was a problem. In a letter to Home Missions Director T. E. Gannon, Brother Paul Markstrom, a fellow Special Ministries missionary, pleaded for financial support for position.

> I believe it is a weakness for Brother McPherson to only spasmodically give time throughout the year. May I recommend that a block

or two of time be utilized (such as 13 weeks) where John would be fully employed to discharge these responsibilities. . . . Since Brother McPherson would be duly representing the American Indian ministry it does appear as though we have a financial responsibility for salary and travel expenses comparable to that of a full-time representative. Therefore, I strongly urge that a budget be established for these financial responsibilities.[84]

Likewise, Indian missionaries formally asked the 1979 General Council to amend the Indian representative job description from "part-time" to "full-time."[85] The minutes, however, do not indicate whether the General Council adopted the proposal.

In the early 1980s, the Indian leaders began to demand that the AG provide funding for the Indian representative. Their plan advocated a 5 percent tithe on missionaries to Indians. This plan would free the Indian representative from his constant fundraising and obligate the Indian missionaries to support him monetarily. The idea never made it to the floor of the General Council, although Indian leaders and others affiliated with Home Missions discussed it. The counterargument was that such a tithe would hurt other divisions of the AG Special Ministries. American Indian leaders had to find a new plan.[86]

During the General Council of 1989, American Indians brought to the floor a resolution to create a Native American Ministry Department. They wanted to develop a separate department just for Indian missions under the auspices of Home Missions. This would change the practice of keeping Indian missions under the umbrella of Intercultural Ministries in Special Ministries and Home Missions (thus run by white missionaries) and would give the Indian leadership more influence in the running of Home Missions. The resolution also called, again, for making the Indian representative position full-time, and it offered several different ways to pay for the proposed department as well as the Indian representative. The proposed means of funding included special contributions designated for Indian missions, one-half of the tithes of nationally appointed home missionaries in Indian work, and a recommended monthly contribution from each Indian congregation. After some discussion, the General Council referred the resolution to a special committee.[87]

The referral of the resolution to committee gave Indian leaders some hope, but a problem immediately arose. The committee did not include a single Indian member. A professor from the American Indian College,

Brother Don Keeter, noticed this oversight and publicly petitioned for Indian input into the committee.[88] But the AG did not rectify this problem. During the 1991 General Council, the committee recommended the rejection of the resolution for three reasons. First, the resolution did not make adequate provision for financial support; second, a Native American Ministry Department would damage the financial and administrative structure that currently existed; and, third, such a department would not solve the problems facing Indian leaders.[89] The committee instead recommended that Indian churches be "encouraged" to give support to the Indian representative so that the position could become full-time and funded. The committee also asked Home Missions to allow the Indian representative to have more national visibility and to encourage the Indian representative to serve as a liaison between Intercultural Ministries and the Native Pentecostal population.[90]

The suggestions of the committee meant that the Indians were back to square one—they were still fighting the same battle that they had been fighting ever since the creation of the Indian representative position. Their representative was still not officially funded or officially full-time. They still had very little control over the policies of Home Missions or Intercultural Missionaries. The quagmire of AG bureaucracy and mistrust of real change left them with little hope. Since Brother Charlie Lee had returned to his reservation in the early 1940s, he and other Indian missionaries had been battling to make their voices heard at the national level. Now, Indian leaders decided to try a new tactic.

During the General Council of 1995, ethnic minority leaders within the AG proposed a resolution to allow for the creation of "fellowships" among certain groups within Intercultural Ministries. Each ethnic and special group would maintain a separate fellowship that would aid in the training and evangelization of their people. Almost as soon as the AG approved the fellowships, Indian leaders seized the opportunity to establish one and use it to implement some of the changes that they envisioned. The Native American Fellowship, established in 1996, was self-funded and self-supporting and existed separately from both Home Missions (now U.S. Missions) and Special Ministries. It was an autonomous space not overseen by any other governing body of the AG. The participants of the fellowship, made up of Native Pentecostal laity and Native leaders, elected the three-member board. Those three board members retained seats on the General Presbytery to speak for Native Americans and also enjoy the opportunity to serve on the Executive Presbytery.[91] The stated goals of the Native American Fellowship were to facilitate evangelism to Native peoples and to encourage leadership opportunities among Native missionaries and pastors.[92]

But the creation of the Native American Fellowship did not solve all of the problems that Indian leaders had been trying to address. As of 2007, the job of Indian representative, now called Native American representative, remained unfunded by the AG and lacked any real influence in Home Missions or Special Ministries. The position was not formally linked to the Native American Fellowship, although the 2007 Native American representative happened to be the president of the fellowship. The Native American representative remained under the jurisdiction of the General Council without specific voting rights, while the members of the Native American Fellowship's board had voting rights within the General Council. The Native American Fellowship remained free from the oversight of Home Missions or Special Ministries. Native Pentecostals raised their own money, ran their own elections, and decided on their own agenda. In 2007, Brother John Maracle sat both as the president of the Native American Fellowship and as the Native American representative.[93] Rodger Cree, a Mohawk and the last of the early AG Native leaders, and Dennis Hodges, a Lumbee, were also on the governing board of the fellowship.[94]

If we compare the goals of the Native American Fellowship to the concerns outlined by Brother McPherson in his letters to Brother Gannon at the time of the establishment of the Indian representative position, we see that they were almost the same. According to Brother Maracle, the Native American Fellowship wished to facilitate the following among the Indian Pentecostal population: indigenous churches (meaning self-supporting with indigenous leadership and staff), more Native leaders and pastors, strong lay leadership programs, and the education of the youth and children.[95] All of these needs remained the same as those highlighted by Brother McPherson. But the creation of the Native American Fellowship made Native leaders hopeful. Although they had not eliminated the problems within the U.S. Missions Department or in the Native American representative position, they finally obtained their own space to work with each other, as well as voting power within the General and Executive Presbyteries. The road for Native leaders had been long and difficult, but while Brother Maracle did not hesitate to say, "I don't see any quick fixes," he also expressed pride that evangelism remained strong among Native peoples.[96]

Conclusion

For American Indian Pentecostals, the struggle for officially recognized leadership within AG and input over the missionary program to their people was a test of their faith in the institution. By the late 1970s, when the AIBI became a part of the official AG Bible school network and Brother Charlie Lee showed that an Indian congregation could become self-supporting and district-affiliated, things seemed to be looking up for Pentecostal Indians. Native missionaries and evangelists had shown the AG that they were capable of innovation and leadership within their ministries. They also hoped to exercise more influence in the running of Home Missions. In order to make their mission public, they lobbied for an Indian representative and received one, but they found the position to be fatally flawed. Conceived in 1977, the Indian representative position proved ill-defined, had little power or influence, and remained part-time and unfunded. This situation left the first Indian representative, Brother John McPherson, with a nearly impossible job.

Over the years, Brother McPherson sought to define the position of Indian representative as well as to expand it so that the position would hold more power and influence as well as funding. Other Native leaders such as Charlie Lee, John Maracle, and Rodger Cree supported him in the 1980s and 1990s and tried at different times to bring their concerns to the fore during the General Council meetings. They also proposed the creation of a Native American Department, to gain influence over the running of the Home Missions Department, but white AG leaders thwarted them. Finally, with the creation of the Native American Fellowship, the Native leadership was able to create its own group, an organization apart from the influence of Home Missions and Special Ministries. The Native leadership relied heavily on the cooperation of progressive white Pentecostals, as well as other ethnic groups (African Americans, Latinos), in order to bring about the creation of the fellowships. With the Native American Fellowship came voting power in the General Presbytery as well as a chance for voting power in the Executive Presbytery. The Native American Fellowship was most certainly not an answer to all the problems that had plagued the Native leadership within the AG, but more than anything else, it offered hope.

Given all the roadblocks and difficulties that the Native leaders faced in their struggle for official recognition and power, and given that many of their efforts met a formidable wall of bureaucratic resistance, it is a tribute to their devotion to their cause that they continued fighting. For many of them, the struggle for official recognition caused heartache and pain. For some, such as the first Indian representative John McPherson, the fight cost them their health. But the Indian leadership within the AG was united in its purpose—they were Pentecostals, members of Assemblies of God, and they demanded to be heard. Leaving the denomination, or just giving up, could have been an easy way out of a difficult and painful situation. But the Indian Pentecostal leadership, including men like Charlie Lee, John McPherson, John Maracle, and Rodger Cree, believed it was possible to be both Indians and Pentecostals, and they held fast to the indigenous principle. By continuing to remain Pentecostals within the AG while attempting to gain more power and recognition, they showed that they were not going to give up on the denomination that they had chosen to join. In their struggle, they solidified the possibility and reality of their Pentecostal Indian identity.

The struggle for institutional power showed just how important the indigenous principle became to Native Pentecostal leaders. The indigenous principle gave them ways to criticize the AG when it was at its paternalistic worst, and in that struggle it became a lived practice. The practice of the indigenous principle came to define Native Pentecostal leaders so strongly because it was the tool that they used to try to carve out their own version of indigenous Pentecostal Christianity—a colonizing theology that was turned against the colonizer to argue for Native autonomy. Although the fight for national leadership and national recognition within the AG remained incomplete as of 2008, the vision of the indigenous principle remained strong. On the Native American Fellowship webpage, as of September 2012, Native leaders continued to make their voices heard by stating, "Native American leadership MUST blaze new trails in evangelism, church planting and leadership development among their own people."[97] Native leaders know that only through the practice of the indigenous principle will they have their voice heard within Pentecostal Christianity, and that only they can bring the indigenous principle to its full fruition as a fully realized form of indigenous Pentecostal Christianity.

American Indian Pentecostals
in the Twenty-First Century

On the afternoon of 10 August 2007, the members of the General Council of the Assemblies of God elected John E. Maracle to the Executive Presbytery.[1] Brother Maracle, a prominent Mohawk evangelist and the national Native American representative, ascended to the ethnic fellowship seat. He joined seventeen other prominent AG leaders in the Executive Presbytery—the most powerful arm of the AG.[2] One hundred one years after the great revival on Azusa Street, Brother Maracle became the first American Indian member of this exclusive governing board. After a long and frustrating twenty-year battle for tangible power and funding for the Native American representative position, Native leaders finally gained a foothold into the AG's main governing body. The nephew of early Mohawk evangelist Andrew Maracle, John Maracle had learned about the importance of the indigenous principle directly from Navajo evangelist Charlie Lee, a beloved teacher and mentor.

On 22 February 2011, I received an email from Darrin Rodgers (the head of the AG archives) saying that the first female Native American presbyter in the AG had been elected. A native Arizonian, Vernice "Cheri" Sampson was a descendant of the original Sampson brothers, the "Pima giants" who Alta Washburn evangelized in the middle of the twentieth century. Sister Sampson headed the Salt River Assembly of God in Scottsdale, Arizona, and was a member of the Pima-Maricopa tribe. In Arizona she was joined by three other Native presbyters who exercise local control in the Arizona district. Sister Sampson acknowledged her historic role as both an Indian and a woman. According to a press statement released online, she stated: "I'm going places that my parents always wanted us to go. My dad and his

Native American contemporaries envisioned our people moving into all areas of leadership. They have all gone [passed away] and I kind of wonder what they would think of my being elected presbyter. . . . I'm excited about this; I'm challenged by it. I feel in one way, I'm over my head, but that's a good place to be because that completely drives me to Christ and I love Jesus Christ."[3] Like Brother John Maracle, she is an example of the power of the indigenous principle, and even more impressively, Sister Sampson managed to overcome obstacles that were placed in front of her as both an American Indian and a woman.

By the autumn of 2012, all of the early Pentecostal leaders mentioned in this work, with the exception of Brother Rodger Cree, had died. Yet the legacies of the first generation of Native leaders lived on in the work and ministry of Brother John Maracle, Sister Cheri Sampson, and in the work of countless other modern Native evangelists, and in the gradual changes in the AG. Although American Indians made up a tiny minority within the Assemblies of God, they were responsible for important changes in the way the AG approached missionary work—specifically missionary work to Native peoples in the United States. Their constant insistence forced the AG to move beyond merely mouthing the indigenous principle and gave Native people the opportunity for autonomy in the denomination.

The heart of this work is the power that the indigenous principle gave Native Pentecostals to engage their own denomination. In Pentecostalism, the indigenous principle was not a radical concept—it was, in fact, rooted deeply in the theology of the movement. But many of the missionaries who carried the Gospel both overseas and among groups in the United States failed to realize the indigenous principle's implications. The AG changed its approach to missions to American Indians only because Pentecostal Indians used the denomination's own theological commitments to challenge its practice. Because any Pentecostal could wield the authority of the Holy Spirit, Native Pentecostals, in theory, held as much spiritual authority as any other Pentecostal. Even though they encountered ethnocentrism and paternalism, they still challenged the AG hierarchy, because as Pentecostals, it was their spiritual right to do so. And even though the AG dragged its feet in developing Native leaders and the structures that allowed for indigenous churches, Native Pentecostals continued to form and re-form their own religious identity in light of their struggle with the AG.

For Native Pentecostals, the indigenous principle became more than just a theology of missions—through their struggle for it, they turned a theology into a practice—a distinctly Native Pentecostal practice. They

lived the indigenous principle in their fight for autonomy within the AG—
it was not simply a theology to be learned as a theory. By viewing the struggle for the indigenous principle as a form of Christian practice, we see how
foundational it was to Native Pentecostal experience. Native Pentecostals
lived out the indigenous principle by promoting, creating, and supporting
indigenous churches, the American Indian College (AIC), and Native leadership. They used Pentecostal methods to do so, but their struggle focused
on Native autonomy—a struggle that is grounded in the American Indian
experience. The process involved pain. Native leaders often mentioned the
long fight against paternalism when talking to me about the project, but
they never wanted to discuss it extensively. They bore wounds from their
internal struggle within the AG. Yet they, like their forbearers, still continued to engage the AG, and they remained within the denomination despite
its difficult history with missions to Native peoples. The generations of
Native peoples who have stayed testify to the fact that, deep down, they
found something within the Assemblies of God that spoke to them and
was worth fighting for.

The long struggle changed the AG. As AG leaders approached the end
of the first decade of the twenty-first century, they expressed regret about
how they carried out missions to Native peoples. When I met with the late
AG historian Gary McGee and first told him of my project over lunch in
2006, he frowned and remarked that the history was "a hard one for the
Assemblies." Jim Dempsey, one of the deans of the AIC in 2008, took great
pains to articulate the history of missions in his writings on American Indians, owning that "genocide, colonialism, bad faith and poor missiolog-
ical practice were prevalent throughout much of this historical period."[4]
He adds, "when Christians have decided to become truly concerned about
Native people, our efforts toward outreach have often been clumsy and
ineffective."[5] Dempsey argued that it is not surprising that Native people
are often indifferent and hostile toward Christianity, given their treatment
by Christians. He acknowledges that Pentecostals have impeded their own
mission, and he reiterates the indigenous principle: "The Native church
is the answer. It must be authentically biblical and authentically Indian.
This means that it must be connected to the body of Christ in America but
must also be a truly Native incarnation of the gospel."[6] No longer a radical
sentiment, Dempsey's words come from a 2008 book on the AIC published
by the Gospel Publishing House. The work of Native Pentecostals forced
the AG to make the indigenous principle front and center in their continuing missionary work. It remains to be seen what further change will

come from the public embrace of this long held theology that underpins Pentecostal missionary work.

The ideal of Native leadership for Native institutions within the AG remained incomplete. In 2009 the AIC gained a new president, David DeGarmo, a white educator who had a long history with the college. The fact is that the AIC, while it did have Native faculty and staff, persisted under a mainly white administration. The main reason given for this was that, while there was growth in Native leaders trained for the ministry, very few Native leaders possessed the advanced degrees necessary to run an accredited college.

As Native leaders fought for the indigenous principle, they provided an answer for a vexed question in both religion and Native American studies: Can an American Indian be both a Christian and an Indian? As this work shows, the answer to that question is complicated, even moving beyond the parameters that the question itself sets up. In her work on Native evangelicals in the modern Christian Right and Promise Keepers movements, Cherokee activist Andrea Smith stresses that trying to understand Native peoples who belong to what have been defined as right-wing Christian groups such as the Promise Keepers "troubles" many long-held assumptions about evangelical Christianity *and* Native peoples. She closes her chapter on Natives in the Promise Keepers movement by noting that "the work done by Native evangelicals through race reconciliation demonstrates that, despite the problems with this movement, the Christian Right is an unstable formation that offers possibilities for progressive rearticulations."[7] Smith argues that as Native participants in the movement continually rearticulate their place and identity as Native evangelicals, the movement itself also undergoes continual change. Smith's point of view reminds scholars that Christianity does not remain frozen in time but instead is constantly redefining itself and its place in the world. With Smith's words in mind, I have intentionally tried to "trouble" how scholars understand modern missionary work to Native Pentecostals, showing how Natives have engaged a historically white Christian denomination through the practice of the indigenous principle.

This book has tried to paint a dynamic picture of both Christianity and Native culture. Native cultures shifted dramatically after contact—often because of Christianity. These changes were often harmful, even devastating, to Native communities. Missionaries wielded Christianity as a way to force the Americanization of American Indians. But the dynamics of conversion, cultural change, and religious identity have always been a two-way street in American religion.[8] As historian James Axtell stressed, Native peoples who became Christian did so under their own authority and for their own reasons.[9] Modern American Indian Pentecostals chose the "Jesus Way" for a variety of reasons, and, in doing so, engaged the AG and carved out a space for their people within a large and powerful white American denomination. Native Pentecostals saw themselves as both American Indians and Christians—that is how they defined their identity. For that reason, it is problematic for any scholar to say that they cannot be both, because to do so would be to impose one's own ideas upon these people, and in the process, second-guess their agency in the shaping of their own religious identity.

As this book shows, the practice of the indigenous principle was also deeply dynamic, and continually shifted and changed in order to meet the specific needs of those who embraced it. It was also a complicated process for believers, one full of difficulties and contradictions. Theology as lived is often very different from theology as an idea contained in books. By understanding the indigenous principle as a lived theology, a communitist theology, and a religious practice, scholars can begin to understand yet another dimension of Pentecostalism among American Indians. Because this work is mostly archivally based, it is hard to know exactly what happened on the ground in the first decades that a Native leadership emerged within the AG. Even modern-day ethnography would not give me the historical answers that I sought or needed in how mid-twentieth-century Native Pentecostals understood their faith. By using the indigenous principle as a prism in which to view the history of the AG and its work with Natives, I was able to uncover bits and pieces of the voices of the Native Pentecostal leadership—all of which may have been obscured by the biases that very much exist in the primary sources.

Understanding the indigenous principle as practice also changes how scholars of American religion view Native American Christians. In the past few decades, the study of Native Christians has expanded and been carried forward by a younger generation of scholars in order to explore the unique ways that Native peoples practice and understand various forms of Christianity. Native people can be Native and Christian too, a sentiment that has been echoed by many scholars. Although the indigenous principle is not unique to missions to Native Americans (or even within Pentecostalism itself), understanding it as a religious practice that became distinctly indigenous (that is to say, Native American) allows us to see just one way that Native Americans have taken Christianity and have begun to dismantle its colonizing roots. No Native Pentecostal leaders have rewritten Melvin Hodges's "The Indigenous Church" from a Native point of view yet, but by their very actions, their lives, their innovation, and their practice of the indigenous principle, they have turned it into something unique. It has become something Pentecostal and Native, a newly indigenous "indigenous principle."

The story of Native Pentecostals also offers a case study in how a small group of people within a larger religious community utilized their religious beliefs in order to enact profound change that challenged the status quo. The history of Native Pentecostals offers scholars a different lens through which to view American Pentecostalism, and specifically the Assemblies of God. As the study of American religion has expanded to include a variety of ethnic groups, the religious history of Native peoples has remained at the margins. This study shows that Native peoples engaged Christianity in often surprising ways, and that they should not be a footnote or briefly mentioned—Native peoples deserve to be fully included in the history of American religion, because their stories and histories are indicative of greater trends in the history of American religion. It is also important to acknowledge that Native Americans continue to be a part of the story. They are not to be relegated to some distant past; they have not "disappeared," but rather they continue to engage modernity as a group and, in engaging modernity, are very much a part of the contemporary American religious landscape. Without the story of Pentecostal Indians, the history of the Assemblies of God is incomplete. If we ignore the work of Lee, McPherson, Washburn, and Maracle, we will never fully understand the shift toward the indigenous principle in home missions due to Native leaders' engagement of the white AG leadership. Instead, scholars might think that it was the result of shifting trends in multiculturalism rather than the product of an internal struggle that forced the AG to pay attention to those trends.

The history of Native Pentecostals within the AG is not a finished history. As the election of John Maracle to the Executive Presbytery shows, the story of American Indians within the AG is a still-evolving history. Native Pentecostals will continue to engage the AG and wrestle with what it means to be both Native and Pentecostal. They will continue to shape the practice of the indigenous principle, which remains a dynamic, living theology. My hope in writing this history of Native Pentecostalism within the Assemblies of God is not to give a single interpretation of the past but to open the windows wide for discussions of Native religious identity and practice. As historians, we have a duty to fully integrate the histories of this nation's Native peoples with the greater narrative—in fact, we need to continue to change and challenge the narrative—to open it up, to shake up the dusty tropes, to look for the meaning behind the silences and biases in the sources, and to privilege the voices of believers, because it is their history that we seek to unearth. So much work remains to be completed regarding the myriad ways that American Indians live out their Pentecostal lives and understand their Native-Pentecostal identities. There are many ways to be Native in America. There are many ways to be a Native Pentecostal.

On a hot Missouri afternoon, in the summer of 2006, I was digging through a dusty box of files when the director of the AG archives, Darrin Rodgers, walked in followed by two Native evangelists. Darrin introduced them as John Maracle and Rodger Cree, both Mohawk, who had come to meet me. As I stood to greet the men, John Maracle said to me, "We have been praying that the Holy Spirit would send us someone to tell our story. We can see now that he has sent you to us for that purpose." I paused, startled, thinking that I made a rather unlikely messenger of the Holy Spirit, but I could see from the look on both men's faces that the sentiment was genuine. The comment reminded me of the Pentecostal worldview: what seems mundane to an outsider may seem providential to a believer. The next day, when I sat with Rodger Cree as he gave his testimony and life story, I listened carefully as the last remaining member of the first generation of Indian leaders related his own personal history. As he talked for more than two hours, sliding gently from English to French and Mohawk, I was struck by how the history of a denomination—something that is often regarded as a monolithic entity—is actually composed of the entwined stories of the people who make up that entity. Without Pentecostal believers, the Assemblies of God would not exist. Without the advocacy, struggle, pain, and stories of Native Pentecostals, the history of the Assemblies of God would be incomplete. Assemblies of God missionaries believed they were giving the ultimate gift of salvation to Native people. At the same time, those Native converts gave important gifts to the Assemblies of God—the audacity to hold the denomination to its deepest theological underpinnings, the innovation to live and practice the indigenous principle, and the example of complex lives lived within a Pentecostal framework that dared to challenge and redefine what it means to be an American Indian and a Pentecostal.

Notes

Abbreviations

AG   Assemblies of God
DMF   Deceased Minister Files
FPHC   Flower Pentecostal Heritage Center, Springfield, Mo.
PE   *Pentecostal Evangel*

Introduction

1. Washburn, *Trail to the Tribes*, 13.

2. Charlie Lee, "Charlie Lee's Testimony," *PE*, 17 August 1955, 10.

3. Clyde Thompson, "Amongst the Indians," *Christian Evangel*, 27 July 1918, 5.

4. Maracle interview. Percentage confirmed by the official AG statistician, Sherry Doty.

5. U.S. Census Bureau, *We the People: American Indians*, 2.

6. The indigenous principle is the official theology of missions in the AG. AG missionary Melvin Hodges gave the theory its name in the 1950s, although its roots can be traced to pre-Pentecostal Protestant missionary work. In its most basic form the indigenous principle is a Pauline approach to missionary work that stresses that Christian missionaries must root their evangelism within the local community that they are serving. In order to do this, they should encourage locally run churches, leadership, and educational systems, and they should be willing, after a time, to turn the mission over to the locals to run on their own. A detailed history of the indigenous principle is in chapter 1.

7. McNally, "The Practice of Native American Christianity," 845.

8. Ibid.

9. See Hodges, *The Indigenous Church*.

10. Treat, *Native and Christian*, 9–10.

11. McNally, "The Practice of Native American Christianity," 835.

12. Ibid., 837.

13. Maffly-Kipp, Schmidt, and Valeri, *Practicing Protestants*, 3.

14. Orsi, *Between Heaven and Earth*, 7.

15. Ibid., 9.

16. Weaver, *Native American Religious Identity*, 22.

17. Ibid.

18. Ibid.

19. See Alexander, *Native American Pentecost*.

20. See Kenyon, "An Analysis of Ethical Issues."

21. Andrea Smith, *Native Americans and the Religious Right*, 75.

22. McGee, *Miracles, Missions and American Pentecostalism*, 156.

23. Poloma, *The Assemblies of God at the Crossroads*, 110.

24. Most of the data I have collected on the gender breakdown among AG missionaries (both white and Native) comes from the AG's deceased ministers files. Most white missionaries were married men. Their wives often helped with their missionary work, but the *PE* rarely mentions them. A notable exception to this rule is Sister Washburn, who was married, and is often referred to by name in the *PE*. I met one of the female missionaries whom she trained, Sister Alma Thomas, by tracking her down through the AG by word-of-mouth, but aside from my interview with her, Sister Washburn is mostly absent from the historical record. There were single female missionaries on the home missions front such as Sister Virginia Kridler—they often evangelized in pairs. Among Native leaders, the numbers were significantly skewed toward men. All of the male Native missionaries were married and occasionally their wives appear in the *PE*, but other than that, the only Native female missionary whom I have been able to confirm is Hilda Cree, sister of Rodger Cree. Charlie Lee, George Effman, and John McPherson were all married to white women.

25. For more information on women and gender roles in missionary history, see Robert, *American Women in Mission*, 240–54.

26. Lewis, *Creating Christian Indians*.

27. See Burkinshaw, "Native Pentecostalism in British Columbia"; Dombrowski, *Against Culture*; Westman, "Understanding Cree Religious Discourse."

28. Wacker, *Heaven Below*, 12.

29. Hinson, *Fire in My Bones*, 3.

30. Cree interview.

31. Wacker, *Heaven Below*, 99.

32. For a brief and basic overview of Native American traditional belief, see Sullivan, *Native American Religions*.

33. See Brusco, *The Reformation of Machismo*.

34. See Sullivan, *Native American Religions*, chap. 1.

35. Cree interview; Lee, "Charlie Lee's Testimony," 10.

36. Several prominent scholars of Pentecostalism have heavily leaned on periodicals for their studies. See, for example, Wacker, *Heaven Below*, and Blumhofer, *Restoring the Faith*.

37. Robert Orsi discusses the import of published testimonials in the preface of his book, *Thank You, St. Jude*.

38. During the rapid growth of home missions to American Indians (from the mid-1950s to the 1970s), the *PE*'s home missions editor was Sister Ruth Lyon, a former missionary to the Chippewa, who held a great interest in missions to American Indians. Before she became editor, Sister Lyon served as a reporter on the home missions front, and she wrote many of the articles on American Indian missions in the *PE*. Thus, she controlled much of the flow of information on home missions. I met with Sister Lyon in August of 2006 in Springfield, Missouri, and she made it clear that she had dedicated her life to bringing publicity to the AG's missions to American Indians. One needs to remember, however, that the AG employed her to bring out the most positive sides of the home missions story. In the interview, she also made it very clear that she believed in the indigenous principle and supported the American Indian leadership within the AG. Sister Lyon passed away before I was able to interview her again.

39. The problem of sources and how Pentecostals were loath to attribute their actions to anything other than the inspiration of God is discussed in the introduction to Wacker's *Heaven Below*.

40. Other historians have wrestled with this problem. Indeed, it is common in Native American missionary studies, and in Native American studies overall. One example of how to approach the source problem is offered by Axtell, *The Invasion Within*, intro.

Chapter 1

1. Clyde Thompson, "Amongst the Indians," *Christian Evangel*, 27 July 1918, 5.

2. Government boarding schools, while ostensibly secular, sought to inculcate the values of white Protestant America in their Native students in the nineteenth and early twentieth centuries. Former Christian missionaries and denominational workers often ran them. While private religious boarding schools were more openly religious, government schools also had religious undertones. For a brief overview of the problematic history of Indian boarding schools, see Adams, *Education for Extinction*.

3. For more on how Christian reformers shaped Indian policy, see Prucha, *American Indian Policy in Crisis*.

4. "Missionaries to Jerusalem," *Apostolic Faith* 1 (1906): 4. Reprinted by Together in Harvest Publications, Foley, Ala., 1997.

5. McGee, *This Gospel Shall Be Preached*, 13–17.

6. A faith mission was a mission undertaken with no guaranteed institutional financial support from a denomination or sending board. Missionaries depended on prayer, personal fundraising, and providence in order to raise the money needed not only to fund the mission but also to pay themselves and support their families.

7. Blumhofer, *The Assemblies of God*, 1:201.

8. Wacker, "The Assemblies of God," 87.

9. Ibid.

10. Ibid.

11. Blumhofer, *The Assemblies of God*, 1:197.

12. Ibid., 1:199.

13. Ibid., 1:201.

14. Ibid., 1:201–2.

15. Ibid.

16. General Council Minutes, 1914, 4.

17. Blumhofer, *The Assemblies of God*, 1:203–4.

18. Ibid.

19. Ibid.

20. Ibid., 1:205.

21. Ibid., 1:204.

22. Ibid., 1:206.

23. Ibid.

24. Ibid.

25. McGee, *This Gospel Shall Be Preached*, 85.

26. Ibid., 86.

27. Ibid.

28. Ibid.

29. Ibid., 87.

30. Blumhofer, *The Assemblies of God*, 1:282.

31. Ibid., 1:285.

32. Ibid., 1:318.

33. Ibid., 1:319.

34. Ibid.

35. Ibid., 1:292.

36. Ibid.

37. For more on this missionary dilemma, see Hutchison, *Errand to the World*, chap. 3.

38. Blumhofer, *The Assemblies of God*, 1:293.

39. Wacker, "Pentecostalism," 937.

40. Ibid.

41. McGee, *This Gospel Shall Be Preached*, 110.

42. Ibid.

43. Ibid., 114.

44. Ibid., 113.

45. Ibid.

46. Lyon, *A History of Home Missions*, 9.

47. For more on early home missions, see ibid., esp. 9–45.

48. Blumhofer, *The Assemblies of God*, 1:334.

49. Ibid.

50. Ibid., 1:339.

51. Ibid.

52. Ibid., 1:333.

53. Charles Lee, from Application from Ordination, DMF, FPHC. 1 Cor. 1:10: "Now I beseech you, brethren, by the name of our Lord Jesus Christ, that ye all speak the same thing, and that there be no divisions among you; but that ye be perfectly joined together in the same mind and in the same judgment." Acts 2:42: "And they continued steadfastly in the apostles' doctrine and fellowship, and in breaking of bread, and in prayers" (King James Version).

54. Lyon, *A History of Home Missions*, 30.

55. Acts 13:43–49: "Now when the congregation was broken up, many of the Jews and religious proselytes followed Paul and Barnabas: who, speaking to them, persuaded them to continue in the grace of God. And the next Sabbath day came almost the whole city together to hear the word of God. But when the Jews saw the multitudes, they were filled with envy, and spake against those things which were spoken by Paul, contradicting and blaspheming. Then Paul and Barnabas waxed bold, and said, It was necessary that the word of God should first have been spoken to you: but seeing ye put it from you, and judge yourselves unworthy of everlasting life, lo, we turn to the Gentiles. For so hath the Lord commanded us, saying, I have set thee to be a light of the Gentiles, that thou shouldest be for salvation unto the ends of the earth. And when the Gentiles heard this, they were glad, and glorified the word of the Lord: and as many as were ordained to eternal life believed. And the word of the Lord was published throughout all the region." Acts 14:3: "Long time therefore abode they speaking boldly in the Lord, which gave testimony unto the word of his grace, and granted signs and wonders to be done by their hands." Acts 16:4–5: "And as they went through the cities, they delivered them the decrees for to keep, that were ordained of the apostles and elders which were at Jerusalem. And so were the churches established in the faith, and increased in number daily." Acts 20:28: "Take heed therefore unto yourselves, and to all the flock, over the which the Holy Ghost hath made you overseers, to feed the church of God, which he hath purchased with his own blood" (King James Version).

56. Hutchison, *Errand to the World*, 87.

57. McGee, "Assemblies of God Mission Theology," 166.

58. Hutchison, *Errand to the World*, 79–81.

59. Ibid., 79.

60. Ibid., 80.

61. Ibid.

62. Melvin Hodges was the first to articulate the phrase "indigenous principle." His predecessors did not use the term. They usually said "Pauline example" or "indigenous church planting."

63. McGee, "Assemblies of God Mission Theology," 166.

64. Ibid.

65. Ibid.

66. Allen, *Missionary Methods*.

67. Ibid., 111.

68. Ibid.

69. Ibid., 112.

70. Ibid.

71. Ibid., 112–13.

72. Ibid., 114–26.

73. Ibid., 190.

74. McGee, "Assemblies of God Mission Theology," 166–67.

75. For more information on Alice Luce and her ministry to the Latino population, see Wilson and Wilson, "Alice E. Luce: A Visionary Victorian," 159–76.

76. Ibid., 166.

77. Alice Luce, "Paul's Missionary Methods," *PE*, 8 January 1921, 6.

78. Alice Luce, "Paul's Missionary Methods, Part 2," *PE*, 22 January 1921, 6.

79. Alice Luce, "Paul's Missionary Methods, Part 3," *PE*, 5 February 1921, 6.

80. Ibid.

81. Ibid.

82. Ibid.; emphasis in the original.

83. Ibid.

84. Sánchez-Walsh, *Latino Pentecostal Identity*, 51.

85. Ibid.

86. Hodges, *The Indigenous Church*, rev. ed., 9.

87. Ibid.

88. Hodges, *The Indigenous Church*, 11.

89. Hodges, *The Indigenous Church*, rev. ed., 31.

90. Ibid., 30–31.

91. Ibid., 31–32.

92. Ibid., 61.

93. Ibid., 71

94. Ibid.

95. Thompson, "Amongst the Indians," 5.

96. Ibid.

97. "Indian Church at Hoopa Now an Assembly of God," *PE*, 5 March 1927, 20.

98. For information on the Nevada mission, see Mr. and Mrs. Warren Anderson,
"Among the Indians," *PE*, 24 September 1927, 11.

99. For examples of such articles, see Mrs. D. L. Brown, "Among the Indians of
California," *PE*, 1 February 1930, n.p.; J. D. Wells "A Veteran Enters the Lord's Army,"
PE, 8 February 1930, 10; "Shall the American Indian Know God?," *PE*, 5 April 1930. 12.

100. J. D. Wells, "Among the American Indians," *PE*, 18 July 1931, 11.

101. Ibid.

102. See Philip J. Deloria, *Playing Indian*, 128–53.

103. Cree interview. Eventually the AG established a mission among the Mohawk, the Eastern Band of Cherokee, and the Lumbees, but all the rest of the AG's missionary work among American Indians took place in the West and Midwest.

104. "A Forward Step to Reach the Navajo Indian," *PE*, 11 July 1937, 9.

105. Mr. and Mrs. W. H. Solmes, "What about Our Neighbors—The Navajo Indians?," *PE*, 9 April 1938, 6.

106. Mr. and Mrs. Sivonen, "Among the American Indians in Washington," *PE*, 22 February 1941, 9.

107. "Kiowa Indian Work," *PE*, 26 April 1941, 9.

108. "Revival among the Apache Indians," *PE*, 8 August 1942, n.p.

109. "Our Home Frontiers: Revivals among the Indians," *PE*, 29 March 1947, 11.

110. "God Moving on American Indians," *PE*, 7 May 1949, 12.

111. "A Forward Step to Reach the Navajo Indian," *PE*, 11 July 1937, 9.

112. George Effman, from Application from Ordination, DMF, FPHC.

113. "First Indian Convention," *PE*, 10 April 1948, 11.

114. Andrew Maracle, from Application from Ordination, DMF, FPHC.

115. McPherson, *Chief*.

116. Cree interview.

117. Washburn, *Trail to the Tribes*, 42.

Chapter 2

1. Ruth Lyon, "Evangelizing the American Indian—Part 1," *PE*, 24 September 1961, 19.

2. Ruth Lyon, "Evangelizing the American Indian—Part 2," *PE*, 15 October 1961, n.p.

3. Washburn, *Trail to the Tribes*, 1.

4. Ibid.

5. Cree interview.

6. Thomas interview.

7. Wacker, *Heaven Below*, 58.

8. Ibid.

9. Ibid.

10. Charlie Lee, "Charlie Lee's Testimony," *PE*, 17 August 1952, 10.

11. Turning Point with David Manse, *The Charlie Lee Story*, 1976, 4, FPHC.

12. Ibid.

13. Lee, "Charlie Lee's Testimony," 10.

14. Manse, *The Charlie Lee Story*, 8.

15. Lee, "Charlie Lee's Testimony," 10.

16. Ibid.

17. Manse, *The Charlie Lee Story*, 10. The official reason that the AG considered it risky that Lee preached in Navajo was because there was some doubt as to whether certain theological concepts would translate correctly. Yet it is probable that white missionaries did not like Lee to preach in Navajo because they had no way of monitoring what he was preaching.

18. Jimmie Dann, "I Received No Peace from the Shoshoni Sun Dance," *PE*, 18 July 1954, 10.

19. For more on the Sun Dance, see Holler, *Black Elk's Religion*.

20. Dann, "I Received No Peace," 10.

21. Ibid.

22. Ibid.

23. Ibid.

24. Ibid., 11.

25. Ibid.

26. Ibid.

27. Andrew Maracle, *From a Log Cabin*, n.p., FPHC.

28. Ibid.

29. Ibid., 7.

30. Ibid., 4.

31. Ibid., 7.

32. Ibid.

33. Cree interview.

34. Ibid.

35. Ibid.

36. Ibid.

37. Ibid. According to Cree, the Methodists waged a fierce battle with the local Pentecostal families because most of the Pentecostal converts came from the Methodist congregations.

38. Ibid.

39. Ibid.

40. Ibid.

41. Ibid.

42. Ibid.

43. This emphasis on language as a marker of culture remains for American Indian Pentecostals and evangelicals. Smith talks about this, pointing out that many twenty-first-century Native evangelicals and Pentecostals fiercely retain their Native languages. Modern Native evangelicals and Pentecostals also feel that it is important to receive the Gospel in their Native languages, mirroring the ideas of Brothers Lee and Cree. Andrea Smith, *Native Americans and the Christian Right*, 97.

44. Cree interview; Dann, "I Received No Peace," 11.

45. Wacker, *Heaven Below*, 69.

46. Poloma, *The Assemblies of God at the Crossroads*, 66.

47. Wacker, *Heaven Below*, 200.

48. Alta Washburn, from Application for Ordination, DMF, FPHC.

49. Norman Rehwinkel, from Application for Ordination, DMF, FPHC.

50. Pauline Nelson, from Application for Ordination, DMF, FPHC.

51. I came to this conclusion after reviewing the Deceased Missionary Files of missionaries who served in this era. Although the AG had about 100 white missionaries to Native peoples during this period, they did not have files on all of the missionaries, so I tried to track down missionaries by using those whose names were mentioned in the *PE* or in other correspondence.

52. It is well established in Pentecostal scholarship that most early Pentecostal missionaries, foreign and home, lacked formal educations. The historian Allan Anderson calls them "Persons of Average Ability" in his work. See Anderson, *Spreading Fires*, 260–89.

53. Alta Washburn, from Application for Ordination, DMF, FPHC.

54. Burt Parker, from Application for Ordination, DMF, FPHC.

55. Virginia Kridler, from Application for Ordination, DMF, FPHC.

56. For more on the early years of AG Bible schools, see Blumhofer, *The Assemblies of God*, 1:313–42.

57. Washburn, *Trail to the Tribes*, 13.

58. Ibid., 17.

59. Ibid., 17–18.

60. "Indian Missions in Wyoming," *PE*, 7 March 1954, 10.

61. "Among the Papagos," *PE*, 18 October 1953, 15.

62. Mildred Kimball, "The Oneidas Build a New Church," *PE*, 8 January 1961, 18.

63. "They Must Wait," *PE*, 26 February 1961, 10.

64. Charles McClure, "The Challenge of the Cattaraugus," *PE*, 26 April 1959, 8.

65. "Thanks from the Reservations," *PE*, 18 March 1950, 18.

66. Emogean Johnson, "Tale of a Tent," *PE*, 27 August 1961, 14.

67. Ibid.

68. "News From Indian Reservations: Report from Hoopa," *PE*, 12 November 1950, 12.

69. Edna Griepp, "The Thirsty River People," *PE*, 23 June 1957, 16–17.

70. Ibid.

71. Herbert Bruhn, "Indian Missions in South Dakota," *PE*, 24 July 1955, 11.

72. J. K. Gressett, "Our Indian Work Is Forging Ahead," *PE*, 6 May 1957, 12–13.

73. Helen Burgess, "Navajo Church Is Crowded Out," *PE*, 25 September 1960, 7.

74. "Indian Congregations Outgrow Present Buildings," *PE*, 20 November 1960, 18.

75. Washburn, *Trail to the Tribes*, 42.

76. Ibid., 42–43.

77. Gene Steele and Betty Steele, "Bearing Precious Seed to the Navajo Capital," *PE*, 17 March 1968, 25.

78. "Medicine Men Find Christ," *PE*, 26 March 1967, 16.

79. "Jail Work among the Apaches," *PE*, 28 October 1956, 15.

80. Ester B. Treece, "Ye Shall Be Witnesses," *PE*, 19 May 1963, 21.

81. Ibid.

82. Washburn, *Trail to the Tribes*, 24.

83. John D. Swank, "Witnessing at an All-Indian Rodeo," *PE*, 31 January 1965, 27.

84. Victor Trimmer, "Summer Indian Camps," *PE*, 10 June 1957, 14.

85. Jane Parker, "I Visited an Indian Camp," *PE*, 31 October 1965, 24.

86. Ibid.

87. Ruth Lyon, "Camp Meeting, Indian Style," *PE*, 11 January 1964, 11.

88. Ruth Lyon, "Smoke-Signals Bear News of Blessing at All-Indian Camp Meetings," *PE*, 28 October 1962, n.p. The missionary's wife was reported to be "shaken up" but unhurt in the incident. The *PE* considered it a small miracle that none of the campers was seriously injured or killed by the tornado.

89. Ruth Lyon, "Emphasis on Youth: In Home Missions Summer Camps," *PE*, 19 May 1968, 26.

90. Lyon, "Camp Meeting Indian Style," 11.

91. The lack of language skills among white missionaries who served Indians is particularly striking in comparison with missionaries who served in foreign missions. Native languages were hard to learn. They were often not written down, and specific theological concepts and phrases had no translation. If missionaries moved among a variety of tribes, as many did, it was not efficient to learn a Native language, since they were all different. For these reasons, many missionaries found it impractical to learn Native languages, although some learned enough to memorize hymns and a few phrases in the local language. Often, however, those who bothered to learn to sing in Native languages were Indian missionaries who were working among a tribe that was not their own, such as Mohawk missionary Rodger Cree who told me that he learned to sing in the Pima language, even though he could not speak or preach in it.

92. According to a *PE* article published in 1961, there were "20 or more American Indian missionaries" out of a total of 170 home missionaries who worked with American Indians. No other hard statistics exist from the 1950–60 period. See Lyon, "Evangelizing the American Indian—Part 1," 18.

93. Because the *PE* was not forthcoming about who actually planned the camp meetings, I spoke with AG mission historian Gary McGee, who told me that standard practice was to have white district officials plan the camp meetings in conjunction with the white missionaries. John Maracle, the national Native American representative, confirmed this and said that he believed that it was an ongoing problem that most camp meetings were controlled by district officials.

94. Ruth Lyon, "Navajo Artist Builds a Church for His People," *PE*, 24 April 1960, 9.

95. Ibid.

96. Ibid.

97. Ibid.

98. Manse, *The Charlie Lee Story*, 15.

99. Ruth Lyon, "Evangelizing the American Indian—Part 3," *PE*, 22 October 1961, 18.

100. Arthur Stoneking, "Indians in Los Angeles," *PE*, 1 December 1959, 12.

101. Lyon, "Evangelizing the American Indian—Part 3," 18.

102. Ibid., 12.

103. "Attractive New Indian Church Erected near Los Angeles," *PE*, 28 February 1965, 16.

104. "Indian Revival Crusades Are Successful," *PE*, 18 June 1967, 26.

105. Ibid.

106. Ruth Lyon, "MF Active on Indian Reservations," *PE*, 27 December 1964, 20.

107. Ibid.

108. Ibid., 21.

109. Leo and Mary Gilman, "These Apaches Serve the Lord Diligently," *PE*, 28 June 1959, 9.

110. Ibid.

111. Alma Thomas, "Phoenix Indian CA's Have Outreach Ministry," *PE*, 10 June 1962, 25.

112. Ibid.

113. McPherson, *Chief*, 127.

114. Initial lobbying for an Indian representative started in 1955, according to John Maracle, who has held the post since 2000. Notably, the General Council minutes did not record the request of Brothers Lee, McPherson, and Andrew Maracle.

Chapter 3

1. McPherson, *Chief*, 48.

2. Ibid.

3. Ibid., 8.

4. Ibid., 9.

5. Ibid., 10.

6. Brother and Sister Norman Rehwinkel, "Indian Missions in Wisconsin," *PE*, 5 June 1955, 13.

7. Higham, *Noble, Wretched and Redeemable*.

8. A survey of the church directory of the *Farmington Times-Hustler* from the 1940s shows that at least six different denominations were engaged in missionary

work among the Navajos in the 1940s. These included Christian Reformed, Methodist, Episcopalian, Catholic, Pentecostal, and nondenominational groups. "Church Directory," *Farmington Times-Hustler*, 23 May 1947, 6.

9. For more on anti-Catholicism in America, see Dolan, *In Search of an American Catholicism*, 56–60.

10. George Bolt, "Signor Mission Ministers to the Chippewas," *PE*, 31 May 1959, 10.

11. Lyon interview.

12. Ruth Lyon, "The Mission Field at Our Front Door," *PE*, 20 July 1958. 14.

13. James Reiner, "Who Is This Man You Call Jesus?," *PE*, 29 June 1961, 9.

14. Betty Swinford, "From Devil Dances to Christ," *PE*, 28 April 1963, 12.

15. Ibid.

16. One important exception to this rule: Alta Washburn always referred to the Indian drums as simply "drums." Her observations on traditional dancing did not have the markers of ethnocentrism in comparison to her other white missionary colleagues.

17. Naomi Johnson, "Among the Papagos," *PE*, 18 October 1953, 15.

18. Ibid.

19. Basso, "Western Apache," 10:478–79.

20. Elva Johnson, "Door in the East: A Report on Our Work among the Navajo," *PE*, 2 October 1957, 16.

21. Ibid., 17.

22. Ibid.

23. "Winning Indians for Christ," *PE*, 26 April 1953, 9.

24. Some peyote users reject Christianity and incorporate peyote within their traditional beliefs, while others embrace certain Christian principals and incorporate peyote in a syncretistic manner as a form of communion with God or Jesus. See Stewart, *Peyote Religion*.

25. Ruth Lyon, "Slaves of Peyote," *PE*, 25 March 1962, 17.

26. Ibid.

27. Luther Cayton, "Peace for the Paiute," *PE*, 17 August 1958, 17.

28. For a more in-depth understanding of the rituals surrounding peyote and the Native American Church, see Stewart, *Peyote Religion*.

29. Ibid., 288.

30. Charlie Lee, "Charlie Lee's Testimony," *PE*, 17 August 1952, 10.

31. Ibid.

32. Turning Point with David Manse, *The Charlie Lee Story*, 1976, 18, FPHC.

33. Cree interview.

34. Manse, *The Charlie Lee Story*, 18.

35. Lee, "Charlie Lee's Testimony," 10–11. Brother Lee did not actively repudiate Navajo religion, and in his later years even consented to illustrate children's

books containing Navajo legends and myths. Windes, "Yel Ha Yah's Second Career—Charles Lee," 15.

36. Charlie Lee's thoughts are mainly recorded through official documents, so it is possible that he was being strategic in his statements to official Pentecostal periodicals like the *PE*. It is also telling that he mentioned that he was illustrating a book of traditional Navajo legends only to *New Mexico Magazine*, a secular periodical, rather than to the *PE*.

37. Andrea Smith, *Native Americans and the Christian Right*, 84.

38. Ibid., 85.

39. Ibid.; see Alexander, *Native American Pentecost*.

40. Andrea Smith, *Native Americans and the Christian Right*, 84–86.

41. Westman, "Understanding Cree Religious Discourse," 95.

42. Ibid., 97.

43. Alexander, *Native American Pentecost*.

44. For more on the great revival in mainstream Pentecostalism, see Harrell, *All Things Are Possible*.

45. Ibid., 5.

46. Ibid., 6.

47. Washburn, *Trail to the Tribes*, 21–22.

48. Ibid.

49. "Healings Reported in American Indian Field," *PE*, 27 June 1965, 27.

50. Ibid.

51. Lemy and Hazel Pike, "Jicarilla Apaches Build a New Church," *PE*, 17 July 1960, 16.

52. Ibid.

53. For another discussion on the use of Pentecostal healings as proof of God's power, see Wacker, "Marching to Zion: Religion in a Modern Utopian Community," 506–26.

54. "Phoenix Indian CA's Believe They Are Saved to Serve," *PE*, 17 July 1960, 21.

55. Ibid.

56. Andrea Smith, *Native Americans and the Christian Right*, 102.

57. McPherson, *The Trail of Tears*, n.p., FPHC.

58. Ibid.

59. For the account of Baptist Missionaries on the Trail of Tears, see McLoughlin, *Champions of the Cherokees*.

60. McPherson, *The Trail of Tears*, last page.

61. Most Navajos who went to Fort Defiance were old men, women, and children. Most of the young warriors were killed in skirmishes with Carson's men, and those who survived hid in Canyon de Chelly with the few sheep herds that escaped government detection. For a readable popular history of Carson and his battle with the Navajos, see Sides, *Blood and Thunder*.

62. Coralie Lee, *The Long Walk*, n.p., FPHC.

63. Ibid.

64. John McPherson and Paul Kinel, "The First Americans," *PE*, 31 August 1958, 14.

65. Ibid.

66. Ibid.

67. George Effman, "The First Are Last," *PE*, 25 February 1962, 12.

68. The language of "Christ giving a new, clean heart" is a striking foreshadowing of similar language that Native evangelical and Pentecostal leaders would use in the twenty-first century during their affiliation with the Promise Keepers. This pattern shows the continuity of rhetoric and theology between modern Native leaders who would join the Christian Right and the early AG leaders who predated them by almost a half a century. Both groups stressed reconciliation and used similar rhetoric when talking about it. Smith calls this trend "performing reconciliation" and points out how it shows that Native peoples defy categorization when it comes to how they employ conservative Christianity for their own uses. For more on this subject, see Andrea Smith, *Native Americans and the Christian Right*, 99.

69. Cree interview.

70. McPherson, *Chief*, 96.

71. Brother McPherson's headdress is on display at the AG's Heritage Museum, which is located on the ground floor of the AG's National Headquarters in Springfield, Missouri.

72. McPherson, *Chief*, 72.

73. Ibid., 74.

74. Ibid., 74–75.

75. Ibid.

76. Ibid.

77. For examples, see the pictures accompanying the following articles: "God's Power Manifested in Sacramento Indian Convention," *PE*, 29 July 1956, 8; Arthur Stoneking "Indians in Los Angeles," *PE*, 12 January 1957, 12; "American Indians Meet," *PE*, 12 June 1955, 10.

78. McPherson, *Chief*, 101.

79. Ibid.

80. Ibid.

81. Ibid.

82. For more on Westerns and how they were used to construct American's popular conception of Indians, see Berkhofer, *The White Man's Indian*, 96–103.

83. Harper, *In the Shadow of the Mahatma*, 140–43.

84. Philip J. Deloria, *Playing Indian*, chap. 5.

85. Ibid., 135.

86. See ibid.

87. Ruth Lyon, "Evangelizing the American Indian—Part 1," *PE*, 24 September 1961, 18.

88. Manse, *The Charlie Lee Story*, 2.

89. Deloria writes about the problems swirling around how modern Native peoples represent themselves and how they are represented in the public by the media in Philip J. Deloria *Indians in Unexpected Places*, 52–108.

90. Washburn, *Trail to the Tribes*, 48.

Chapter 4

1. Sister Washburn gives no date for this incident in her autobiography. Because it happened while she was working in Phoenix, we can safely assume it took place sometime between 1950 and 1956. Washburn, *Trail to the Tribes* 47–48.

2. Ibid.

3. Ibid., 48–49.

4. Ibid.

5. Ibid.

6. Dempsey and Saggio, *American Indian College*, 113.

7. Ibid., 134.

8. "Navajo Indian Church Becomes Indigenous," *PE*, 10 August 1979, 8–9.

9. Alta Washburn's Bible school bore many different names over the years. It began as the All-Tribes Bible School. When it was formally taken over by the AG, the denomination renamed it the American Indian Bible Institute, then later the American Indian Bible College. In 2009 its name was the American Indian College of the Assemblies of God.

10. For the balance between the pragmatist and primitivist impulses in Pentecostalism, see Wacker, *Heaven Below*.

11. L. F. Wilson, "Bible Institutes, Colleges, Universities," 59.

12. Ibid., 58.

13. Ibid., 59.

14. Blumhofer, *The Assemblies of God*, 1:313.

15. Ibid., 314.

16. Brereton, *Training God's Army*, 12–13.

17. Blumhofer, *The Assemblies of God*, 1:316.

18. In 1920 the AG attempted to found its first Bible College in Auburn, Nebraska, but the Midwest Bible School failed almost immediately because of problems with the physical plant and a lack of funding. The Central Bible Institute was the first successful General Council Bible school. See Blumhofer, *The Assemblies of God*, 1:316.

19. Ibid., 1:318.

20. Ibid., 1:319.

21. Ibid.

22. Ibid., 1:325.

23. Ibid., 2:125.

24. Ibid., 2:128.

25. For an example of how the difficulties of (non-Pentecostal) Bible school life prepared students for faith missions, see Austin, "Hotbed of Missions," 134–51.

26. Washburn, *Trail to the Tribes*, 49.

27. No first names appeared in the document with the exception of Elva Johnson.

28. "Notes on Planning Meeting of 2 June 1956," 1, FPHC.

29. Ibid.

30. Ibid., 2.

31. Ibid.

32. The emphasis on "Bible Training School" probably meant that the AG thought (or hoped) that Washburn's college would follow the short-term Bible school model, rather than the ministerial training institute model.

33. "Notes on Planning Meeting," 2.

34. Ibid.

35. Ibid., 3.

36. Washburn, *Trail to the Tribes*, 50.

37. Thomas interview.

38. "Notes on Planning Meeting," 3.

39. Ibid., 4.

40. Ibid.

41. Ibid., 5.

42. Washburn, *Trail to the Tribes*, 49–50.

43. Ibid., 50.

44. Ibid., 51.

45. Ibid.

46. Ibid.

47. Ibid., 52.

48. Ibid.

49. Ibid.

50. Ibid.

51. Dunn, *Trail of Beauty*, 5.

52. Robert, *American Women in Mission*, 246.

53. Ibid., 248.

54. Ibid., 252.

55. The importance of women in supporting indigenous leadership and the education of indigenous converts was not limited to Pentecostalism. In the nineteenth century, the Presbyterian Church established a mission to the Dakota Indians with women as the main evangelists. These women, like Sister Washburn, built their own ministerial training school for Dakota Christians so that they could train potential Native leaders for the Presbyterian Church. This shows that despite the limitations

placed on women within evangelical denominations (nineteenth-century Presbyterians did not ordain women; the AG encouraged women to become missionaries rather than pastors and did not ordain large numbers of women), the flexibility of missionary work allowed women to innovate within their denominations' constraints. Lewis, *Creating Christian Indians*. The most notable Pentecostal example of a woman who founded a Bible school for the training of nonwhite pastors was Alice Luce and her work with Mexican and Mexican American evangelists. Luce founded the Latin American Bible Institute in San Diego, California, in 1926. For more on Luce, see Wilson and Wilson, "Alice E. Luce: A Visionary Victorian," 159–76.

56. See also Tucker, "Female Mission Strategists," 73–88.

57. Poloma, *The Assemblies of God at the Crossroads*, 110.

58. Low tuition marked Bible schools. See Brereton, *Training God's Army*, chap. 9.

59. Washburn, *Trail to the Tribes*, 55.

60. Ibid.

61. Ibid., 54.

62. Ibid.

63. Ibid.

64. Ibid.

65. For more on the intricacies of the Pentecostal testimony and miracle story, see "Testimony," in Wacker, *Heaven Below*.

66. The few existing published testimonies of students who attended All-Tribes bolsters this point. All of them emphasize how the school, in the guise of its students, teachers, and staff, acted as a substitute family for them. For more, see "Alumni Reflections," in Dempsey and Saggio, *American Indian College*, 353–84.

67. Washburn, *Trail to the Tribes*, 57.

68. Brereton, *Training God's Army*, 132.

69. Ibid., 134.

70. Ibid.

71. Dempsey and Saggio, *American Indian College*, 304.

72. Many alumni affectionately referred to the school as "American Indian Bridal College." Ibid., 310.

73. McPherson, Lee, and A. Maracle were all from the first generation of native Pentecostal evangelists, and all attended various Bible schools before AIC opened. They never attended a Bible school where they might meet a fellow Pentecostal Native woman.

74. Washburn, *Trail to the Tribes*, 60.

75. Ibid.

76. Ibid.

77. Ibid.

78. Dunn, *Trail of Beauty*, 6.

79. Washburn, *Trail to the Tribes*, 55.

80. Dunn, *Trail of Beauty*, 7.

81. Washburn, *Trail to the Tribes*, 56.

82. Ibid., 55.

83. Washburn, *Trail to the Tribes*, 56; Dunn, *Trail of Beauty*, 8.

84. Washburn, *Trail to the Tribes*, 68–70.

85. Ibid., 71.

86. Ibid.

87. Dunn, *Trail of Beauty*, 10–12.

88. Ibid., 12.

89. Ibid.

90. Ibid., 16.

91. "New Campus Site for Indian Bible School Dedicated," *PE*, 28 April 1968, 14.

92. "Indian Bible School Planning New Campus," *PE*, 16 April 1967, 18.

93. "American Indian Bible Institute Dedicated," *PE*, 12 December 1971, 17.

94. Ibid.

95. The building project of 1968–71 could not accommodate the student body, so in 1977 ground was broken for another building complex, housing a chapel, classrooms, offices, and a library. "Indian Bible School Building a New Chapel," *PE*, 12 December 1971, 17.

96. Dunn, *Trail of Beauty*, 25.

97. Ibid.

98. Ibid., 28–29.

99. Ibid., 35.

100. Ibid., 36.

101. Ibid., 37.

102. Ibid.

103. Ibid., 38.

104. Ibid., 44–45. As of 2013, this was the name still in use.

105. Dempsey and Saggio, *American Indian College*, 376.

106. "Church Directory," *Farmington Times-Hustler*, 20 September 1946, 6.

107. For an in-depth review of stock reduction and its impact, as well as the history of how the federal government tried to dissolve the Navajo Tribal Council in order to implement the Indian Reorganization Act (Wheeler-Howard Act), see Parman, *The Navajos and the New Deal*. For an overview of stock reduction and its impact on the Navajo, see Iverson, *The Navajo Nation*. For a review of the politics of the BIA and how it affected the Navajo, see Kelley, *The Navajo Indians and Federal Indian Policy, 1900–1935*. For a general view of twentieth century Navajo history, see Bailey and Bailey, *A History of the Navajos*.

108. For a biased but factually correct portrait of J. C. Morgan, see Parman, "J. C. Morgan: Navajo Apostle of Assimilation," 83–96.

109. Historians still argue over the various reasons that Navajos voted down the Wheeler-Howard Act, but many agree that it was because Morgan successfully exploited Navajo anger toward the U.S. government and linked stock reduction to the

Wheeler Howard Act. For more on the intricacies of the Wheeler-Howard Act (also called the Indian New Deal or Indian Reorganization Act), see Prucha, *The Great Father*, 2:965.

110. Allotment, as enacted by the Dawes Act of 1887, destroyed the reservation system by breaking the traditional communal/familial way of living. It divided up reservations into plots meant to serve nuclear families (chiefly through farming) and allowed Native peoples to sell off their plots to whites if they wished after a period of time. One provision of the Wheeler-Howard Act was to stop the allotment of reservation land.

111. For the argument that stock reduction reduced the Navajo from self-sufficiency to dependency, see White, *Roots of Dependency*, 236–55. The government implemented stock reduction because they believed that the Navajo lands were being overgrazed and because they wanted the Navajos to focus their attention on wool production. Later studies have shown that the government was primarily concerned with the sediment runoff caused by desert flash floods that filled the gullies and streams and eventually clogged the Hoover Dam, thus threatening the water supply for large western cities. The government blamed the overgrazing in the high deserts of Arizona and New Mexico for contributing to the sediment runoff. For this reason, the government viewed the extra sheep, horses, and goats as pests. What the government did not realize was that Navajos kept the extra goats and horses as a social welfare system—if a neighbor or family member was going hungry, it was better to give them a goat or horse to slaughter than to kill a sheep, which had commercial value. Once the extra horse and goat herds diminished because of stock reduction, Navajos were often forced to eat their sheep so they would not go hungry. This cycle tended to impoverish smaller sheep-holding families, which ended up eating their wool-producing sheep, leaving them without wool or mutton to sell. Although the Navajos did not have a cash-based economy, the people were able to take care of themselves and each other thanks to their tribal subsistence system.

112. Ibid.

113. "Church Directory," *Farmington Times-Hustler*, 23 May 1947, 6.

114. J. C. Morgan, "Missionary J. C. Morgan Tells How He Became Engaged in Gospel Work among His People," *Farmington Times-Hustler*, 30 May 1947, 4.

115. "J. C. Morgan Is Officer in Eastern Indian Rights Association," *Farmington Times-Hustler*, 12 April 1946, 1.

116. J. C. Morgan, "Navajo Protests Growing Use of the Peyote Narcotic," *Farmington Times-Hustler*, 4 April 1947, supplement, n.p.

117. John E. Hamilton, "Navajo Tribe Should Have Public School System on Their Reservation," *Farmington Times-Hustler*, 20 September 1946, n.p.

118. E. L. Butler and Orval Ricketts, "Legislature Attempts Disenfranchisement of Navajos," *Farmington Times-Hustler*, 14 March 1949. 1.

119. Ibid.

120. Stewart, *Peyote Religion*, 296.

121. Barrett, Kurian, and Johnson, *World Christian Encyclopedia*, 1:787.

122. Ibid., 2:229.

123. "American Indian Bible Institute Graduates Largest Class," *PE*, 25 August 1968, 14.

124. On the cover of the magazine, Brother Lee appeared in a 1970s era suit.

125. "Navajo Indian Church Becomes Indigenous," *PE*, 10 September 1978, 8.

126. Ibid., 9.

127. Ibid.

128. Ibid. Lee was probably referring to the popularity of Dee Brown's "new Indian history," *Bury My Heart at Wounded Knee*, along with the emergence of American Indian scholar-activist Vine Deloria Jr. and his early works, including *Custer Died for Your Sins*. Lee was also certainly aware of the American Indian Movement and its leaders as well as its emphasis on traditional Native religion during this time. Brown, *Bury My Heart at Wounded Knee*; Vine Deloria Jr., *Custer Died for Your Sins*. For more on AIM during the late 1960s and early 1970s, see Smith and Warrior, *Like a Hurricane*, Some might think that Lee was mainly influenced by AIM, but his work on indigenous churches well predates the movement and traces back to his experiences as a Navajo, as I argue in the following pages. (While I argue that AIM was not Lee's main influence, I do not deny that he and other Pentecostal Indian leaders could have drawn some inspiration from the movement.)

129. "Navajo Church Becomes Indigenous," 9.

130. The Lumbees claimed the first indigenous church in Shannon, North Carolina, in 1969, but the Navajos are significant because the Shiprock church ranked as the first among a federally recognized tribe.

131. "Navajo Church Becomes Indigenous," 8–11.

132. Janice J. Freeland, "Indigenous Indian Church Expands Its Borders," *PE*, 21 October 1979, 20.

133. Ibid.

134. "Navajo Church Becomes Indigenous," 11.

Chapter 5

1. T. E. Gannon to John McPherson, 2 December 1977, FPHC.

2. John McPherson to T. E. Gannon, 15 December 1977, FPHC.

3. Ibid.

4. Throughout this chapter, when "Home Missions" is capitalized, it refers to the Department of Home Missions. When uncapitalized, it refers to "home missions" in general.

5. Maracle interview. (I searched the General Council Minutes of that year without success.)

6. Resolution sent to T. E. Gannon, n.d., FPHC.

7. Ibid.

8. Ibid.

9. Confidential Memo, 15–16 September, 1977, FPHC.

10. Ibid.

11. Ibid.

12. Home Missions Administrative Committee Memo, 11 November 1977, FPHC.

13. Memorandum to T. E. Gannon, Re: American Indian Representative, 7 December 1977, FPHC.

14. Ibid.

15. Tommy Crider to T. E. Gannon, 25 October 1977, FPHC.

16. Ibid.

17. Ibid.

18. Ibid.

19. Turning Point with David Manse, *The Charlie Lee Story*, 1976, FPHC.

20. Memorandum to T. E. Gannon, Re: American Indian Representative, 7 December 1977, FPHC.

21. John McPherson to T. E. Gannon, 21 March 1978, FPHC.

22. T. E. Gannon to John McPherson, 5 April 1978, FPHC.

23. Ibid.

24. Ibid.

25. For the period between 1 April 1977 and 31 March 1979, the budget for Home Missions was $3,956,652 and the budget for Foreign Missions was $32,692,473. The national Indian representative position remained unfunded not because of a lack of money but because the AG did not want to shift money from its other endeavors. "Audit Report, April 1, 1977 to March 31, 1979," in *General Council Minutes and Reports, 1914–1999*, 8–9.

26. Report of National Representative/American Indian, 18 September 1978, 1, FPHC.

27. Ibid.

28. Ibid.

29. Ibid., 2.

30. Ibid.

31. Ibid.

32. Ibid.

33. Ibid., 3–4.

34. Ibid., 5.

35. Ibid., 6.

36. Brother McPherson's talking points are undated and lay among a jumble of his papers that had not yet been cataloged by the AG archives. Even though we do not know where or when this forum or speech took place, the existence of these talking points indicates that there were grumblings in Indian Pentecostal ranks.

37. Position Statement/Nat. Rep. (Indian), n.d., 1, FPHC.

38. Ibid.

39. Ibid.

40. Ibid.

41. Indian Representative Job Description, August 1979, FPHC.

42. Ibid.

43. The letters do not reveal where the colloquy was held or when.

44. John McPherson to T. E. Gannon, 18 December 1979, 1, FPHC.

45. Ibid.

46. Ibid.

47. Ibid.

48. Ibid.

49. Census figures show that a higher proportion of American Indians than of the total U.S. population lives in poverty. Overall, about 30 percent of American Indians live in poverty, with the Sioux, Apache, and Navajo tribes having the highest percentages (32%) and the Creek, Cherokee, and Lumbee having the lowest (18%). The average median earned income for American Indian adults is $28,900 for men and $22,000 for women. U.S. Census Bureau, *We the People: American Indians*, 11–12.

50. Ibid.

51. Manse, *The Charlie Lee Story*, 4.

52. T. E. Gannon to John McPherson, 28 December 1979, 1, FPHC.

53. Ibid.

54. Ibid.

55. Ibid., 2.

56. Ibid.

57. Ibid.

58. T. E. Gannon to Charlie Lee, 8 April 1980, FPHC.

59. Vine Deloria Jr., *Custer Died for Your Sins*, 127, 125.

60. Daily, "Vine Deloria's Challenge to the Episcopal Church, 1968–1974," 3.

61. Ibid., 4.

62. Ibid.

63. Ibid.

64. Ibid.

65. Quoted in ibid., 6.

66. Ibid., 7.

67. Deloria's engagement with the Episcopal Church was inspired by his own father's fight to help Native peoples within the church to gain more control over the missionary program. Vine Deloria Sr. was an Episcopal priest and the first Native director of the national mission program in the 1950s. Deloria Sr. also encountered political obstacles within the Episcopal Church and eventually resigned his post to return to regular parish life. For a short overview, see Philip J. Deloria, "Vine Deloria Sr.," 79–98.

68. Manse, *The Charlie Lee Story*, 18.

69. The white female missionary champion of Latinos (specifically Mexicans) was Alice Luce. She founded the Latin American Bible Institute in 1926 and was a forerunner to Alta Washburn. Like Washburn, Luce preached autonomy, but she also remained maternalistic in her approach toward supervising Latino evangelists and pastors in the field. (It appears that Washburn might have been similar to her in this, but the sources that remain do not say much on this subject.) For more information on Luce and the LABI, as well as the development of Latino Pentecostal identity, see Sánchez-Walsh, *Latino Pentecostal Identity*.

70. Blumhofer, *The Assemblies of God*, 2:173.

71. Sánchez-Walsh, *Latino Pentecostal Identity*, 3, 5.

72. See ibid., esp. chaps. 4 and 5.

73. Andrea Smith, *Native Americans and the Christian Right*, 94.

74. Blumhofer, *The Assemblies of God*, 2:173–74.

75. Sánchez-Walsh, *Latino Pentecostal Identity*, 122.

76. Ibid.

77. Kenyon, "An Analysis of Ethical Issues in the History of the Assemblies of God," 84.

78. Raybon, "Race and the Assemblies of God Church," 114.

79. Ibid., 151.

80. Ibid., 190.

81. Ibid., 217.

82. "Native American Churches," 21 July 1989, FPHC.

83. Maracle interview.

84. Paul Markstrom to T. E. Gannon, 20 October 1980, FPHC.

85. General Council Minutes, 1979, 63, FPHC.

86. Maracle interview. Maracle was present at all the General Council meetings during the 1980s and recollected events that were not included in the official AG minutes.

87. General Council Minutes, 1989, 93–96, FPHC.

88. Maracle interview.

89. General Council Minutes, 1991, "Study Committee Report: The Feasibility of a Native American Department," 56, FPHC.

90. Ibid.

91. One representative was chosen through a vote from all of the representatives of the various ethnic fellowships (Native American, African American, Latino, Gypsy, and Jewish) for a seat on the Executive Presbytery. According to John Maracle, who as of 2009 was President of the Native American Fellowship, from 2004 to 2006 the fellowship leaders chose the African American Fellowship president as their voice on the Executive Presbytery.

92. Maracle interview.

93. The Native American Fellowship president position was an elected position. The representative job was an appointment from U.S. Missions.

94. Maracle interview.

95. Ibid.

96. Ibid.

97. See http://agnaf.com/.

Epilogue

1. "General Council Minutes," *Minutes of the 52nd Session of the General Council of the Assemblies of God*, Indianapolis, Ind., 8–11 August, 2007, 44.

2. The leaders of the Ethnic Fellowships elected John Maracle to the Executive Presbytery seat. Most of the seats on the Executive Presbytery were defined by U.S. region: Northwest, Southwest, North Central, South Central, Great Lakes, Northeast, Southeast, and Gulf. The three nonregional seats in 2007 were Ethnic Fellowships, Language–Spanish, and Language–other.

3. "First Female Native Presbyter Elected," http://ag.org/top/News/index_article detail.cfm?targetBay=c97d4d5c-a325-4921-9a9e-e9fbddd9cdce&ModID=2&Process= DisplayArticle&RSS_RSSContentID=18712&RSS_OriginatingChannelID=1184&RSS_ OriginatingRSSFeedID=3359&RSS_Source=.

4. Dempsey and Saggio, *American Indian College*, 388.

5. Ibid.

6. Ibid., 389.

7. Andrea Smith, *Native Americans and the Christian Right*, 113.

8. Albanese, "Exchanging Selves, Exchanging Souls: Contact, Combination and American Religious History," 224–26.

9. Axtell, "Some Thoughts on the Ethnohistory of Missions," 35–41.

Bibliography

Primary Sources

Archival Sources Held at the Flower Pentecostal
Heritage Center, Springfield, Mo.

FILED UNDER JOHN MCPHERSON–INDIAN REPRESENTATIVE
Confidential Memo, 15–16 September, 1977.
Crider, Tommy, to T. E. Gannon. 25 October 1977.
Gannon, T. E., to John McPherson. 2 December 1977.
Gannon, T. E., to John McPherson. 5 April 1978.
Gannon, T. E., to John McPherson. 28 December 1979.
Gannon, T. E., to Charlie Lee. 8 April 1980.
Home Missions Administrative Committee Memo. 11 November 1977.
Indian Representative Job Description. August 1979.
Markstrom, Paul, to T. E. Gannon. 20 October 1980.
McPherson, John, to T. E. Gannon. 15 December 1977.
McPherson, John, to T. E. Gannon. 21 March 1978.
McPherson, John, to T. E. Gannon. 18 December 1979.
Memorandum to T. E. Gannon, Re: American Indian Representative.
    7 December 1977.
Position Statement/Nat. Rep. (Indian). Undated.
Report of National Representative/American Indian. 18 September 1978.
Resolution sent to T. E. Gannon. Undated.
Zimmerman, Thos. F., to Rev. E. R. Anderson. 10 March 1980.
Zimmerman, Thos. F., to Earl Vanzant. 10 March 1980.

OTHER ARCHIVAL DOCUMENTS
"Native American Churches." 21 July 1989. Uncatalogued.
"Notes on Planning Meeting of June 2, 1956."
General Council Minutes. 2007. From *Minutes of the 52nd Session of The General Council of the Assemblies of God*. Indianapolis, Ind., 8–11 August, 2007.

Books, Pamphlets, and Missionary Tracts Held at the
Flower Pentecostal Heritage Center

Dunn, Pauline. *A Trail of Beauty: A Short History of the American Indian Bible College.*

Lee, Coralie. *The Long Walk.* Distributed by AG Home Missions.

Turning Point with David Manse. *The Charlie Lee Story.* 1976.

Maracle, Andrew. *From a Log Cabin: An Autobiography of the Life and Ministry of Rev. Andrew Clifford Maracle.*

McPherson, John, with Phil Taylor. *Chief: My Story.* Tulsa, Okla.: Carbondale Assembly of God, 1995.

———. *The Trail of Tears.* Distributed by AG Home Missions.

Washburn, Alta. *Trail to the Tribes.* Springfield, Mo.: self-published, 1990.

Deceased Minister Files (from Applications for Ordination),
Flower Pentecostal Heritage Center

Herbert Bruhn

Ralph Buchanan

Clyde Buck

Lois Carruthers

Luther Cayton

Manuel Cordova

George Effman

Vera Eldridge

James England

Pearl Foster

Albert Gomes

Pearl Habig

Lorraine Hampton

Virginia Kridler

Charles Lee

Andrew Maracle

John McPherson

Pauline Nelson

Burt Parker

James Pepper

David Phillips

Norman Rehwinkel

Silas Rexroat

Virgil Sampson

Charles Slater

Caleb Smith

Arthur Stoneking

Oliver Treece

Alta Washburn

Robert Wheeler

Lyle Wolverton

Heritage Digital Documents

General Council Minutes, April 1914. From *General Council Minutes and Reports, 1914–1999.* FPHC.

General Council Minutes, 1979. From *General Council Minutes and Reports, 1914–1999,* 63. FPHC.

General Council Minutes, 1979. "The Audit Report, April 1, 1977 to March 31, 1979." From *General Council Minutes and Reports, 1914–1999,* 8–9. FPHC.

General Council Minutes, 1989, Resolution 11. From *General Council Minutes and Reports, 1914–1999*, 93–96. FPHC.

General Council Minutes. 1991. "Study Committee Report: The Feasibility of a Native American Department." From *General Council Minutes and Reports, 1914–1999*, 56. FPHC.

Interviews by the Author

Cree, Rodger. Springfield, Mo., 8 August 2006.

Lyon, Ruth. Springfield, Mo., 11 August 2006.

Maracle, John. Via telephone, 1 August 2007.

Thomas, Alma. Phoenix, Ariz., 11 June 2010.

Periodicals

Apostolic Faith. Reprint. Foley, Ala.: Together in Harvest Publishing, 1997.

Christian Evangel (complete digital file held at the Flower Pentecostal Heritage Center, Springfield, Mo.).

Farmington Times-Hustler (microfilm held by the University of New Mexico).

Pentecostal Evangel (complete digital file held at the Flower Pentecostal Heritage Center, Springfield, Mo.).

Secondary Sources

Adams, David Wallace. *Education for Extinction: American Indians and the Boarding School Experience 1875–1925*. Lawrence: University Press of Kansas, 1997.

Albanese, Catherine L. "Exchanging Selves, Exchanging Souls: Contact, Combination and American Religious History." In *Re-Telling U.S. Religious History*, edited by Thomas A. Tweed, 200–226. Berkeley: University of California Press, 1997.

———. *Nature Religion in America: From the Algonkian Indians to the New Age*. Chicago: University of Chicago Press, 1990.

Alexander, Corky. *Native American Pentecost: Praxis, Contextualization, Transformation*. Cleveland, Tenn.: Cherohala Press, 2012.

Allen, Roland. *Missionary Methods: St. Paul's or Ours?* Mansfield Center, Conn.: Martino Publishing, 2001.

Anderson, Allan. *Spreading Fires: The Missionary Nature of Early Pentecostalism*. New York: Orbis Books, 2007.

Axtell, James. *The Invasion Within: The Contest of Cultures in Colonial North America*. New York: Oxford University Press, 1985.

———. "Some Thoughts on the Ethnohistory of Missions." *Ethnohistory* 29 (1982): 35–41.

Baily, Garrick, and Roberta Baily. *A History of the Navajos: The Reservation Years.* Santa Fe: School of American Research Press, 1986.

Barrett, David B., Greg T. Kurian, and Todd M. Johnson. *World Christian Encyclopedia: A Comparative Survey of Churches and Religions in the Modern World.* 2nd ed. 2 vols. Oxford: Oxford University Press, 2000.

Basso, Keith. "Western Apache." In *The Handbook of North American Indians*, vol. 10, *Southwest*, edited by Alfonso Ortiz, 462–88. Washington, D.C.: Smithsonian Institution, 1983.

Berkhofer, Robert J. *Salvation and the Savage: An Analysis of Protestant Missions and the American Indian Response, 1787–1862.* Louisville: University of Kentucky Press, 1965.

———. *The White Man's Indian: Images of the American Indian from Columbus to the Present.* New York: Alfred A. Knopf, 1978.

Blumhofer Edith L. *The Assemblies of God: A Chapter in the Story of American Pentecostalism.* 2 vols. Springfield, Mo.: Gospel Publishing House, 1989.

———. *Restoring the Faith: The Assemblies of God, Pentecostalism, and American Culture.* Chicago: University of Illinois Press, 1993.

Bowden, Henry Warner. *American Indians and Christian Missions: Studies in Cultural Conflict.* Chicago: University of Chicago Press, 1981.

Brereton, Virginia. *Training God's Army: The American Bible School.* Bloomington: Indiana University Press, 1990.

Brown, Dee. *Bury My Heart at Wounded Knee: An Indian History of the American West.* New York: Holt Books, 2001.

Brusco, Elizabeth. *The Reformation of Machismo: Conversion and Gender in Colombia.* Austin: University of Texas Press, 1995.

Burkinshaw, Robert. "Native Pentecostalism in British Columbia." In *Canadian Pentecostalism: Transition and Transformation*, edited by Michael Wilkinson, 142–70. Montreal: McGill University Press, 2009.

Daily, David W. *Battle for the BIA: G. E. E. Lindquist and the Missionary Crusade against John Collier.* Tucson: University of Arizona Press, 2004.

———. "Vine Deloria's Challenge to the Episcopal Church, 1968–1974." Paper presented at the American Society of Church History, Washington, D.C., 5 Jan. 2008.

Deloria, Philip J. *Indians in Unexpected Places.* Lawrence: University Press of Kansas, 2004.

———. *Playing Indian.* New Haven: Yale University Press, 1998.

———. "Vine Deloria Sr." In *The New Warriors: Native American Leaders Since 1900*, edited by R. David Edmunds, 79–96. Lincoln: University of Nebraska Press, 2001.

Deloria, Vine, Jr. *Custer Died for Your Sins.* New York: Avon Books, 1969.

Dempsey, Jim, and Joseph J. Saggio, eds. *American Indian College: A Witness to the Tribes.* Springfield, Mo.: Gospel Publishing House, 2008.

Dolan, Jay P. *In Search of an American Catholicism: A History of Religion and Culture in Tension*. Oxford: Oxford University Press, 2002.

Dombrowski, Kirk. *Against Culture: Development, Politics and Religion in Indian Alaska*. Lincoln: University of Nebraska Press, 2001.

Dunch, Ryan. "Beyond Cultural Imperialism: Cultural Theory, Christian Missions, and Global Modernity." *History and Theory* 41, no. 3 (October 2002): 301–25.

Harper, Susan Billington. *In the Shadow of the Mahatma: Bishop V. S. Azariah and the Travails of Christianity in British India*. Cambridge: William B. Eerdmans, 2000.

Harrell, David. *All Things Are Possible: The Healing and Charismatic Revivals in Modern America*. Bloomington: Indiana University Press, 1975.

Higham, C. L. *Noble, Wretched and Redeemable: Protestant Missionaries to the Indians in Canada and the United States, 1820–1900*. Albuquerque: University of New Mexico Press, 2000.

Hinson, Glenn. *Fire in My Bones: Transcendence and the Holy Spirit in African American Gospel*. Philadelphia: University of Pennsylvania Press, 2000.

Hodges, Melvin. *The Indigenous Church*. Springfield, Mo.: Gospel Publishing House, 1953.

————. *The Indigenous Church and the Missionary: A Sequel to The Indigenous Church*. South Pasadena: W. Carey Library, 1978.

————. *The Indigenous Church Including The Indigenous Church and the Missionary*. Rev. ed. Springfield, Mo.: Gospel Publishing House, 2009.

————. *A Theology of the Church and Its Mission: A Pentecostal Perspective*. Springfield, Mo.: Gospel Publishing House, 1997.

Holler, Clyde. *Black Elk's Religion: The Sun Dance and Lakota Catholicism*. New York: Syracuse University Press, 1995.

Hughes, Richard T., and C. Leonard Allen. *Illusions of Innocence: Protestant Primitivism in America, 1630–1875*. Chicago: University of Chicago Press, 1988.

Hutchison, William R. *Errand to the World: American Protestant Thought and Foreign Missions*. Chicago: University of Chicago Press, 1993.

Iverson, Peter. *The Navajo Nation*. London: Greenwood Press, 1981.

Jacobsen, Douglas. *Thinking in the Spirit: Theologies of the Early Pentecostal Movement*. Bloomington: Indiana University Press, 2003.

Kelley, Laurence C. *The Navajo Indians and Federal Indian Policy, 1900–1935*. Phoenix: University of Arizona Press, 1968.

Kenyon, Howard N. "An Analysis of Ethical Issues in the History of the Assemblies of God." Ph.D. diss., Baylor University, 1988.

Lewis, Bonnie Sue. *Creating Christian Indians: Native Clergy in the Presbyterian Church*. Norman: University of Oklahoma Press, 2003.

Lyon, Ruth. *A History of Home Missions of the Assemblies of God*. Springfield, Mo.: Division of Home Missions, 1992.

Maffly-Kipp, Laurie F., Leigh E. Schmidt, and Mark Valeri, eds. *Practicing Protestants: Histories of Christian Life in America 1630–1965*. Baltimore: Johns Hopkins University Press, 2006.

McGee, Gary. "Assemblies of God Mission Theology: A Historical Perspective." *International Bulletin of Missionary Research*, October 1986, 165–168.

———. *Miracles, Missions and American Pentecostalism*. New York: Orbis Books, 2010.

———. *This Gospel Shall Be Preached: A History and Theology of Assemblies of God Foreign Missions to 1959*. Springfield, Mo.: Gospel Publishing House, 2003.

McLoughlin, William G. *Champions of the Cherokees: Evan and John B. Jones*. Princeton: Princeton University Press, 1990.

———. *The Cherokees and Christianity, 1794–1870: Essays on Acculturation and Cultural Persistence*. Athens: University of Georgia Press, 1994.

McNally, Michael. *Ojibwe Singers: Hymns, Grief, and A Native Culture In Motion*. New York: Oxford University Press, 2000.

———. "The Practice of Native American Christianity." *Church History* 69 (December 2000): 834–59.

Orsi, Robert. *Between Heaven and Earth: The Religious Worlds People Make and the Scholars Who Study Them*. Princeton: Princeton University Press, 2006.

———. *Thank You, St. Jude: Women's Devotion to the Patron Saint of Hopeless Causes*. New Haven: Yale University Press, 1996.

Parman, Donald. "J. C. Morgan: Navajo Apostle of Assimilation." *Prologue: The Journal of the National Archives* 4 (Summer 1979): 83–96.

———. *The Navajos and the New Deal*. New Haven: Yale University Press, 1976.

Poloma, Margaret M. *The Assemblies of God at the Crossroads*. Knoxville: University of Tennessee Press, 1989.

Porter, Andrew. "Cultural Imperialism and Protestant Missionary Enterprise, 1780–1914." *Journal of Imperial and Commonwealth History* 25, no. 3 (September 1997): 367–91.

Prucha, Francis Paul. *American Indian Policy in Crisis: Christian Reformers and the Indian, 1865–1890*. Norman: University of Oklahoma Press, 1976.

———. *The Great Father: The United States Government and the American Indians*. 2 vols. Lincoln: University of Nebraska Press, 1984.

Raybon, Joel. "Race and the Assemblies of God Church: The Journey from Azusa Street to the 'Miracle of Memphis.'" Ph.D. diss., University of Memphis, 2005.

Robeck, Cecil M., Jr. *The Azusa Street Mission and Revival: The Birth of the Global Pentecostal Movement*. Nashville: Thomas Nelson, 2006.

Robert, Dana. *American Women in Mission: A Social History of Their Thought and Practice*. Macon: Mercer University Press, 1998.

———. "From Mission to beyond Missions: The Historiography of American Protestant Foreign Missions since World War II." In *New Directions in American*

Religious History, edited by Harry S. Stout and D. G. Hart, 362–93. Oxford: Oxford University Press, 1997.

Sánchez-Walsh, Arlene. *Latino Pentecostal Identity: Evangelical Faith, Self, and Society*. New York: Columbia University Press, 2003.

Sides, Hampton. *Blood and Thunder: An Epic of the American West*. New York: Doubleday, 2006.

Smith, Andrea. *Native Americans and the Christian Right: The Gendered Politics of Unlikely Alliances*. Durham: Duke University Press, 2008.

Smith, Paul C., and Robert A. Warrior. *Like a Hurricane: The Indian Movement from Alcatraz to Wounded Knee*. New York: New Press, 1996.

Stewart, Omar Call. *Peyote Religion: A History*. Norman: University of Oklahoma Press, 1987.

Sullivan, Lawrence E., ed. *Native American Religions: North America*. New York: Macmillan, 1989.

Synan, Vinson. *The Century of the Holy Spirit: 100 Years of Pentecostal and Charismatic Renewal, 1901–2001*. Nashville: Thomas Nelson, 2001.

———. *The Holiness-Pentecostal Tradition: Charismatic Movements in the Twentieth Century*. Grand Rapids: Eerdmans, 1997.

Tinker, George. *Missionary Conquest: The Gospel and Native American Cultural Genocide*. Minneapolis: Fortress Press, 1993.

Treat, James, ed. *Native and Christian: Indigenous Voices on Religious Identity in the United States and Canada*. New York: Routledge, 1995.

Tucker, Ruth. "Female Mission Strategists: A Historical and Contemporary Perspective." *Missiology* 15, no. 1 (January 1987): 73–88.

———. *Guardians of the Great Commission: The Story of Women in Modern Mission*. Grand Rapids: Academie Books, 1988.

U.S. Census Bureau. *We the People: American Indians and Alaska Natives in the United States*. Washington, D.C.: Dept. of Commerce, 2000.

Wacker, Grant. "The Assemblies of God." In *Encyclopedia of Religion In the South*, edited by Samuel Hill, Charles Lippy, and Charles Reagan, 85–89. Macon: Mercer University Press, 2005.

———. *Heaven Below: Early Pentecostals and American Culture*. Cambridge, Mass.: Harvard University Press, 2001.

———. "Marching to Zion: Religion in a Modern Utopian Community." *Church History* 54 (December 1985): 506–26.

———. "Pentecostalism." In *The Encyclopedia of the American Religious Experience: Studies of Traditions and Movements*, edited by Charles H. Lippy and Peter W. Williams, 3:933–46. New York: Charles Scribner's Sons, 1989.

———. "Playing for Keeps: The Primitivist Impulse in Early Pentecostalism." In *The American Quest for the Primitive Church*, edited by Richard T. Hughes, 196–219. Chicago: University of Illinois Press, 1988.

Weaver, Jace, ed. *Native American Religious Identity: Unforgotten Gods*. New York: Orbis Books, 1998.

Westman, Clinton. "Understanding Cree Religious Discourse." Ph.D. diss. Alberta 2008.

White, Richard. *The Roots of Dependency: Subsistence, Environment and Social Change among the Choctaw, Pawnee and Navajo*. Lincoln: University of Nebraska Press, 1983.

Wilson, Everett A., and Ruth Marshall Wilson. "Alice E. Luce: A Visionary Victorian." In *Portraits of a Generation: Early Pentecostal Leaders*, edited by James R. Goff Jr. and Grant Wacker, 159–76. Fayetteville: University of Arkansas Press, 2002.

Wilson, L. F. "Bible Institutes, Colleges, Universities." In *Dictionary of Pentecostal and Charismatic Movements*, edited by Stanley M. Burgess and Gary McGee, 57–65. Grand Rapids: Regency Reference Library, 1988.

Windes, Vinda. "Yel Ha Yah's Second Career—Charles Lee." *New Mexico Magazine*, July 1977, 15.

Index

missionary efforts by, 2–3, 22, 26–31, 40–43; early years of, 23–26; ethnic fellowships within, 149, 201 (n. 91), 202 (n. 2); evolution of, 2–3, 27; Executive Presbytery of, 3, 25–26, 28, 42, 140, 147–48, 150, 152–59, 171, 176, 202 (n. 2); and faith missions, 27, 43–44; female missionaries' role in, 10, 17, 43, 57, 124–25, 180 (n. 24), 194–95 (n. 55); foreign missions of, 2, 28–30, 199 (n. 25); founding of, 24–25; General Presbytery of, 166–67, 168; Home Missions of, 22, 30–31, 45, 143, 147, 148–52, 158, 168; and indigenous principle, 3, 8, 32, 144, 175; and Latinos, 9–10, 160–61; Native American changing of, 4, 9, 144, 173–76; Native American empowerment in, 5–8, 10, 39, 78, 143, 144–45, 163, 172; Native American Fellowship within, 164–69, 201 (nn. 91, 93); Native American membership in, 2; and other Pentecostal denominations, 1, 4, 17; paternalism within, 45, 71, 152, 163; racism within, 9–10, 163; white male power structure of, 10, 26. *See also* Indian representative, Assemblies of God; Missionaries, Native; Missionaries, white; Native American Pentecostals; Pentecostalism
Assemblies of God Theological Seminary, 120
Axtell, James, 175
Azusa Street Mission, 23, 24, 171

Bell, E. N., 25
Bell Gardens Assembly of God, 73
Berean Bible Institute, 119
Berkhofer, Robert, 12
Bible schools, 134–37; AG network of, 26, 168; curricula of, 119, 121–22;

funding of, 124, 126, 128, 134; and indigenous principle, 133, 136, 137, 173; role of in Assemblies of God, 118–20; Washburn and, 2, 10, 108–9, 115–16, 117, 120–33, 136–37, 144. *See also* All-Tribes Bible School; American Indian Bible Institute; American Indian College of the Assemblies of God; Central Bible Institute
Blumhofer, Edith, 119
Boarding schools, 22, 181 (n. 2)
Bolt, George, 83
Brereton, Virginia, 128
Brown, Dee, 198 (n. 128)
Brown, D. L., 41
Bruhn, Herbert, 123
Bryant, Brother, 124
Burgess, Helen, 62
Burkinshaw, Bob, 11
Burnette, Marco, 137
Bury My Heart at Wounded Knee (Brown), 198 (n. 128)

California Bible College, 119
Callings, 1, 47–48, 57–59
Camp meetings, 67–71, 188 (n. 93)
Canadian first peoples, 17
Canyon Day Apache Mission, 74, 75
Canyon de Chelly, 19
Carruthers, Brother and Sister, 124
Carson, Kit, 100, 191 (n. 61)
Catholics: missionary work by, 140, 190 (n. 8); Pentecostals and, 82–83, 88
Cattaraugus reservation, 60
Cattle industry, 66
Cayton, Luther, 47, 88, 91
Central Bible Institute (CBI), 51, 120, 193 (n. 18); creation of, 27–28, 119
Cherokee, 98–99, 102
Chisolm, Robert Benjamin, 26

Gannon, T. E., 147, 153, 154, 157–58
Gardiner, Ruth, 124
Gila River reservation, 51, 86–87
Gospel Publishing House, 27, 173
Gressett, J. K., 62, 120, 121–22, 123
Griepp, Edna, 61

Habig, Pearl, 58–59
Hampton, Lorraine, 58–59
Harper, Susan Billington, 105
Harrell, David, 95–96
Healing: in Maracle conversion narrative, 53–54; Native missionaries' emphasis on, 98, 101, 102–3, 107; traditional religions on, 14, 85; white missionaries and, 95–98
Herd, Eugene, 135
Higher-Life Pentecostalism, 25
Hinson, Glenn, 13
Hispanics. See Latinos
Hobby Indians, 105, 106
Hodges, Dennis, 167
Hodges, Melvin: and Allen, 33, 36; and development of indigenous principle, 5, 37–38, 44, 118, 179 (n. 6); *The Indigenous Church*, 37–40, 176; Lee and, 40, 51, 143
Holiness movement, 24, 25, 28, 162
Holy Ghost powwows, 67–71
Holy Spirit, 8, 43, 51; and AG missionary work, 36, 44, 69; baptism in, 24–25, 26, 27, 48, 55, 66; messages and signs from, 129, 177; Pentecostalism's primacy of, 12, 13, 56, 172
Home Missions Board, 147, 148, 150–51, 152, 158
Home Missions Committee, 150–51, 152
Home Missions Department, 22, 30, 45, 148–49, 168, 199 (n. 25)
Hoopa tribe, 41, 61
Hutchison, William, 32

Identity: language and customs as definition of, 55, 186 (n. 43); of Native American Pentecostals, 45, 88, 128, 162, 175; traditional customs and, 75, 88
India, 33, 105
Indian Institute, 156
Indian representative, Assemblies of God, 147–65; appointment of, 3, 42, 78, 140, 145, 147–48, 150, 152, 171, 176, 189 (n. 114), 202 (n. 2); funds lacking for, 153, 155, 159, 165, 168, 199 (n. 25); institutional support lacking to, 152–53, 154–55, 168; job description, 156; as part-time position, 153, 155, 165, 168; vagueness of responsibilities, 152, 153–54, 156, 168. *See also* Leadership, indigenous
The Indigenous Church (Hodges), 37–40, 176
Indigenous church movement, 3, 71–72, 130, 144, 148, 151, 152, 168, 198 (n. 130); and indigenous principle, 116–18, 137–38; Mesa View Assembly of God and, 137–43
Indigenous principle: Allen on, 33–35; Anderson and, 31–33, 44; Assemblies of God changed by, 4, 9, 144, 173–76; central idea of, 5; as communitist theology, 8–9, 175; Cree on, 116, 169; development of, 31–40, 44; dynamic nature of, 82, 175; ethnocentrism and, 5, 8, 23, 45, 81–82, 145; and fight for national power, 147–69; halfway, 48–49, 67, 71, 77, 81; Hodges on, 5, 37–40, 44, 118, 179 (n. 6); implementation of, 40, 48, 77, 117; Indian Bible schools and, 118, 133, 136, 137, 173; indigenous church movement and, 116–18, 137–38, 173; institutionalizing, 115–45; Lee and, 31, 51, 116–17,

McPherson, 77; missionary-convert interdependence in, 37; among Navajos, 42, 60–61, 62, 64, 68, 189–90 (n. 8); by other denominations, 140, 190 (n. 8); success in, 2, 141–42; in urban areas, 73–74

Mohawks, 41, 53, 54–55, 131

Morgan, Jacob C., 138, 139

Mormons, 140

National American Indian Defense Association, 139

National Indian Committee, 159

Native American Contextual Movement, 93–94

Native American Fellowship, 169, 201 (nn. 91, 93); creation of, 164–69

Native American Pentecostals: Assemblies of God changed by, 4, 9, 144, 173–76; and community, 8; divisions among, 151–52; empowerment of, 5–8, 10, 39, 78, 143, 144, 145, 163, 172; evangelization and conversion of, 49–71, 77–78, 175; identity of, 45, 88, 128, 162, 175; and indigenous church movement, 61, 71–72, 117–18, 137–43, 148, 151–52, 168; indigenous principle used by, 2, 3, 5–6, 7–9, 23, 81, 169, 172–73; rise to leadership of, 2–3, 22, 23, 145, 147–69; scholarship on, 11–12; and supernatural, 12, 13, 14, 56; terminology, 17; and traditionalist Indians, 86–87; and traditional religions, 87–95, 107–8, 141. *See also* Indigenous principle; Leadership, indigenous; Missionaries, Native

Native Americans: boarding schools for, 22, 181 (n. 2); and Christianity, 5–7, 173, 174–76; diversity of, 101; dressing up as, 103–7; Hollywood portrayal of, 41, 82, 104, 106; identity of, 45, 55, 75, 88, 128, 162, 186 (n. 43); injustices suffered by, 19, 98–100, 102, 138, 191 (n. 61), 196 (n. 107); Latinos compared to, 161–62; and "playing Indian," 105–6; portrayed as "savages," 55, 69, 80–81, 84–85, 100; and poverty, 69, 139–40, 157, 200 (n. 49); racism toward, 9–10, 54–55, 71, 80, 81; stereotypes of, 6, 12, 100, 101, 103–7; terminological use of, 16–17. *See also* Traditional customs and practices

Navajos: government injustice toward, 19, 98, 100, 138, 191 (n. 61), 196 (n. 107); indigenous church of, 71–72, 117, 142, 151, 198 (n. 128); missionary work among, 42, 60–61, 62, 64, 68, 189–90 (n. 8); and Navajo language, 51, 72, 152, 186 (n. 17); poverty and inequality among, 139–40; religious diversity among, 140; stock reduction program and, 138–39, 197 (n. 111); traditional beliefs and customs of, 86, 131, 140, 191 (n. 36); and Wheeler-Howard Act, 138, 143, 196–97 (nn. 107, 109, 110)

Nelson, Pauline, 57

Nelson, Roy, 62

Oneness congregations, 37

Oral traditions, 93

Orsi, Robert, 8

Paiute reservation, 62

Papago, 17, 60, 84–85

Parham, Charles, 24

Parker, Burt, 57

Paternalism, 23, 33, 34, 37, 71, 94; Allen on, 33, 35, 40; within AG power structure, 45, 71, 152, 163; of dressing up Indian, 107; Hodges on, 38–39, 40; Native Pentecostals' fight against, 8, 23, 45, 87, 138, 141, 143, 145, 161, 173; of white missionaries, 2, 40, 43, 49, 67, 70, 76, 141, 157

Paul, Saint, 22, 36; and Pauline example, 29, 31, 33, 35, 183 (nn. 55, 62)

Pentecostal Evangel (*PE*): conversion narratives in, 49, 66–67; ethnocentrism and paternalism of, 80, 140–43, 163; as flagship AG periodical, 27; mentioned, 30, 36, 106, 134, 157; on miraculous healings, 97–98; Native missionaries' use of, 98, 99, 100, 101; as publicity and fund-raising vehicle, 16, 63, 181 (n. 24); reports on reservation missions in, 60, 62–63, 65, 69, 74, 75, 80; as source, 15–16, 40–42; traditional religions demonized by, 83–84

Pentecostal Indians. *See* Native American Pentecostals

Pentecostalism: and Catholicism, 82–83, 88; converts to, 49–59, 63–65, 70, 76, 77–78; and Devil, 82; early years of, 24, 44; egalitarianism within, 15; and faith missions, 27, 43–44; "great revival" within, 95–96; groups within, 4; Holy Spirit's primacy in, 12, 13, 56, 172; indigenous principle and, 9, 22, 44, 172, 179 (n. 6); mentioned, 81, 99, 162; Methodist church and, 55, 186 (n. 37); and miracles, 13–14; Native American impact on, 2, 4, 108, 169; oral traditions of, 93; pragmatism of, 71, 119, 125, 137; and prophecy, 4, 9, 10, 13, 14, 26, 67, 101; restorationist impulse of, 62, 88, 97, 101, 102, 117; theology described, 13–14, 24–25, 26; tongue speaking in, 4, 9, 13, 26, 67, 126, 133. *See also* Assemblies of God; Missionaries, Native; Missionaries, white; Native American Pentecostals

Pepper, James F., 106

Pershing, C. E., 103

Peter, Simon, 135, 151

Peyote, 87–88, 140, 190 (n. 24)

Phillips, James, 47

Pima, 62, 63–64

Piper, William H., 24

Playing Indian, 105–6

Poloma, Margaret, 56

Poverty: of Bible school, 126, 128; of Native Americans, 69, 139–40, 157, 200 (n. 49)

Powwows, 67–71

Pragmatism: of Pentecostalism, 71, 119, 125, 137; of Washburn, 48, 130, 144–45; of white missionaries, 63, 67, 76–77

Presbyterians, 11, 194–95 (n. 55)

Prisoners, 65–66, 76

Promise Keepers, 174, 192 (n. 68)

Prophecy: Pentecostalism and, 4, 9, 13, 14, 67, 101; women and, 10, 26

Racism, 9–10, 54–55, 71, 80, 81, 163

Ramsey, Don, 134

Red Power movement, 159, 160. *See also* American Indian Movement

Rehwinkel, Norman, 57, 80

Relocation program, 73

Reservations: social conditions on, 61–62, 69, 101, 139–40, 157, 200 (n. 49); traditionalist-Christian rift on, 86–87; white missionaries in, 59–67

Robert, Dana, 125

Rodeos, 66

Rodgers, Darrin, 171, 177

Rosebud reservation, 61

St. Arneault, Brother, 54

Salvation: in conversion narratives, 51, 54; Native Pentecostals and, 8–9,